A Passion to Oppose

A Passion to Oppose

John Anderson, philosopher

Brian Kennedy

Melbourne University Press
1995

Melbourne University Press
PO Box 278, Carlton South, Victoria 3053, Australia

First published 1995

Typeset by Syarikat Seng Teik Sdn. Bhd., Malaysia in 11/13.5 point Plantin
Printed in Malaysia by SRM Production Services Sdn. Bhd.

National Library of Australia Cataloguing-in-Publication data

Kennedy, Brian, 1942–
A passion to oppose: John Anderson, philosopher.
Bibliography.
Includes index.
ISBN 0 522 84683 1.
1. Anderson, John, 1893–1962. 2. Philosophers—Australia—Biography. 3. Intellectuals—Australia—Biography. I. Title.
199.94092

To Sandy, with gratitude.

Contents

Illustrations

Unless otherwise attributed, all photographs are reproduced with permission of the University of Sydney Archives

Prelude

> It is literally true . . . that God has specially appointed me to this city, as though it were a large thoroughbred horse which because of its great size is inclined to be lazy and needs the stimulation of some stinging fly . . . and all day long I never cease to settle here, there, and everywhere, rousing, persuading, reproving every one of you. You will not easily find another like me, gentlemen.
>
> *The Apology of Socrates.*[1]

AT NOON ON 4 May 1987 I was one of three thousand people, black and white, crowded into the main public place of the University of the Witwatersrand to hear the university's most famous student, Mrs Winnie Mandela, speak on the coming South African elections. Above the amphitheatre rose the Greek temple façade of the Great Hall, while flanking us were the two modern library buildings. Earlier that day the students had requested the Johannesburg magistrate for permission to hold the meeting since the chief speaker was a 'banned' person. There was no reply. We all waited anxiously and expectantly. Many watched at a safe distance and height from the windows and parapets of the Wartenweiler Library. Winnie Mandela was to give her views on whether whites should vote or not in the national elections. The choice of political party, Nationalist or P.F.P., was not an issue on the radical campus, since all blacks were denied the vote.

Suddenly, without warning, hundreds of riot police descended on the student mass, down the steps to the public place. As they surrounded the amphitheatre and charged into the crowd, behind plastic shields and wielding their quirts, students fled, rushed for cover or gingerly gathered in small groups here and there. Unrelenting, the police pressed their advantage, arresting and sjambokking students, until blood stained the steps and panic swept the university. Then, as if by chance, a few academics appeared in the crowd, wearing gowns, coloured hoods and caps, smoking, chatting and promenading up and down, to and fro. Gradually and imperceptibly a measure of calm returned to the throng and the police retired *en masse*. Students began to don black gowns over their jeans and re-assembled on the dry lawn for an afternoon of sombre protest and vigil.

This vignette from a recent study leave describes a dramatic incident in the life of one great university. However specific and localised the setting, there are elements common to universities everywhere. Even the classical portico suggests the university's debt to ancient Greece, the Academy and the Socratic injunction to 'know thyself' at whatever cost in public contention and acrimony. The action was unusual for its violence and brutality, but the actors, both as individuals and groups, were drawing on powerful symbols, beliefs and traditions. In the midday light of the high veld, the physical assault revealed a fundamental clash of ideas, beliefs and values; and evoked in that near-Mediterranean setting of golden sun, sere grass and Greek temple the life and death of Socrates.

The crisis of one strife-torn university may serve as a paradigm for the crisis of all universities today. Peter Scott, the British writer on universities, wonders whether the traditional ideals of the liberal university—a community of scholars, the cultivation of the mind, and the disinterested pursuit of knowledge by methods of free inquiry—can survive in the post-modern, specialised and fragmented world of the 1990s. For Scott, however, the threats are as much within as without the institution, and he presents a formidable catalogue of them:

> . . . the process of disciplinary specialisation in the modern university has led to its loss of a common intellectual language. The different branches of knowledge find it increasingly difficult to regard the modern university as in any sense an organic academic society rather than simply as a shared bureaucratic environment, a common material framework of buildings, jobs, careers, and equipment which

> can be exploited for a variety of more or less cognitive activities that have little in common with each other. If this is true, it has important and depressing implications for the ability of the university to maintain its traditional autonomy and so for the ability of society to organise its intellectual effort under conditions of freedom.[2]

Another influential critic of the modern university also directs his analysis to the inner life and academic values of the university because 'the university, of all institutions, is most dependent on the deepest beliefs of those who participate in its peculiar life . . . Thought is all in all for universities. Today there is precious little thought about universities, and what there is does not unequivocally support the university's traditional role'.[3] In a bold synoptic essay, Allan Bloom surveys the history of the 'philosophic experience' as the key to the university's existence. Contemplation of Socrates has been a central task of philosophy through the ages. The ironical tension of the philosopher viewing life in the light of death—'Is not the love of wisdom a practice of death?' asked Socrates—is an essential element in disinterestedness and criticism, the probing of all 'opinion' and conventions. In his controversial book, *The Closing of the American Mind*, Bloom presents his agenda for a real university—serious thinkers, great books, sensitive souls, friendship and a spiritual community. It is Athens Revisited and his prescriptions for reform are unrepentantly élitist, generalist and intellectual. But given the present educational chaos, subject rivalries and loss of nerve in the principal disciplines, what hope is there for the ideal of a liberal humane education? Not surprisingly, Bloom is despondent: 'These great universities—which can split the atom, find cures for the most terrible diseases, conduct surveys of whole populations and produce massive dictionaries of lost languages—cannot generate a modest program of general education for undergraduate students. This is a parable for our times'.[4]

Australia has not been immune from contention and controversy about 'the university's vocation'. The rapid changes to the tertiary education sector initiated in 1988 by John Dawkins, the Minister for Employment, Education and Training, are symptomatic of a drive in many industrialised countries to harness higher education to the tasks of restructuring the economy and reskilling the workforce. In the Australian context, financial deregulation, the deficit and mounting national debt have encouraged Treasury, the minister and the bureaucrats to 'rationalise' and 'restructure' the administration and financing of the universities and the higher education system. Their rhetoric is frankly economistic and boasts of increased 'efficiency' and 'accountability', but pays scant regard to the idea of a liberal university and general culture:

> The society we want cannot be achieved without a strong economic base. In Australia, this now requires a greatly increased export income, a far more favourable balance of trade than at present and a considerable reduction in our external debt. It also requires a shift in the traditional profile of our economic activity. Our industry is increasingly faced with rapidly changing international markets in which success depends on, among other things, the conceptual, creative and technical skills of the labour force, the ability to innovate and be entrepreneurial.[5]

In response to these challenges and the circumstances of public austerity, Peter Scott calls for a 'remoralisation' of the university and a return to 'its broader social responsibility', including 'the cultivation of rationality within society'. He concedes the validity of some of the political demands for greater efficiency and public accountability, but insists that governments must also respect the diversity and variety of educational institutions and their traditional right to freedom of inquiry and criticism.

John Anderson, the subject of this biography and the Scottish philosopher who professed his subject at the University of Sydney for more than three decades, would certainly have endorsed these claims. From his arrival at Sydney in 1927, he fought countless battles to prevent the university from becoming a bureaucratised factory devoted to the churning out of 'trained personnel' to meet the most shallowly conceived needs of 'society'. His words as a student editor at Glasgow in 1918 are as prophetic as ever:

> And signs are not wanting that there will be a still stronger movement in the near future towards the thorough commercialising of the University, placing it under State regulation, and subordinating it to some misty ideal called 'the needs of the community'. The University is itself a community, with its own needs and purposes, which are not lightly to be set aside. It must be *co-ordinated* with other institutions, but not in such a way that it will lose its own free and independent spirit.[6]

Socrates' life and death provided Anderson with the essential model of the philosophic task—to find a way of life, 'to inculcate the spirit of criticism, to encourage the questioning of received opinions and traditions'; as Socrates said, 'the uncriticised life is not worth living' because 'to lead such a life is to be in the lowest state of ignorance, ignorant even of one's own ignorance'.[7] The Socratic practice of dialectic or criticism led by a process of questioning to the acquisition of true knowledge in place of opinion, and revealed the interrelatedness of all culture. 'Fields of study', Anderson wrote, 'are not cut off from one another but mingle just as peoples do. And to treat each as a separate "world" is to fall into contradictions'.[8] Anderson attacked narrow specialisation, and he strongly challenged the distinction between 'scientific' and 'cultural' subjects. His early training in mathematics and physics gave authority to his assertion that 'such subjects as philosophy, language and literature are essentially scientific and experimental; they can only be really studied in terms of living problems'.[9] 'What this involves', he goes on, 'is that there is a single logic which applies to all the sciences, a single way of being which all their objects have'.[10] Such an integrated view of knowledge recalls the Greeks, and Anderson held that Greek civilisation of the fifth century was the first great expression of the classic spirit when 'objectivism, criticism and intellectual detachment' flourished. As he summed up at the end of a long career, 'Classicism, in short, stands for the unity of culture against all forms of subjectivism and interestedness, and for the unity, the common principles, of criticism against specialism and *ad hoc* devices'.[11]

Anderson's view of education was both liberal and classical, for education 'enables us to live *freely*. It is a training, not for a particular job or service, but for a whole life'.[12] He thus rejected all utilitarian and 'instrumentalist' theories that justified education in terms of some extrinsic end, whether economic growth or personal well being. Such theories were opposed to the intrinsic 'goods' of inquiry and criticism, which, following Socrates, he took to be the true definition of education: 'The classicist recognises the natural opposition between disinterestedness and interestedness, between concern with the ways of working of things themselves and concern with what we can get out of them'.[13] Likewise, he rejected all 'service' theories of education, be it service to the community, business or the state, because they failed to distinguish between education and training. They were 'servile', misguided and unfree. Education does not serve other ends but has its own ways of working and intrinsic qualities. It involves 'a general grasp of the scientific, artistic and social activities of mankind' and not uncommonly leads to '*the finding of a way of life*, as contrasted with the mere acquisition of a number of arts or accomplishments'.[14]

According to Anderson, a university is the institution that pre-eminently embodies the educational 'goods' of inquiry and criticism in a continuous tradition. It is a corporation 'invested with the privilege of maintaining and spreading culture', with a strong claim 'to speak in the counsels of the nation'. This conception of the university received eloquent expression in the submission of Anderson and his colleagues to the Murray Committee in 1957:

> Following the traditional British view of a university and its functions, we consider the principal functions of any Australian university to be the preservation, the extension and the transmission of knowledge in a number of fields where a special kind of demand is made upon human understanding and judgement. In serving these ends, the university provides a liberal education, that has no specific vocational aim, as well as a thorough preparation for those professions which rest firmly on the basic fields of knowledge with which a university should be concerned.[15]

There has been in my generation a marked tension between the demands of a vastly changed society and the claims of a liberal education for the cultivation of the mind. Was Anderson quixotic and unrealistic in his uncompromising insistence on 'the disinterested pursuit of knowledge by methods of free inquiry', the inter-relatedness of all knowledge, and liberal general education? Did he ignore the competing claims of vocationalism, specialisation and research? Did he also fail to see the dangers of 'mass civilisation' in the 'inclusive' democracy he championed as a Marxist in the 1930s?

During three decades at Sydney, Anderson saw the university grow fourfold in population and become much more concerned with professional training, a range of new disciplines and postgraduate research. 'Science poses the major problem of education because of the very magnitude of its success', Ian Clunies Ross reflected on the university's centenary in 1952, 'so that the ceaseless and bewilderingly rapid proliferation of knowledge forces its votaries into ever-narrowing specialisms'.[16] The relationship with the state also changed as governments increased their grants to the university to compensate for the declining value of private endowments and fees. Yet, throughout his career, Anderson was an unsparing critic of vocational and utilitarian 'ends' in education and of state interference, fearing that they would subvert the 'primacy' of 'investigation, discussion, exploration and rigorous thinking' in the central disciplines. Learning was not 'a commodity to be bought and sold' but 'one of the mainsprings of life'. On democracy and mass education, he did change his mind from the 1940s when, disillusioned with Marxism, he perceived a growing threat of 'declining standards' and 'mediocrity' in the 'unlearned mass'. But his commitment to interdisciplinary general culture, as expressed in his view of classicism and 'humane studies', remained undimmed to the end and bore a strong resemblance to John Henry Newman's view of a liberal education as a good in itself:*

---

* Of course, Anderson would have condemned Newman's view of theology and metaphysics out of hand, but they are allies on the inter-relationship of subjects and disciplines, and the intrinsic value of knowledge as a good.

> Truth is the object of knowledge of whatever kind; and when we inquire what is meant by truth, I suppose it is right to answer that truth means facts and their relations, which stand towards each other pretty much as subjects and predicates in logic. All that exists, as contemplated by the human mind, forms one large system or complex fact, and this of course resolves itself into an indefinite number of particular facts, which, as being portions of a whole, have countless relations of every kind, one towards another. Knowledge is the apprehension of these facts, whether in themselves, or in their mutual positions and bearings. And, as all taken together form one integral subject for contemplation, so there are no natural or real limits between part and part; one is ever running into another; all, as viewed by the mind, are combined together, and possess a correlative character one with another.[17]

Why have I chosen at this time to write a biography of John Anderson? The answer is complex and not entirely clear to me, but it is tied up with the myth of the great man that still lingered in my distant student days, and the philosophers who taught and impressed me at Kensington, among them Ray Walters, Eric Dowling and Jack Thornton, all students of Anderson. Of course, there is also the urgency of 'time's wingéd chariot' as colleagues and former students join the master carousing on Olympus, and there is the sense of threat to the academic institutions and way of life that Anderson strenuously fought for. It is my fond hope that Anderson's story and the values for which he struggled will inspire a younger generation to wage war for those same values on crass utilitarians and present-minded philistines.

Perhaps at this point I should state my own position as a biographer. I am neither an Andersonian nor a Sydney libertarian, nor even a philosopher. Others have been more than willing to help me with the technical aspects of Anderson's realist philosophy, and A. J. Baker's *Australian Realism* provides an excellent exposition of Anderson's general position.[18] Of the many philosophers who have assisted me in my task—too numerous to name individually—I am particularly obliged to John Anderson's son, Sandy. This biography could not have been written without his many vital contributions as critic, informant, counsellor and philosopher. It is a pleasure more than a duty to dedicate this book to him. Of course, the interpretations and judgements are my own as are, unfortunately, all its errors and shortcomings. I also wish to thank Professor Eugene Kamenka for his countless suggestions and amendments to early drafts, and for his hospitality on the two occasions when I was a Visiting Fellow in the History of Ideas Program, Division of Historical Studies in the Australian National University. Professor David Armstrong has helped considerably in the later stages of writing.

In defence of the general biographer, it should be noted that Anderson was always more than just a technical philosopher. To misquote Kipling, what do they know of Anderson who only Anderson know? His public role as a controversialist, stirrer and Socratic gadfly stinging the bourgeoisie about such topical matters as censorship, sex, Communism and religion demands consideration of the whole man in his time and society—Scotland and Australia, Glasgow and Sydney. Whatever else, Anderson possessed moral stamina, intellectual courage and span. He has also provided the biographer with the aesthetic yardstick to measure his art in the objective criteria of realism, relevance, coherence, structure and thematic development:

> Seize hold of things, hammer out the issues, abjure dilettantism in any shape. This is the true attitude of the artist, whose mind . . . permits no ideals or taboos to come between him and a direct handling of things themselves. No sentimental attachments, no higher meanings, no irrelevant antecedents or consequences, are allowed to affect the positive treatment of things, their presentation as a balance of forces or sequence of phases.[19]

Anderson's wide range of intellectual interests, his hellenism and commitment to general culture stemmed, in large measure, from the architectonic character of Scottish education. In fact, there is a direct link between his ideas and the educational theory of John Burnet, the Professor of Greek at

St Andrews from 1892 to 1926; George Davie has explored this in *The Crisis of the Democratic Intellect: The Problem of Generalism and Specialisation in Twentieth Century Scotland.* Anderson lived through a time of fierce educational debate and controversy in Scotland, during which Burnet became the champion of a generalist education for all Arts and Science students based on the trinity of classics, mathematics and philosophy. As Davie comments,

> Throughout the whole length of the ten-year conflict—from his graduation year at Glasgow in 1917 to his departure for the Sydney Chair in 1927—Anderson had, by a fortunate coincidence, been personally associated as student, as lecturer, and as creative thinker with three of the professors most deeply involved in the Scottish educational conflict: George Gibson of Glasgow, under whom he had got a First in mathematics with philosophy, Norman Kemp Smith of Edinburgh whose department he joined in 1920, and John Burnet of St Andrews whose work in Greek philosophy was to be a major influence in his intellectual formation.[20]

A renaissance in Scottish historical and cultural studies over the past two decades has provided me with much new material on the 'intellectual baggage' that Anderson brought with him to the chair at Sydney. It is important to locate John Anderson firmly in the context of Scottish culture and ideas because, unlike Pallas Athena, he did not come fully formed and in full armour out of the sea or the head of Zeus. In my efforts to research the Scottish background, I owe special debts to the Anderson and Baillie families, especially to John Anderson's nieces at Edinburgh, Lesmahagow and Sheffield, and to Jenny Anderson's brother and sister at Hamilton. It would have been a duller book without their contributions.

But though Scotland bred Anderson, Australia made him. If he had remained in Britain, it is unlikely he would have found a chair. Anderson's radical politics, known publicly after the General Strike, would have been held against him by his more conservative colleagues. More serious was the knowledge that a textbook he had written on Freud and logic had been rejected as eccentric by the standards of the time. If Anderson had stayed on in Scotland, he would have had to write detailed technical articles of a kind he never produced until the logic articles of the 1950s, and his general essays on Marxism, aesthetics, cultural criticism and ethics would never have been tolerated by the professionals. Without Australia, the John Anderson we know and admire would never have happened.

In important ways, Anderson's philosophical career and success in Australia bear out the Hartz theory of cultural colonisation.[21] Briefly, Hartz argued that a fragment of Europe breaks away from the mainland and lodges in much more favourable circumstances in the 'new world'; because it does not have to contend with resistances and the 'dialectic' of a well established and complex intellectual life, it is free to flourish in its new environment, unconfined and, for the most part, unopposed. After an early struggle to establish his 'school' of realism, Anderson vanquished the idealists at Sydney and was free to develop his philosophy in a thorough and systematic way that would not have been possible in canny Scotland. Of course, the small departments and god-like authority of the professor of that generation required Anderson to perform single-handedly in many fields—logic, classical philosophy, ethics, aesthetics and political philosophy—but he not merely performed, he excelled, and each field was made part of a greater whole or system.

Today, Scottish cultural and philosophical historians are anxious to re-appropriate Anderson as one of the great exponents of the Scots 'conception of education as humanist, theoretical and critical'. In *The Eclipse of Scottish Culture*, Craig Beveridge and Ronald Turnbull, while lamenting the drab utilitarian character of so much modern education in post-Thatcher Britain, take courage from the many achievements of John Anderson in the struggle against narrow specialisation, present-minded relativism and a crude instrumentalism.

> Anderson is a powerful ally, providing the rigorous, worked-out position which those who attempt to defend humanist education seem mostly to lack. We desperately need his eloquent insistence that education is not training

> or a form of psychotherapy; that there are higher goals than the acquisition of useful skills; that 'the finding of a way of life', and not preparation for everyday life, is the essence of education.[22]

Perhaps we, too, still have much to learn from John Anderson.

SCOTTISH PARTICLE, 1893–1927

A fig for those by law protected!
Liberty's a glorious feast!
Courts for cowards were erected,
Churches built to please the priest!

Robert Burns

1

The 'Dominie'

JOHN ANDERSON liked to believe that he was descended from a gypsy tribe which lived on the Lammermoors, and that this accounted for his striking black eyes and his wanderlust. He thought he found support for this opinion in George Borrow's description of a gypsy:

> The tallest, and, at the first glance, the most interesting of the two, was almost a giant, for his height could not have been less than six feet three. It is impossible for the imagination to conceive anything more perfectly beautiful than were the features of this man, and the most skilful sculptor of Greece might have taken them as his model for a hero and a god. The forehead was exceedingly lofty,—a rare thing in a Gypsy;—the nose less Roman than Grecian,—fine yet delicate; the eyes large, overhung with long drooping lashes, giving them almost a melancholy expression; it was only when they were highly elevated that the Gypsy glance peered out, if that can be called glance which is a strange stare, like nothing else in this world. His complexion—a beautiful olive; and his teeth of a brilliancy uncommon even amongst these people, who have all fine teeth.[1]

Men and women, especially women, have felt the power of John Anderson's stare and smile, and a gypsy alliance or misalliance would make a pretty story to begin. Alas, there are other stories told by members of the Anderson family. John's brother Willie claimed that his father was an elder of the kirk and descended from good Covenanting stock. Gypsies or Covenanters? The Scottish dualism is already at work in family lore and legend.

The dark-haired black-eyed Romany at war with the world sits uneasily with the stern Covenanter fighting and dying for religious liberty, but such clashing images do point to unusual conflicts in the life and struggles of John Anderson. There is the clash of passion and intellect, theory and practice, the romantic and the classicist. Perennial and never-ending conflict was at the heart of John Anderson's view of himself, his philosophy and the world; and the thinkers he most admired—Heraclitus in the ancient world and Hegel, Marx and Freud in the modern—placed conflict and struggle at the centre of their systems. The Scottish city and university that moulded Anderson was also the scene of deep conflicts and tensions. Was it true of his family?

Many roads lead to Alexander Anderson M.A., the schoolmaster and father, and few tracks go beyond him, at which point legend, hearsay and myth-making begin. Alexander was born in 1863 at Aberlady on the Firth of Forth, about twenty miles east of Edinburgh, although it is unlikely that he spent many years there. William, his father, was a shepherd who worked on the Lammermoors and Soutra Mains or Hill, some fifty miles to the south-west, and young Alexander, the child of elderly parents, grew up in the Scottish border country. His love of the countryside, his lifelong interest in botany, Sir Walter Scott's ballads and sheep-dog trials, all stemmed from this border background. With no brothers or sisters, he became self-contained, resourceful and independent, excellent qualities for the 'lad o' pairts' he was to become as he climbed the Scottish educational ladder. During the week he boarded away at school, but on Friday nights he walked the many miles home in all weathers, ringing the changes on the multiplication table for amusement. Mathematics remained his favourite subject.

From the time of John Knox and the Reformation, Scotland had aspired to the ideal of 'a school system which would put religious education and the element of literacy within reach of the whole population through the provision of a school in every parish'.[2] The village school was to afford opportunities to the able so that poverty should be no barrier to talent, and individuals from whatever background should be able to proceed to the university. The three parts of the educational system—parish schools in the countryside, burgh schools in the towns and the universities—were to form a national system, with no social barriers between them:

> Nor Faction's voice nor Dives' nod,
> Nor class nor caste she owns,
> And Peer and Peasant both have trod
> Her well-worn cobble stones.[3]

To bring this democratic ideal closer to reality in a rapidly industrialising society, the Education Act was passed in 1872. This act, the first major incursion by the state into the field of education, established compulsory schooling for children between the ages of five and thirteen. Many handsome new schools were built to be administered by local school boards, and the salaries of schoolteachers raised to make teaching a more attractive career for increasing numbers of men and women.

In 1884 Alexander Anderson took advantage of the educational career open to all talents, and enrolled as an Arts student at Edinburgh University. Latin, Greek and mathematics comprised the core of the traditional general degree, but students were also required to take some classes in mental and moral philosophy as well as science or 'natural philosophy'. During the nineteenth century the tradition of a general education based on the classics and philosophy was being challenged by new specialised subjects of a scientific or commercial character. Yet it is remarkable how strong was the Scottish commitment to the classics, general culture and breadth of study. 'Behind the old Arts curriculum, which held its ground from 1860 to 1892', reflected the Professor of Greek at Aberdeen,

> there lay an Educational idea nothing short of this, that the faculties of the students' mind should be exercised over a diversity of subjects so chosen as to secure that on the conclusion of his University course the whole field of human thought and knowledge should lie open to the graduate.[4]

Alexander graduated M.A. in 1888 to embark on a long career in schoolteaching, first at Port Logan, a fishing village in the Rhinns of Galloway, then in 1892 at Stonehouse in Lanarkshire.

On 31 December 1888 at Glasgow, Alexander also embarked on a long and fruitful marriage with Elizabeth Brown. The Browns hailed from Fauldhouse in West Lothian, where Eliza was one of a large, close-knit family. She taught for some years after completing teacher-training at the Glasgow Normal School, and two of her brothers were also schoolteachers. Eliza was a fine pianist and brought a love of music and gardening to the marriage, tempering Alexander's stern intellectualism with a lively wit and literary sensibility. Children soon arrived. William was born at Kirkmaiden in 1889, Katherine at Stonehouse a few years later, John on 1 November 1893, 'wee Alex', a sickly baby who was carried off by pneumonia in infancy, and Helen, John's favourite sister, in 1897. As the second son, John was named after his mother's father, John Brown.

Stonehouse, where the Anderson children grew up, was a weaving and coal-mining village in Lanarkshire some thirty miles south-west of Glasgow. The working of the Lanarkshire coal seams gave Stonehouse and its neighbouring towns, Blantyre, Larkhall and Lesmahagow, a modicum of prosperity in the mid- to late-nineteenth century. The schoolmaster and his family lived in a comfortable stone schoolhouse on a grassy rise above the grubby town. Perhaps its situation near the kirk symbolised the 'dominie' or schoolmaster's strained position in local society as an outsider with authority. Until the mid-1860s schoolmasters were compelled to sign the Westminster Confession of Faith, and after 1867 they promised 'never . . . to teach or inculcate any opinions opposed to the divine authority of the Holy Scriptures, or to the doctrines contained in the Shorter Catechism'.[5] As the dominie with a position to uphold, Alexander was capable of practising 'occasional conformity' and Victorian decorum to placate the minister and the School Board. Not all the family were so obliging, however. When one Sabbath a lugubrious preacher kept on intoning 'for we like sheep have gone astray', Kate Anderson made bleating sounds. Alexander was publicly affronted and confined her to her room for the day.

The large, two-storeyed stone school in Camnethan Street was imposing for such a small stinted town and all the Anderson children went there, rubbing shoulders with the children of miners, weavers and labourers. The democratic ethos of Scottish education was grounded in gritty reality. To discipline unruly children, the dominie made use of his commanding physical presence, a domineering manner and, when all else failed, a

Map of Anderson's Scotland

good belting with the tawse. He operated with power and venom. One 'Camnethan bound' pupil later recalled:

> Authority over staff, dominance over pupils, unpredictable in mood, he veered like the winds, with blasts of the wilder not experienced here, we rarely enjoyed the full balmy day, if only a gentle breeze was astir we were lucky. His control over us was absolute, parents approved liberal use of the strap, and the namby-pamby sympathetic ear was not yet attuned, being at the moment deaf to juvenile complaint . . . One peculiar, but certain, sign, by which all could read him like a barometer, seemed determined by the growth of his beard; when newly trimmed his eye sharpened, the jaw protruded, he acted as grumpily and huffily as a bear with a sore back, gradually mellowing with the process of growth, until reaching his best when at his fuzziest.[6]

At home, where disputation and argument flourished during meals, the Anderson children knew a softer side to the man—his infectious curiosity about most things but especially the countryside, plants and animals, his delight in reading and giving presents, usually second-hand books bought from the Glasgow Barras or weekend market, and his penchant for organisation and radical causes. The latter was not to everyone's taste.

His attitude to religion is a case in point. Whatever his earlier beliefs and practice (and some of the family claim he had once aspired to be a minister), as John grew up his father cast off conventional religion to espouse a doctrinaire socialism of a strongly secular character. He became an active member of the Independent Labour Party, founded by Keir Hardie in 1893. On Sunday afternoons, in hat, suit and tie, the dominie strode the several miles to address the crowds on socialism at Garrion Brig, a local market and fairground in the Clyde Valley. Young John could not have escaped his father's strenuous life of political and social commitment—what Anderson male would have wanted to?—but more than this, he exulted in the affection and notoriety of being his father's close accomplice and associate in unpopular causes, often accompanying him on his expeditions to the Brig. By the age of ten John Anderson was a convinced socialist and 'no longer wanted to be good'. He felt no diffidence or twinges of embarrassment about his father's radicalism and political causes. Years later in Australia he addressed a meeting of unemployed men in Newcastle in the depths of the depression. When they asked the visiting professor from Sydney why he was a socialist, Anderson pondered before replying, 'Well, I suppose it is because my father was'. It was more than just a shrewd answer.

In later life, when John, his brother and sister had emigrated, Alexander was to leave the Labour Party to become an ardent Communist. Thorough in everything, the retired teacher worked indefatigably as an organiser and party speaker, becoming known in the small mining town of Lesmahagow as 'Old Trotsky'. Perhaps it was the grizzled beard and rimless spectacles that suggested a resemblance. Like Trotsky, too, Alexander Anderson was no ordinary worker, for while a framed portrait of Lenin, 'the workers' only friend', occupied a prominent place in his study, there was also a black bust of Plato. His wide intellectual interests and active curiosity remained constant, the number of his books grew to fill all the walls of a large study, and he became a benign if catechising grandfather to the children of his youngest daughter, who grew up next door at Lesmahagow. Among many things, he taught them to sing the 'Internationale'. A dominie, a free-thinker and a Communist. Was his father William, the border shepherd, the connecting thread between Alexander's rural past and the local miners, whose sons and daughters he had taught and who were now the hope of the world?

Eliza Anderson was a gentle and cultivated person who sometimes found Alexander a difficult man to live with. A Fabian socialist with wide literary and musical interests, she tried to share her husband's political enthusiasms until she became disenchanted with the Communist Party. There must have been some difficulties in the marriage, but whether the dominie helped to drive his wife to a nervous breakdown during the First World War when her favourite son, Willie, was away at the front, and to intermittent periods in an asylum, remains another tantalising family 'secret'. She was certainly absent from home for an extended period in 1918 and John believed she was undergoing psychiatric treatment, an experience which may have greatly stimulated his interest in Freud.

Did Eliza also find John a demanding and difficult son to nurture? It seems she preferred the more phlegmatic first-born William, and long mourned the loss of her fourth child, 'wee Alex', whose death may have clouded relations with the nearest child to him. Did John turn to his father out of his mother's seeming indifference and rejection of him, and was the strong bond between father and son meant in some way to punish her? 'Earth hath no hate *but* love to hatred turned, and hell no fury but a baby scorned'.[7] Such intriguing speculations form the stuff of psycho-history and, while there is no finality in the matter, there is evidence to point to some underlying tensions in the family and an uneasy pattern of authority. The carefully posed family portrait of 1905 suggests some of these difficulties, particularly the young John's insistent relationship with his father. But at this stage oedipal rivalry was less important than sibling rivalry between the brothers. John supported Celtic because Willie barracked for Rangers. In academic matters, it was to be a fruitful tension, for in John's passionate efforts to outvie his older brother he won distinctions, bursaries, medals and prizes—all necessary to scale the heights of the Scottish educational system. One of them enabled him to attend Hamilton Academy, a private fee-paying school in the main centre of North Lanarkshire and the seat of the Dukes of Hamilton. There, between 1907 and 1910 he completed his secondary education and assiduously prepared himself for entrance to the university, specialising in English, higher mathematics and higher Greek. But did his mother see through the defence mechanism to the inner uncertainty? When in 1911 John won first place in the bursary competition to Glasgow University, she said, 'Our Willie won the second prize and so John had to go one better'. Hardly warm praise. No matter; prizes were means to an educational end, an end that was embodied in his father's fierce and productive character. Alexander was undoubtedly the single greatest positive influence on the young John

Anderson. He provided a compelling model of the disinterested pursuit of truth, whatever the cost in human and conjugal happiness. Thus fortified and encouraged, the gypsy-scholar with the dark eyes and willowy good looks set off to join the educational flagship in the second city of the British empire. It was to become the object of Anderson's most intense desire and loyalty.

2

Gypsy City—Divided Mind

GLASGOW was originally two small but closely linked settlements. One clustered round the twelfth century cathedral, built above the tomb of St Mungo, and it comprised the houses of churchmen, those who worked for them, and those who traded with them. The other grew up around a ford to the south, the lowest crossing of the Clyde. Concentration of traffic across the river at this point resulted in the growth of a small trading village, while some of the villagers also fished for salmon to sell to the cathedral. Soon the path between the two settlements was lined with houses. As prosperity increased, large stone houses were built nearby for rich merchants and a university or 'College' was established by Bishop William Turnbull in 1451 mid-way between the commercial and ecclesiastical centres.

The city began to rise from its medieval slumber in the seventeenth century but even in 1723 its green meadows and open spaces impressed Daniel Defoe, who described it as 'one of the cleanliest, most beautiful, and best built, cities in Britain'. During the eighteenth century its success was built on a thriving trade with the colonies—sugar from the West Indies, tobacco from Virginia and slaves from West Africa. At this time the commercial hub of the city moved west to George Square, where 'tobacco lords' and merchants built elegant townhouses and solid warehouses. Above a grid street plan the commercial city rose, monumental, handsome and uncompromising in sooty stone. Alexander 'Greek' Thomson and other busy architects of the nineteenth century gave the Victorian city a surfeit of churches, banks, railway stations and hotels built in a medley of historical styles, from Egyptian and Greek Revival to Scots Renaissance. A municipal palace of granite and marble towered over George Square and its statues of Sir Walter Scott, Sir John Moore, Sir Colin Campbell, James Watt and Robert Burns.

Merchants, enterprise and the river dominated the future and from the late eighteenth century the Clyde was regularly dredged and widened to allow large ships to approach the city. Glasgow's great successes in the industrial revolution were based upon cheap energy and abundant raw materials. The new textile, chemical and shipbuilding industries also required a vast influx of labour, and population grew rapidly from 28 000 in 1765 to 202 000 in 1831 and 547 000 in 1871. Much of the increase came from the Highlands after the clearances and from Ireland after the famine, making Glasgow a peculiarly Celtic city. Its ethos, so unlike the ancient capital in the east, was a strange compound of nobility and vulgarity, respectability and vice, of lowlands prudence and Gaelic recklessness. Immigrants crowded into the decayed old town and neighbouring suburbs south and east of Glasgow Common. South of the river, the Gorbals soon became a byword for urban squalor, disease and overcrowding; yet tenement life also bred the amazing human warmth and resilience of 'Glesca'. In the gypsy life of the shawled dishevelled poor, shifting for shelter in the 'wynds' or alleys of the slum, the pawnbroker was as necessary for survival as the corner pub. On Saturday nights bouts of heroic drinking preceded the sober, gloomy Sabbath. Glasgow without whisky was as inconceivable as Glasgow without sermons.

The city's topography reinforced the class divide as the wealthy took advantage of new forms of transport to escape the congested centre and busy river for the amenities, fresh air and fine views of hilly Kelvinside. The leafy middle-class suburbs were all in the west. In 1870 the university also moved from its old cramped quarters in the High Street to a spacious site above the river and gardens at Kelvingrove; along the summit of Gilmorehill Sir George Gilbert Scott built his vast and dour

Gothic pile surmounted by a high turretted tower and spire, and flanked by a row of professor's houses.

When John Anderson went up to the university in 1911, Scott's stone buildings comfortably accommodated the five faculties and their professors. Lecture halls, laboratories and a library served over two thousand undergraduates, most of them young men. For students and townspeople, this was the university; yet the institution that the young Anderson joined was much older than the mock Gothic buildings. Scottish universities were founded in late medieval or renaissance times and looked to the Continent for their intellectual sustenance and traditions. Something of the medieval map of knowledge—the *quadrivium* and *trivium*—still persisted in the general degree of the Faculty of Arts, 'seven compulsory subjects and no nonsense', comprising Latin, Greek, mathematics, natural philosophy, logic, moral philosophy and English. In its reforming ordinance of 1908 Glasgow sought to preserve the architectonic character of this curriculum by insisting that all Arts students study logic or moral philosophy, mathematics or a science, and a language.

In the fierce educational controversies of the next decade, Professor John Burnet of St Andrews became the staunch defender of the Scottish tradition of general education with philosophy as the corner-stone:

> It seems clear to me that in one form or another Philosophy ought to hold the central place in the stage of education we are now considering. That is in accordance with Scottish tradition, and I am convinced it was just this that enabled Scotland to do as well as it did in the past . . . It is the study of philosophy alone that can help a young man to approach all other studies aright, and can save him from the narrowing influences of special study. In many cases it can bring about a change of spirit almost as great as a religious conversion.[1]

The 'truly democratic ideal of *la carrière ouverte aux talents* [the career open to talent]' was another tradition lauded by Burnet, who became one of Anderson's heroes.

Unlike Oxford or Cambridge, Glasgow was not a collegiate or residential university. Students lived at home or in lodgings, fees were cheap, and the university more accessible to the wider community. Hence, Glasgow attracted a much higher proportion of working-class students than Edinburgh. Some of them became socialists and schoolteachers, which was an important ingredient in the making of 'Red Clydeside' during the war. The Union was the real centre of student life, and Union Nights fostered a strong debating tradition among male students. Although many students worked over the long summer vacation to pay for the winter session, bursaries and the new Carnegie Trust scholarships enabled the brightest and best to attend the university without having to work. John Buchan was one of the fortunate:

> Things have changed now, but in my day a Scottish university still smacked of the Middle Ages. The undergraduates lived in lodgings in the city and most of them cultivated the Muses on a slender allowance of oatmeal. Every morning I had to walk four miles to the eight o'clock class through every variety of the winter weather with which Glasgow fortifies her children . . . fog like soup, drenching rains, winds that swirled down the cavernous streets, mornings that dawned bright and clear over snow . . . My summers were spent in blessed idleness, fishing, tramping and bicycling up and down the Lowlands. But my winters were periods of beaver-like toil and monkish seclusion. I returned home early each afternoon and thereafter was at my books until midnight.[2]

Above all, the authority of the professor was absolute. The pattern was to appoint a notable scholar, provide him with a gaunt classroom, and to require him, in professorial isolation, to educate his men by delivering a course of lectures from October to March. There were no tutorials to soften the formality of the system, and much depended on the lectures that were delivered slowly and with great deliberation to facilitate note-taking. Lectures began promptly at five minutes past eight with a prayer: 'Almighty God, with whom are hid all the treasures of wisdom and knowledge, Enlighten us with the vision of truth, inspire us with the love of wisdom, And enable us to find freedom in our knowledge of Thee'. Gilbert Murray recognised dangers in the system, particularly the temptation for professors to become 'dignitaries', isolated from their students, but often strong teachers attracted 'something akin to hero-worship' in their students.

The pride and confidence of the university was vindicated by much high thinking, hard work and solid achievement. During the Enlightenment, to take a striking example, the chair of Philosophy was occupied by Thomas Reid, Francis Hutcheson and Adam Smith. Moreover, Scottish universities were regarded as 'national institutions', established by law, supported from public funds, and supervised by the authorities of church and state. As the Principal of St Andrews declared, 'The Scottish Universities are not private corporations—they are national seats of learning, existing for the nation, and controlled by the Parliament of the nation. And the Universities have no wish to become independent of the State, or to be removed from the control of the State'.[3]

That professors of philosophy, if not quite philosopher kings, should still exercise a dominant influence on the university and its students is no surprise, given the central role of philosophy in the Scottish curriculum and the importance of the Arts Faculty in the university. In addition, the incumbents at Glasgow had abilities of a high order and attractive and forceful personalities. Edward Caird, a quiet Scot with 'massive dignity and reserve of character and of speech', held the chair from 1866, while his brother was Principal or Vice-Chancellor. Both were Hegelians and orthodox Christians. According to Gilbert Murray, who took up the chair of Greek in the early 1890s, 'the two Cairds compelled one's admiration and respect—Edward, the great philosopher who was afterwards Master of Balliol, and John, the Principal, who was a famous preacher in the old dignified school of eloquence'.[4] In these years Thomas Carlyle's influence was at its zenith and the waters of the Rhine flowed strongly into the Clyde. It was important to be earnest.

Caird's successor was the fiery and combative Henry Jones, who, from 1894 to his death in 1922, carried on the tradition of Absolute Idealism at Glasgow. Jones was the self-made philosopher and professor under whom John Anderson studied and against whose doctrines the young man passionately reacted. Born in 1852 in the village of Llangernyw in Wales, Jones was the son of the shoemaker. After leaving the village school he worked in his father's shop and became an enthusiastic member of the Calvinistic Methodist chapel. At that time, Jones said, 'I had two mastering ambitions, both of them at once strong and steady. One was to become a first-rate shoemaker, and the other was to be made an elder in the little Calvinistic Methodist chapel, when I was a man'.[5] Some years later he taught as a pupil teacher in Welsh schools and then a 'calling' to the Wesleyan ministry led him to apply for a scholarship to the University of Glasgow, which he won in 1875. At the university he came under the spell of Professor Edward Caird, who impressed him with 'the openness of his mind, the breadth of his outlook, the sincerity and depth of his convictions, the impressiveness of his personality'. As Jones himself confessed, 'I was born in Llangernyw in 1852, and born again in 1876 in Edward Caird's classroom'.[6]

Caird and Jones blended Hegel's system with their own ethical and religious concerns to promote a secularised and liberal version of Protestant Christianity for their students, many of whom were destined for the ministry. Drawing on a wide range of literary, historical and philosophical sources, Jones developed his rhetorical style of address. Of spare and wiry physique, his eyes ablaze, he spoke to his students with the stirring vehemence and fervour of a missionary out to make converts:

> Hegel and Goethe, Carlyle and Wordsworth—the poetic imagination in them catching first the rosy light of the new dawn and their philosophy following and broadening the light into clearness and calm of the common day—these poet-philosophers, I say, are unique amongst their peers; and they are unique precisely in this—that they teach the world as it was never taught before, in any age, how sacred it all is and how interfused with the light divine.[7]

At the most fundamental level, idealists maintained the primacy of consciousness or mind in all forms of knowledge: 'Philosophy is an attitude of mind, rather than a doctrine. It is the experience of the world becoming reflective, and endeavouring to comprehend itself. Hence a final philosophic theory is not to be attained, and a fixed system is not to be sought'.[8] Evolutionary assumptions were built into the unfolding dialectic of 'becoming', a seemingly blind process which culminated in the emergence of Spirit or Absolute Mind. In his lectures, Jones preached the immanence of God in history and nature: 'If man is to find God he must find Him in the world he knows, as its very substance and essential being'.[9] But Jones was too independent and unorthodox a thinker to satisfy his fundamentalist countrymen. 'They are told', said a friend, 'that you deny the divinity of Christ'. 'I!', exclaimed Jones, 'I deny the divinity of Christ! I do not deny the divinity of any man'.[10] Jones' religion of humanity closely followed the views of Strauss and Feuerbach, and naturally aroused suspicion in the evangelical circles from which he sprang. In 1881 Professor Robertson Smith had been tried for heresy and dismissed from his teaching post by the Free Kirk because of his sympathy with the 'higher criticism' of German biblical scholarship. Jones was a self-reliant Protestant and no one's catspaw.

Freedom was the leading theme of his political philosophy, as befitted a Welsh Liberal and a staunch friend and supporter of Lloyd George. Although an impassioned expositor and populariser, Jones was not an original thinker and drew heavily on the work of T. H. Green and Bernard Bosanquet. Following closely in the steps of Hegel, he traced the development of the idea of freedom from the Greek city-state through the Reformation to the French Revolution and the modern world. According to one of his students, the central theme of the whole course was the idea of freedom:

> He sought to show how that idea passed from the negative meaning of absence of external restraint, through the notion of self-determination, to the positive conception of the self's discovery of its kinship with the objective structures of the physical and moral worlds, and of its self-realisation through participation in them. His course was for his students a searching and often a difficult experience.[11]

Jones stressed the ethical side of this process, and resolved the conflict between the individual and social duty in terms of a higher, inner obedience to the state as 'the Kingdom of Heaven on Earth'. 'It is life *within* the State; it is the life *of* the State within its members, for his duties to himself are duties to the State'.[12] Such doctrines were to exact a heavy price in the coming world war.

Jones took his public and political duties very seriously to become a dominant influence in Wales and the west of Scotland. In 1912, on Lloyd George's instigation, he accepted a knighthood 'for little Wales' and the recognition of his subject. His lectures on 'Social Responsibilities' proclaimed his gospel to an audience of shrewd Glasgow businessmen gathered in the city:

> the State or the city and its citizens have only one life . . . In other words, the Individualist must be brought to see that his dependence on society is much more close than he deems, and the Socialist that the welfare of society depends on providing for the individual the means for the most vigorous growth of an independent personality—means which include, amongst other things, full rights of private property and full scope for private enterprise.[13]

In arguments about the relationship between the individual and society, Jones drew on the Scottish 'common sense' view of their mutual interdependence and on the new liberalism with its criticism of unfettered individualism and *laissez-faire* economics. Such criticisms were sorely needed in the second city of the empire.

In the late nineteenth century Glasgow's population doubled from half a million in 1871 to about a million in 1914. This growth was dependent on an economic base of iron and steel and heavy engineering. Shipbuilding was the great success story and by the turn of the century 'the Clyde was responsible for one-third of British tonnage and one-half of its engine power'.[14] Famous firms like Beardmores and Browns were run on family lines and benefited greatly from the skills and enterprise of independent foremen and craftsmen. Trade unions were beginning to emerge, but were comparatively weak because of craft traditions and the pool of cheap unskilled labour.

Glasgow was a gypsy city when it came to housing. Homeownership was lower than in any other major British city, although urban densities were very much higher. By 1914 no less than 700 000 people lived in three square miles at the centre, thus creating the most densely populated city in Europe. While the world of the four- or five-storey tenement had its close-knit human side, moonlight flits to avoid the factor or rent-collector became common practice. Poor and congested housing conditions were at the root of the city's social and public health problems. In 1917 a royal commission described the situation:

> . . . insufficient supplies of water, unsatisfactory provision for drainage, grossly inadequate provision for the removal of refuse, widespread absence of decent sanitary conveniences, the persistence of unspeakably filthy privy-middens . . . gross overcrowding and huddling of the sexes together . . . occupation of one-room houses by large families, groups of lightless and unventilated houses in the older burghs, clotted masses of slums in the great cities.[15]

Such housing conditions contributed to high rates of infant mortality, tuberculosis, alcoholism, and mass ill health among schoolchildren.

In the years that John Anderson attended the university, Glasgow became one of the major centres of labour unrest and socialism in the United Kingdom. As T. C. Smout writes:

> The younger generation were offered a rich variety of red-blooded socialist things to do . . . One might begin at a very tender age as a member of a socialist Sunday school or join the Clarion Scouts distributing ILP [Independent Labour Party] literature, or subscribe to *Forward*, Tom Johnston's lively ILP newspaper founded in 1906, or attend one of the innumerable lectures and meetings in the Glasgow halls where the principles of the ILP, or the SDF [Social Democratic Federation], or the SLP [Socialist Labour Party], or the syndicalists, or the secularists, or the anarchists, were propounded. For the most serious-minded there were the evening classes of the Workers' Educational Association, and, most rigorous of all, those of John MacLean, Govan schoolteacher and member of the SDF, anti-militarist, revolutionary, whose teaching of 'Marxian

> economics' at times attracted classes of over a thousand. Then there was the artistic side, drawn from old connections with William Morris' Socialist League in the 1880s, which attracted men like the young poet Edwin Muir at the time of the First World War. *Forward* advertised piano lessons, and Hugh Robertson's Glasgow Orpheus Choir became in the 1930s the most famous amateur choir in the world; it was the most important manifestation of the cultural aspects of the ILP.[16]

Anderson's father was one of those schoolteachers who became a socialist and anticleric, challenging what was being taught in the state schools. The depressing experience of teaching children in the slums contributed significantly to political awareness and radicalism. A young graduate wrote about his first school:

> The playground was a small area laid with concrete. The rooms were overcrowded, and the children were ill-clad. Looking back now, I realise that the majority of them were obviously suffering from malnutrition and some of them from actual hunger. Some came to school with no breakfast, and others with only tea and bread and butter. Going round between the seats one could see the lice crawling on their heads and on their clothing. We were supposed to teach them grammar, arithmetic and all the other subjects in the educational curriculum. I went home the first night feeling physically sick and very depressed.[17]

Other experiences in Glasgow confronted the young Anderson with the plight of the poor, unemployed and thriftless. A university settlement had been established by Henry Drummond in Possil Park, one of the worst slums in Glasgow, to involve students in the life and problems of the poor. It began in the 1880s as an attempt to evangelise the urban masses but, with the encouragement of Caird and Jones, it acquired broader aims of social amelioration and information-gathering. Both William and John Anderson lived in the settlement for lengthy periods. The settlement occupied a four-storey tenement near a distillery and the dozen students in residence enjoyed 'the warm smooth smell of burnt barley which wrapped you around'.

Philosophy was a dominant interest so that 'Kant's Critique and the screech of tram-wheels on tram-lines' were inextricably mixed.[18]

The settlement conducted educational classes in the neighbourhood and Professors Jones and Latta were regular speakers. A medical dispensary was set up and free legal advice given. Students visited local families and encountered at first hand the dirt, smells and overcrowding of Glasgow's notorious 'single-ends'. Entire families lived in one-room apartments, often a kitchen, off a 'close' or narrow courtyard, and inspectors 'ticketed' the smaller houses in an effort to prevent unhealthy crowding. Most families were over the limit and had to hide children with neighbours when the inspector called. A settlement student, William Boyd, was asked to conduct the funeral of a small girl who had fallen into boiling water; 'as she lay in her coffin, her eyes were closed with coins'.[19] The two Andersons, as settlement students, interacted with Glasgow's seamy side on a daily basis, as they attended the university at Kelvinside and pondered the lofty ideals of Professor Jones. The latter exhorted his audience to 'do their best to bridge the gulf that separated the well-to-do from the poor, and foster mutual understanding and goodwill by social intercourse; so that the nation might be one body and its members bound together in one fellowship'.[20] Perhaps such noble thoughts and confident hopes seemed more real in Miss Cranston's art nouveau tea rooms in Sauchiehall Street than in the spirituous fumes and grimy fetid neighbourhood of the settlement.

3

The Undergraduate

JOHN ANDERSON won first place in the University bursary competition of 1911 and came to Glasgow a shy and awkward lad with brilliant prospects. But John's successes were soon overshadowed by his brother's golden achievements. On 16 November 1911 William Anderson graduated Master of Arts with first class honours in moral philosophy, 'one of the best . . . candidates we have had for a long time', according to his professor.[1] One year later he joined Professor Robert Latta's department as a junior lecturer in logic. Academic rivalry with his brother was for John a spur to success, and would be an element in his relationship with the woman he was to woo and marry.

There are problems in understanding Anderson's undergraduate career, both in the formal academic sense and in terms of his personal development and interests. John Anderson was unusual in doing *two* honours degrees, not a combined degree, one of them in mathematics and natural philosophy, the other in logic and moral philosophy. After first year Greek, Latin and mathematics, he spent three years studying mathematics and natural philosophy, with some laboratory work; and then embarked on another three years of moral philosophy, logic and political economy. Hence his academic record embodied to an exceptional degree the generalist character of Scottish education. It also helps to make sense of his strong interest in science and mathematics in his philosophical development.

Anderson's two degrees account for the length of his stay at university—seven years or academic sessions, including his 'sabbatical' year in experimental psychology after graduation in 1917, compared to the mandatory four years for the M.A. degree. In other words, he became something of a professional undergraduate. Seven years in university parlance means two student generations, so that Anderson's career spanned the pre-war and war generation of students, an important distinction. He felt keenly the frailty of the university as an institution and its loss of certain vital traditions in wartime. Without the buoyant pre-war experience of university life, however, John Anderson may have been less of a champion of the intellectual values of the university, and less concerned about the encroachment of military, commercial and vocational pressures. There was a war to be waged within the university no less than on the Somme, and Anderson thought the outcome of one could well affect the other.

John's somewhat unusual degree path is curious in the light of his brother's more straightforward degree in philosophy and raises a number of questions. How far did John embark on a mathematics and science degree out of genuine interest in the subjects, how far to succeed in a field of his own? Excel he certainly did, winning first place in the mathematics honours class and the Cunninghame gold medal in 1915. Having achieved that feat, did John then join the philosophy stream to match his brother on his home ground, even if it was the unappealing terrain of idealism and Sir Henry Jones, or was he simply captivated by philosophy in academic mid-stream? The irony is that by this time, 1915, fate and the First World War intervened to change the competitors, rules and prizes of the struggle. William, a member of the Officers' Training Corps, enlisted in the Army Ordnance Corps and was called up for military service early in 1917. The university granted him leave. John, it seems, failed his medical test through poor eyesight, but one wonders how genuine was his desire to join the army and what he would have done if he had been conscripted. While he wore uniform at classes, his attitude to the war was complex and ambiguous. A strong anti-war and pacifist movement existed in 'Red Clydeside', led by Guy Aldred and John

MacLean, but Scottish Idealism and Sir Henry Jones pointed in another direction. Outwardly, the young Anderson subscribed to this latter position in a prize essay:

> The present war would seem to be an unsettling of the conditions of concerted action by the European powers. But it is not to be regarded simply as a conflict of two interests within the whole. It would appear, rather, under the category of rebellion, one nation endeavouring to act independently of the society of nations, or trying to bring that society under its domination as the State of States. And so the action of the Allies might be compared to punishment, or to the putting down by a state of an attempted rebellion. The defeat of Germany would bring about once more the conditions of social peace.[2]

The questions posed here about Anderson and the war are important because in the long run the war experience was to undermine British Idealism and liberalism and to bring socialism nearer centre stage. Of course, Anderson was not to know all this in 1917—though it was the year of the Russian Revolution, and Anderson saw more clearly ahead than many. In these circumstances it is useful to employ a distinction between the 'public' and 'private' Anderson—the 'public' student, contending for the glittering prizes and the favour of Sir Henry Jones, and the 'private' undergraduate, criticising and challenging the orthodoxies of the day. It is a familiar phenomenon, but in someone as intellectually ambitious and as ambivalent about authority as John Anderson, it is very striking. For John Anderson, the winner of the university's prestigious silver medal, the Edward Caird and Thomas Logan prizes, the Ferguson scholarship and the Shaw Fellowship, was also the iconoclastic editor of the *Glasgow University Magazine* during the war years. 'You have got to humour your professors', counselled a contemporary, and to a close friend Anderson confided some amusing thoughts on doing philosophy under Professor Jones:

> There is a kind of atmosphere about it (which I might call 'religious' or perhaps 'poetical') which gets on my nerves. Yesterday I was listening to Sir Henry in a state of mental anguish and, as he was looking intently at me all the time,

> I had to try to get my features to represent intelligent interest combined with rapt admiration. Consequently by the end of the hour I was in a state of collapse.[3]

Turning aside from the formidable academic achievement, what influences at the university and in Glasgow helped to make the private undergraduate into a rebel? Anderson began his active involvement in student life in second year, when he was a boarder with a family in Hillhead. His first appearance was at a Union debate. 'Mr. J. Anderson was earnest and Socialistic', commented the student paper, 'He must learn to appeal to the imagination as well as to the reason'.[4] Within a short time he found his niche in the disputations of the Philosophical and Fabian Societies, and in November 1914 was elected to represent the Arts students on the Students' Representative Council.

In numerous articles to the university magazine John Anderson began to assume the persona of 'Jude'. The association with the tragic hero of Hardy's novel that so outraged Victorian society a decade before was clearly present in the mind of Anderson and his contemporaries. 'I had almost forgotten to tell you about my pseudonym', he wrote to a friend. 'The reason why I use it is that it is pithy and expressive, and has the literary connection of Hardy's "Jude the Obscure" '.[5] Jude is the quintessential outsider, rustic atheist, scourge of Victorian conventions, and excluded forever from the colleges of Christminster. The mask helped Anderson cultivate a certain wry detachment from the hothouse atmosphere of academic life and competition, and gave him licence to goad sacred cows. 'Jude' regularly mocked temperance advocates as narrow-minded prigs; like Burns, he celebrated the social pleasures and conviviality of drinking and the public house. In one philosophical piece, he cleverly used drinking to bring out the difference between a realist and idealist view of the world:

> The wise man drinks his beer, he absorbs it, he makes it part of himself. He is in the realm, not of the ideal, but of the real, for he knows what he is getting, and he makes sure that he gets it. The foolish youth gazes at the pictures [in the cinema], and thinks he is sharing a pleasure with his fair companion, that he is taking part in a joint ex-

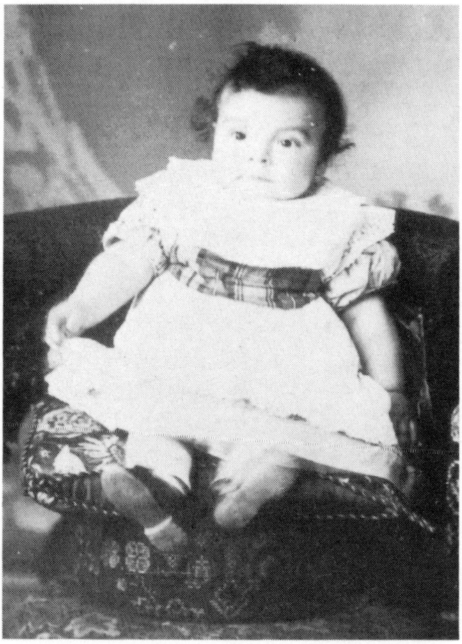

The young John Anderson, at about twelve months

The Anderson family: (left to right) *John's paternal grandmother Ellen, brother Willie, father Alexander, John, sister Katherine (Katie), mother Elizabeth, sister Helen (Nellie). John seems to lean insistently towards his father.*

The 'Dominie', Alexander Anderson M.A., as a young man

The schoolhouse at Stonehouse was home to the Anderson family

The school in Camnethan Street, Stonehouse

Rubbing shoulders with the proletariat at Camnethan Primary School. John is second from the right, second row.

The winners of the bursary competition, 1911: (left to right) *'Little John' Kennedy, Janet (Jenny) Baillie, J. A., Selby Campbell, Ellen Hill, Arthur Robertson*

The crème de la crème*: the matriculation class at Hamilton Academy. John is on the left, front row.*

> perience. He deceives himself, for he can only experience things for himself. He is an Idealist, and he is deservedly damned.[6]

In another playful piece about Nietzsche's influence on the university, Jude wrote in December 1914, just after the outbreak of war:

> The innate sense of duty in the breast of every student must prompt him to come to the aid of his country, and, at the same time, of his University. Revenue is urgently required. Every man must have asked himself, 'What can I do?' To this we unhesitatingly reply 'DRINK BEER!' Thus can a man best serve his University, his country and humanity.[7]

Among the idealists, T. H. Green had been a strong advocate of state intervention to regulate the sale and distribution of liquor on the grounds of the 'common good' and the vulnerability of the poor to alcohol—their need to be protected from their worst selves. Professor Jones, influenced by his Wesleyan background, endorsed this position and during the war vigorously campaigned for severe restrictions to the drink trade in the Clyde Valley. Anderson the student was taking some risk in ridiculing the prigs and wowsers.

Jude's writings were not all of a piece—sometimes the undergraduate frivolity and satire gave way to a mood of ironic pessimism, as in the following example:

> Hjalmar Madwig lived with his mother in a lonely house by the side of a fjord. He was a solemn child, but industrious and obedient. On week-days he rose early in the morning and trudged off to school, five miles away, and on Sundays he accompanied his mother to the little church beside the fjord. One evening he returned from school with a puzzled look in his eyes, and said, 'Mother, who am I?' 'Alas', replied his mother, 'I do not know'.
>
> The next morning his body was found floating peacefully in the fjord.[8]

Anderson's favourite objects of ridicule were pomposity, conceit, hypocrisy and stupidity, qualities he usually associated with organised religion. 'I object to any religion whatever', he wrote early in 1917. Jude was also a shortened form of Judas. In a portrait of a Lancashire philanthropist, Joseph Makepeace, Jude exposed the self-serving platitudes of the unctuous businessman. Through a system of spying and informing, Makepeace exercised a near total control over the lives of his workers. He opened a temperance club at night:

> And there of an evening they might amuse themselves with draughts or dominoes instead of cards and sporting papers, and drink coffee instead of beer and whisky. A carefully selected list of the most respectable English periodicals was also supplied, but the reading of books was discouraged as tending to subvert religion and morality. Another achievement of Joseph's was the erection of a chapel for his workmen . . .

When the worm turned, however, and the men went out on strike, Makepeace was astonished:

> What did they want? he demanded, taking careful note of the identity of his interviewers. More wages? Had they not the club? Had they not the church? Had they not the multifarious advantages of his system? What could they want more wages for, except for gambling and drink? And that he could not allow.

An unfortunate accident resulted in his premature death. 'The philanthropist finds no reward in this world', Jude reflects, 'But surely he finds it in heaven'.[9]

To develop his more extended philosophical themes of scepticism, nihilism and despair, Anderson turned to allegory. A particularly notable example, written in December 1917 after he had graduated, enabled him to engage in much more adventurous speculations of an anti-idealist kind. Anderson called this piece 'A Fable':

> There was once a young man who wondered about Life. He was for ever trying to find out what it meant and what it was for. Yet he was not a Russian; far from it . . . In point of fact, he read far too much. That was his complaint. But being as God had made him, he spent his time wonder-

> ing about life and endeavouring to find out what was the good of it. His books did not help him . . . they merely fostered in him a critical and dissatisfied spirit, and *that* did not cut much ice in the affairs of the world. But it drove him to go about asking questions in order to discover what different people took as their aim in life . . . For he was of opinion that the glittering show meant *something*, if only he could get at it.

Those who explained the end of life as wealth, position, power and success failed to satisfy the young man, 'for he saw that none of these things could be good in itself; they were all instrumental, or at least incomplete . . . so that the end was still to seek, because it was still to be discovered what a man was to use his wealth or power or position for'. Others defended pleasure as their goal, but this did not satisfy him either because 'he could not think that pleasure was their aim, if pleasure by its very nature was incapable of being an aim'.

Cultured folks pointed to beauty and art and love. Their explanations were also found wanting 'because love was always love of something, and they had not told him what that was'. The men of science pleased him better, 'for they told him that the end of life was knowledge'. But their practice was much less convincing. 'It was the same everywhere he went'. Moralists could not define freedom. Humanists could not justify their service to humanity. 'No one could explain on what principles he governed his life, nor how *any one* could lead a rational life'. Not even a priest could help. He only accused the young man of rationalism and 'bade him begone'.

> Thus the young man did not find out from any one what was the purpose of life, nor could he discover it for himself. But he did not despair and die, like the hero of a Russian novel. No, he went up and down lecturing to people to show them the inadequacy of their views and the foolishness of their lives. And he was handsomely paid for it.[10]

The fable was not just a young man's exuberant *jeu d'esprit* but also a pointer to important themes in the later life. It almost seems to anticipate his controversial role at the University of

Sydney. There was the task of the Socratic gadfly, stinging the complacent, the philistines and experts, the sharp wit and irony of the social critic, the distinction between intrinsic and extrinsic ends, and the tough-minded realist conclusion.

As editor of the university magazine, Anderson greatly enjoyed the Bohemian atmosphere and late-night sessions that characterised the enterprise of student journalism. G. K. Chesterton's cheerful pugnacity and love of paradox directly influenced him. So too did Bertrand Russell's essays. In all these high spirited activities, his hero and model was Alfred Richard Orage of the *New Age*, who exemplified the ideal of a cultural alliance between advanced intellectuals and the workers. In important ways, Anderson remained a journalist-*manqué*, working to deadlines in a hurry, and relishing the coterie atmosphere and hedonism of a literary Bohemia. But what did other students think of their young editor? A magazine piece gives the following impression:

> And surely Jude is of the true Italian stock. He stands in dignified silence, as one who, near some great crossing in the city, might churn his portable organ, looking out into the infinite . . . His is the great tragedy of a civilisation that has gone by, he is bowed under the yoke of a glorious past, remembered but not to be brought back. Yet we who have not that heritage cannot pity him. He has looked on things which we shall never see, and the memory lights up his face with tragic intensity. Thinkest thou of Rome, dark Southerner?[11]

Anderson's favourite maxim, like Marx's, was Terence's '*Homo sum; humani nihil a me alienum puto* [I am a man; nothing human is alien to me]' and he liked to quote Hegel's dictum that the owl of Minerva or philosophy only emerges at the 'dusk' of a great civilisation. Does that suggest a tendency to self-consciousness, self-dramatisation, even self-pity? If it does, it was probably little more than a pose and affectation.

John Anderson was not only a brilliant student in his chosen discipline, but an enterprising, lively and popular member of the student body, caught up in the varied life of many student societies and activities. He was editor of the university magazine during the years 1915–16 and 1917–18, and in December 1916 was elected Vice-President of the Students' Representative Council. A pose of world-weary sophistication could be an amusing asset for a shy undergraduate from the country, finding his feet in an unfamiliar and intensely competitive world. But the mask of precocious aesthete was soon cast aside as Glasgow and the university were overtaken by the war and its insatiable demands. The public role of his combative father was more appropriate for this new struggle.

The university was reeling under the pressures of war: staff and student numbers had declined dramatically, morale was low, and many student societies had collapsed. With so many students and staff at the front, the university was cast into gloom. A brooding anxiety pervaded the place and, as the casualties of the Somme mounted, all felt the pall of the young dead about them. Students able to pursue university degrees had their confidence sapped by the patriotic fervour. Should they be at the university at all? The editorship of the *Glasgow University Magazine* in the critical years of 1917 and 1918 gave John Anderson an unusual opportunity to be the voice of his generation. He now spoke cogently on their behalf: 'we think that those students who are at present taking an Arts course should be given the greatest possible encouragement. Exempted from service on account of comparative or absolute unfitness, they are entitled to every advantage that can be obtained from a University Course'.[12]

In 1917 the 23-year-old Anderson was completing his final honours work in moral philosophy. He had been rejected as medically unfit for war service and there is no reason to suppose he was ever a pacifist or conscientious objector, like Bertrand Russell, and some reason to think he supported the allied cause against Germany. His prize essay of 1917 largely accepted Jones' view that the state is a moral agent: 'the State is the end and aim of the citizen, and the citizen the end and aim of the State, just because both are moral and therefore ends in themselves'. Certainly, his father was almost belligerent in his views about the war and early in 1917 his brother, Willie, was called up. The war nearly caused the university to close down—male student numbers had halved since 1914—and there was a strong move to concentrate on the 'service' faculties of Medicine and Science. University authorities were in favour of subordinating everything to the war effort, and professors like Jones clearly disapproved of fit young men attending classes unless they were in military uniform. He regarded John Anderson as an 'invalid' or 'a lost sheep'.

In spite of the depressing circumstances, Anderson refused to wear sackcloth and ashes; in fact, he wielded his formidable power as editor to inject new life and spirit into the student body. When the university Court or governing body postponed awarding bursaries and scholarships for Arts students because of the war and high enlistments, Anderson boldly attacked its action as a form of punitive discrimination: 'The principle seems to be that of balancing one setback by another; because some have been totally or partially thrown out of their course, others are to suffer likewise, simply to show them what it feels like. This pious doctrine is also known as "equality of sacrifice" '. In another editorial he issued a rousing manifesto to combat student despond and despair:

> In short, what we say to the general body of students is this, shout, sing, kick up a row, get drunk, get locked up—do anything except creep about the quadrangles and the Union like 'pale, forpynèd ghosts', moving sluggishly from yesterday to to-morrow. You are not here for nothing. Your activities are necessarily restricted, but remember that you are alive, and let people know it.[13]

Challenging the instrumental view of the university—that we are here 'for the patriotic purpose of keeping up the supply of doctors, engineers, teachers, ministers etc. and that we should confine ourselves to that'—Anderson asserted that 'it is absolutely essential that we should maintain the traditions of the University as far as we can, so that the continuity may not be lost; so that when peace comes, we may revert to our old life'. In his editorials Anderson elaborated a theory of the university that emphasised its distinctive role as the disinterested pursuit of truth and, as a condition of that activity, the necessity for autonomy or a measure of independence from state and society.

He began to attack 'the commercial spirit', vocationalism and state control:

> Instead of the disinterested devotion to science which ought to characterise it, which provides it with a value of its own, and which is at once the source and the bond of connection of all the other elements of University life, we have the commercial spirit, reducing the institution to a mere machine for turning out professional men. And signs are not wanting that there will be a still stronger movement in the near future towards the thorough commercialising of the University, placing it under state regulation, and subordinating it to some misty ideal called 'the needs of the community'. The University is itself a community, with its own needs and purposes, which are not lightly to be set aside. It must be *co-ordinated* with other institutions, but not in such a way that it will lose its own free and independent spirit.[14]

A common student life was essential for morale, and Anderson welcomed the resumption of such activities as university dances. But his support of student societies stopped short of the 'Services Club' because of its exclusive membership and its failure to maintain the intellectual traditions of the university.

Throughout his career, whenever Anderson and the university were assailed by hostile forces, a similar pattern emerged. At Sydney in the fierce public controversies of 1931 over war memorials and free speech, in 1943 over religion and education, and in the Orr case of the 1950s, Anderson was provoked and antagonised into asserting his manhood as a warrior against the enemy host. Indeed, the university itself became in his mind the battleground of competing and conflicting forces, of goods and evils. John Anderson found his Somme and Passchendaele in academia.

During the war years Glasgow rapidly acquired a well earned reputation for political radicalism as 'Red Clydeside'. Years of agitation and educational work by socialists and schoolteachers like James Maxton, John MacLean and Alexander Anderson bore fruit in industrial militancy, when the ranks of the labour aristocracy were threatened by the dilution of skills, unemployment and the requirements of mass production. The perennial problem of dense, overcrowded and unhealthy tenements also became acute as an influx of munition workers caused housing shortages and rent increases. Rapid inflation contributed to widespread discontent, and a general rent strike in 1915 began a period of great turbulence. When the syndicalist propaganda of the socialists fused with the craft struggle of shop stewards against the deskilling of labour and the anti-war sentiments of the masses, the authorities deported the leaders of the Clyde Workers' Committee, suppressed the socialist newspapers, and arrested John MacLean, James Maxton and others on charges of sedition. They were found guilty and forced to serve harsh sentences in an Edinburgh prison. In January 1919, fearing a 'Bolshevist rising' in the 'Leningrad of the West', Lloyd George sent troops and tanks to Glasgow, and police baton charged crowds of workers during a rally at George Square. The political movement culminated in the return of ten Labour M.P.s in the general election of 1922. In explaining the victory, the *Times* wrote:

> No-one can make even a cursory investigation of the methods of propaganda pursued by the Labour Party on the Clyde without discovering in them the real foundation of victory. Year in and year out, in season and out of season, the Clyde area has been saturated with socialist teaching.[15]

From 1916 John Anderson had the bracing experience of living at the University Students' Settlement at 10 Possil Road, Garscube Cross, in the heart of an overcrowded slum. The fifteen or so students usually in residence ran the settlement themselves with the assistance of a warden, often a senior student. In the years that Anderson lived there, politics and economics increasingly claimed the attention of students and the working-class residents. He helped to conduct a small reading circle in economics, political philosophy and literature. The warden summed up the experience:

> In the background of my studies was the life of the Students Settlement and its friendships and differences and its constant stimulus . . . in these years I was living intensely in the society of a very varied group of young fellows with a purposeful attitude to life, and . . . I had always before me

> in my comings and goings a reminder of the hard way of life for many of those in whose neighbourhood I was living and was forced to consider the problems of social life.[16]

The fortnightly meetings of the Philosophical Society also played an important part in Anderson's intellectual development. During 1918 Professor Samuel Alexander, the Australian-born Jewish philosopher from Manchester, lived at the university for several months while he delivered the Gifford lectures. He frequently attended meetings of the society and canvassed the realist arguments of 'Space, Time and Deity' in informal meetings with students and staff. The young man liked the affable and avuncular Alexander and had a number of discussions with him:

> Samuel Alexander had none of the concern for analysis of the English establishment, none of the preachiness of the Scots moralists. The system he unfolded before his audience was a bold speculation that hung together and took in its stride the findings of the nineteenth century biologists, with modern references to Einstein and Freud. The pattern of this philosophical achievement enthralled the young Anderson.[17]

Sir Henry Jones, by comparison, was quite 'hopeless', Anderson confided to the young woman whom he was now passionately courting.

4

A Philosopher in Love

JENNY BAILLIE was born on 5 November 1892 at the mining village of Larkhall, about five miles from Stonehouse, the first child of William Baillie, a coal miner, and his wife Janet.* Her mother was twenty-two and two months' pregnant when she married William Baillie—scarcely an unusual condition in a Lanarkshire mining town of the late nineteenth century. That Janet's own mother was born out of wedlock to a woman who never married because the father, a miner, already had a wife and family in the town emphasises the thread of marginality in the Baillie family. It also points to certain class and psychological contrasts between the Anderson and Baillie families. As one of the Andersons confided, 'There's nae frivolity about them'. Janet Baillie, whose father was a cousin of David Livingstone, was a power-loom weaver at the local silk factory at the time of her marriage. William continued to be a miner until he developed the 'black spit' and was forced to retire from work, uncompensated, in the late 1920s. All were staunch unionists and socialists, through circumstances as well as conviction.

---

* She was christened and always known as Janet by her own family, but John Anderson used the Scots pet-form of Jenny. To avoid confusion with her mother, I have decided to use Jenny throughout the text, though the Baillies will not approve. To them she resolutely remains Janet, for as the first daughter she was named, in the Scots manner, after her mother's mother, the matriarchal Janet. Jenny herself adopted John's name after the marriage, and so she was known in Australia. To what extent the young John's Marxist persona influenced his choice of the name—Marx's wife was another Jenny—is an interesting speculation.

William and Janet Baillie leased a house in Church Street, one of a miners' and weavers' row, and Janet's mother lived next door. The kitchen was the largest of the three rooms since it was where the weaving was done. Life in Church Street was stoical, stinted and hard. Water was not laid on and the family had to use a neighbouring well. Janet Baillie was a hard-working housewife, conscientious to a fault about laundry, starching and house-cleaning. A woman who did not have fine white starched linen on her table and bedstand was a 'brazen slut'. She went regularly to the nearby Congregational Church. So, too, did William until a strike split the congregation and disenchanted him with the minister, who sided with the mineowners. Every New Year's Day William and Janet dispensed a bottle of whisky and port wine to callers, the only alcohol that ever passed the Baillie threshold. Drink and sex were kept at a very safe distance.

The eldest daughter, Jenny, was a bright child and attended Larkhall Academy. There, one of the teachers spotted her talent and objected when her parents wanted her to leave school and take a job at the silk factory, persuading them to continue her education at Hamilton Academy, despite the financial sacrifice. Against considerable odds—odds that John Anderson never faced—Jenny mastered higher Latin in two years and won third place to John's first in the university bursary competition of 1911. They were not close friends at this stage. Dux girl of Hamilton Academy, she was the second girl from Larkhall to go to the university.

Financial constraint and a strong sense of family obligation hindered her full participation in university life. Commuting by train from Larkhall, where she lived at home, may have saved money but it consumed valuable time and prevented her involvement in the night-time life of clubs and societies. Her parents' financial sacrifices and high expectations put her under a strong obligation to do well and not to fail. To make sure she would have an acceptable teaching qualification she first completed an ordinary degree before proceeding to do honours work in English. Illness appears to have marred her examination performance in the finals, and in 1915 she gained a second-class honours degree. In August 1916, after completing a year's teacher-training, she took up her first teaching post at Buckie, a fishing town east of Inverness. It was a happy and stimulating time. From mid-1917, however, she returned to Larkhall to live at home with her ailing mother and to teach at Hamilton Academy. Professionally and personally, there was a narrowing of horizons.

John and Jenny first met as academic rivals at Hamilton Academy, and the note of rivalry never quite left the relationship. Later, at the university, there were occasional meetings at classes or at the Literary Society and chance encounters on the train or tramcar travelling home from Glasgow. John invited her to one or two cinemas, followed by tea, but there was little more when Jenny left Glasgow to teach at Buckie. John later claimed to have been more interested in gaining experience from 'affairs' with women at the university. Was this a case of the double standard, self-dramatisation or both?

There was a revival of the 'friendship' in the summer of 1916, when Jenny was home on holiday. In plotting the ebb and flow of the affair, one soon notices that winters were for strenuous work during the short Scottish academic session, while summers were for love and leisure in the long twilight hours. John was encouraged by their walks and talks around Larkhall and Stonehouse to resume a vigorous correspondence with Jenny on her return to Buckie. She was flattered by his attentions and, a little in awe of him, welcomed his 'sincere friendship'. But it is likely that Jenny was also being courted by a young man called Smillie from Larkhall, who was more popular with her family.

On a long evening walk to Larkhall Fair in the summer of 1917—a turning point in the relationship—John expressed his dissatisfaction with mere friendship and asked Jenny for something more intimate. It took another year of almost daily correspondence for Jenny 'to open her heart' and tell John on 'the Fairholm night' in the summer of 1918 that she loved him. Kisses and caresses followed on dark nights under 'our fir-tree' at Thinacre, 'with the moon just peeping through the trees and the topmost branches sighing in the wind'. Soon after, John left Glasgow, laden with prizes, to take up his first appointment at the University College of South Wales in Cardiff. The correspondence continued with renewed vigour: 'And what is that new world we have come into, Jenny? It is a world of infinite tenderness, of slow contemplation and swift emotion, of sweet sympathy and austere unworldliness. Always your loving, John'.[1]

John and Jenny became engaged in the summer of 1919 and at Christmas, while at home on leave, John made his first serious sexual proposals, which provoked a major crisis in the relationship. Jenny was much perplexed by John's insistence: 'And if you spent about half of your life ignoring a thing: it isn't quite comprehensible all at once, especially when all the ways of approach to it that you had ever any contact with, were tacitly condemned'. Jenny confessed her 'muddled' thoughts on sex, her Puritan upbringing, her 'resistance' to John's demands and her own 'suppressed' sexuality. The situation led to an emotional confrontation between the couple and Mrs Baillie, who was more concerned about marriage than love and freedom, and anxious to impose limits on the times and activities of their courting. John was adamant and maintained his pressure on Jenny to resist her mother. Reluctantly, Jenny 'capitulated' to John and agreed to some sexual experimentation. John soon reassured her: 'almost the whole time I have known you has been a time of trial, testing, probation of love. We could not have begun with a full assurance'.[2]

During 1921, while John climbed the next step of his academic career at 'kirky' Edinburgh, Jenny grew extremely despondent: 'For I think, dear, that I had lost with you the sense of companionship that I found with Ishbel in Buckie, and that I had with you in the earlier days of our intimacy but which came only fitfully and then disappeared in these latter days'.[3] Over several months she suffered a serious mental and emotional crisis due to the unrelenting demands of John and the relationship: 'I had got so tired of conflicts both within and without, that I *had* thought . . . that I would need to let you go, not because I did not love you, but because I wanted peace'.[4] Her near-collapse was in part the outcome of deep inner conflicts over sex, fear and guilt, but it was also the result of John's insistence that she shed all emotional baggage—career, friends and family—for his sake and career: 'it seemed as if there was the family on one side with all its claims and you on the other, with yours, so that there was nothing for me but to satisfy one or the other, or to go right away'.[5] Echoing Nietzsche, he announced their love was a 'transvaluation of all values' and that 'we've still to learn "to live dangerously" '. Thus encouraged, she gave up her teaching career in May 1922 and on 30 June 1922 they were married in a civil ceremony at Glasgow. 'A sanctimonious ceremony or civil contract is nothing to the fact', wrote the impatient groom.[6] Alexander (Sandy), their one child, was born on 14 November 1923.

What ideas did John Anderson bring to the relationship and how did they change? Certainly, John claimed that he gained much from Jenny's love. In October 1918, he wrote, 'I couldn't connect philosophy with my life until there was something *real* in it; but finding reality in our love I have come into closer touch with reality in general'.

An important discovery of the letters is that, while still an undergraduate student of Sir Henry Jones, John Anderson was busy forming and formulating a general anti-idealist position. The three major elements of that position were 'realism' in philosophy and psychology, 'objectivism' in ethics, and 'modernism' in aesthetics. Of these three, the least developed was his aesthetic theory, especially as it concerned literature, art and music, and he was to benefit considerably from Jenny's more extensive knowledge and critical grasp of the issues. 'You have certainly led me to extend my acquaintance with literature and to appreciate many things that I had not noticed before', he wrote in June 1917.

Two of Anderson's principal concerns as a philosopher will make clear his emotional and intellectual debt to Jenny—first, his notion of love as a good, and secondly, the role of comedy, or the play of the mind about real ideas, as a dispeller of illusion. For Anderson, the 'simple goods' were knowledge, beauty, creation, love and freedom, and with G. E. Moore and Samuel Alexander, Anderson believed that these were objective goods. He also agreed with Aristotle that a mixture of goods, such as the creative love of truth (or a passion for discovery) were preferable to and of greater value than a simple good. For the attainment of these goods, there was need for co-operation, adventure, risk and experiment, all marks of the productive life:

'Explorer=Producer=Free Man=Realist . . . The good thing is the courage and freedom shown in taking the risk . . . The really free mind makes opportunities and laughs at hindrances'.[7] Significantly, Anderson thought that creation and the pursuit of knowledge were male activities, while the appreciation of beauty and love were female ones. In an effusive tribute he wrote of how Jenny's love had enabled him to live a fuller and better life: 'I think I have changed quite a lot . . . in the last three years: and I think I have gradually become more capable of that certainty, that possession of love that we now have: more capable of appreciating and understanding you'.[8] But he also wrote that, since love was only one good and many goods were preferable to one, they should use their frequent separations to produce other goods in thought and action. In one sense, the letters are a remarkable testimony to those activities and a godsend to the intellectual biographer. Yet did Jenny find the doctrine very comforting as she taught and corrected schoolwork at Hamilton, wrote her many letters at all hours, and drudged at home for an ill and demanding mother?

At least Jenny's long absences and letters stimulated John to develop and refine his idea of the producer and the 'comic spirit'. Borrowing ideas from George Meredith's essay on comedy, John argued 'it is comedy that contains the universal spirit' because it exposes illusions and hypocrisy. Freud's theories already interested him, and he saw comedy and psychoanalysis as performing the same essential function—to expose illusion, error and 'suppressions'. As in Schiller's *Letters on Aesthetic Education*, play was to mediate between the sensuous, empirical self, subject to space, time and the laws of science, and the moral self bound by duty and the categorical imperative. The comic spirit would thereby liberate and enrich the human personality to the full:

> Thus, if one begins by being a supporter of the working-class, and holds to that then there will follow the idea of 'the producer' with its full ethical application, and finally from that will come the 'comic spirit'. I feel that I am ever so much further on than I was when I came down here, and that progress has been made almost entirely through our letters.

> And so, Jenny, it isn't just that we *possess* one another: but that we can participate more and more fully with one another and become ever nearer to truth and understanding of things: and so from one another we have the more with which we can participate with other people and live a full life.[9]

To that end, John offered to analyse Jenny's dreams, to help expose her illusions, 'suppressions' and confusions. He had already liberated her from religious illusion—'I wouldn't consider my philosophy worth a rap, if it hadn't something to say on such matters'—and with the help of Dr Freud he now turned to the citadel of her sexuality. The several dreams that Jenny supplied to John illuminate the stresses and conflicts of the relationship during these years. One of them was about a bull threatening Jenny in a field. Somehow John had to control and tame the beast, but, simultaneously, John had to master himself, for he was also the beast. Evidently, aspects of John's personality still frightened her and required curbing. She spoke of drink but implied other things as well, above all John's sexual demands and her own disturbing needs:

> I have been so miserable. This business of sex has something to do with it. I feel that it is all round me somehow, hemming me in, stifling me: that it won't let me just accept it, it keeps bothering and clamouring for my attention, so that I seem to hear no other voice but its. It has got all out of harmony with our love again, so that the song of it seems to have gone from my heart.[10]

In another letter, John discussed Jenny's 'inhibitions, illusions and errors' in terms of her 'conventional' upbringing and her censorious ignorant mother and grandmother. 'For you see, Jenny, I have often felt that it was for me to rescue you from your home-life', he confided to his 'dearest Jenny' on 21 June 1921 during a crisis with her mother,

> And what you told me brought to my mind most intensely the thought of you living with your mother and drinking in, half involuntarily, all her superstitions, having your imagination quenched by her lack of it, and thinking through

John Anderson, c. *1918*

Jenny Baillie on her graduation, November 1915

Jenny's miner father William (c. 1940) and mother Janet (c. 1915), and their family home in Church Street, Larkhall

*John's mother Elizabeth (*c. 1920*); his father on their world cruise (*c. *1924); and together at home in Lesmahagow*

John and Jenny on their honeymoon in Ayrshire in July 1922

> it all that you were compensating for something that you owed her: laying waste your future for the impossible sake of her past.[11]

All 'resistances defences and rationalisations' would have to be overcome and yield to the new love, no matter how painful the process: 'It is not that I think our love is irreconcilable with your staying at home, but it cannot be reconciled with your being "one of the family" '. In an acutely depressed state and physically ill, Jenny vented her frustrations with the exclusive attachment and John's impossible standards. She accused him of pharisaism and 'Olympianism', of a lack of appreciation for ordinary human beings, like her own 'folk' and friends; and a dismissal of all aspects of herself that were not 'part and parcel' of him: 'I cannot ask you to share my work or anything like that, dear, and it seems to me that all the time you've wanted me to share with you, while you wouldn't share with me—at least with any kind of good grace'.[12] It was a rare and painful moment of insight. How near Jenny Baillie came to a nervous breakdown at this point remains a disquieting speculation.

As in all intense and intimate relationships, the balance of power and attraction changed over time. Quite early we encounter John's passionate nature, his ego and will to power, his unrealistic expectations and demands, his need for an exclusive attachment and a certain unscrupulousness, possibly even desperation, in his wooing of Jenny. It was a 'thrawn' kind of loving, twisted and conflicted by John's Pygmalion complex. His desire for the paragon convert and agreement on all fundamentals was almost as strong as the need for a woman to love and marry.

The protracted wooing, covering several years, was intense and occasionally stormy. Jenny's letters speak at times of a stubborn 'resistance' to John's emotional and intellectual demands as well as an intermittent sense of inadequacy, depression and emotional withdrawal. There is oscillation between elation and hope on the one hand, and dour resignation and despondency on the other. Clearly, Jenny needed much wooing, but did she want to believe too much? 'In fact, John', she wrote on

7 February 1922, 'I believe that I sometimes act—though maybe I don't admit it to myself—as if you were omniscient . . .'

There was a price to be paid for such an illusion. For one thing, there was the sacrifice of emotional and economic independence as a successful teacher; for another, there was the painful loss of family and friends as she changed from dutiful daughter and elder sister to estranged critic and family outsider. Tensions with her mother and sister were much exacerbated by John and, in the end, Jenny had to give up the close family circle for John. There was also the transition from the solidarity and bustle of the miner's cottage and mining village to the lonely elevation of a professor's pedestal, no matter how respectable. Sadly, this was to be her fate when the Andersons moved to Australia in 1927. Exile merely made explicit what was implicit in the relationship.

Finally, why did they marry and why did the marriage persist? The central irony is that the institution of marriage, which Anderson strenuously questioned as a philosopher, proved convenient for both of them—up to a point.

For John, marriage provided a stable base for his academic career, a curb on too much self-indulgence, on socialising, drinking and early morning lethargy. It was an essential aid to work, a discipline and a spur. At times, he needed mothering and perhaps an intellectual helpmeet.

For Jenny, marriage provided a respectable and secure base for motherhood. Did the fear of illegitimacy, abandonment by the father and poverty play on the mind of the newly educated miner's daughter as it surely preyed on her mother's? Marriage and John's brilliant career would remove those hindrances.

Both had gone too far to retreat. Both passionately believed in their love and ideas. Marriage offered them independence and autonomy, attractive goals for young lovers: 'There *is* communication: there are connections, and new communications can be opened—new things held in common. So, Jenny, we come back to things themselves: objective goods as against sentimental "self-realisation" and servile externality'.[13]

5

The Making of a Realist

JOHN ANDERSON, the student, was strongly influenced by the life and philosophy of Sir Henry Jones, perhaps more than either of them realised or cared to admit. Anderson's prize essay that won the university silver medal in 1917 was on a topic chosen by the patriotic professor—Is the state a moral agent?—and provides tangible evidence of that influence. The essay is argued powerfully and persuasively within the Hegelian system and employs all the familiar idealist categories of the 'state', 'community', 'individual' and 'absolute mind'. Following the professor's line, Anderson developed the ideas of T. H. Green and Bernard Bosanquet to criticise utilitarian theories of the state and individualism, and to argue for the social nature of the individual and the moral nature of the state:

> The State, like the individual, has its 'hazards and hardships'. But has it that 'stability and security' which the individual finds in religion, according to Bosanquet, or which we may say he finds in the achievements of absolute spirit, Art, Religion and Philosophy? This achievement may be represented as the end of all action, for it is not itself action but something attained through it. Just as the subjective mind of the individual would be meaningless without its objectification in society, so the social system of individuals and institutions only takes its meaning from the achievements of spirit in and through it. The action of the State has its full meaning only within that system and consequently only in relation to that end.[1]

Anderson's thoroughness, complexity and intellectual power are already evident in the arguments of the essay, but the mould is quite clearly Hegelian:

> The result of our analysis is to show that a community is a mind, which can think, act and feel. To regard the State as the active faculty has a certain degree of truth. But this action is the action of the community. And from this point of view we may say that the State is the community, and is supremely a moral agent.[2]

When Anderson comments on war and *realpolitik* his arguments are tough-minded and realist, and more than compatible with the full prosecution of the present war and conscription:

> Certainly, as Hegel points out, war emphasises the real nature of the State and the rights established within it . . . Thus the action of the State in war demonstrates by a dialectic movement the real nature of rights and their place in the social system. The individual is not valuable in himself, but only as attaining to absolute ends; property is not to be upheld for its own sake, but only as a necessary expression of individuality in the system through which these ends are achieved.[3]

In passing, Anderson justified the recent allied intervention in Greece and found no difficulty endorsing British rule in India: 'Lovers of peace ought to show due gratitude . . . to the "pax Britannica", which would come to a speedy end were India left to the Indians'.[4] Such neat and pithy judgements indicate a lack of sympathy with 'cant phrases' and humanitarian sentiment, but they also suggest a certain canny bending to the wind. After all, the judge of the essay competition was known to be Professor Jones, who in 1917 received leave from the university to campaign for recruitment and national savings, and to lecture and write about the war. With a favourite son in Burma, he was a firm believer in Britain's 'civilising mission' in the East. John Anderson was torn between a public persona as academic success and prize-winner, and an unofficial self as iconoclast and rebel. The strain took its toll and at one point in 1917 the frustrated student wrote to Jenny castigating idealists as 'state mongers'—'the good of the State is one's own good. Prussianism! The Servile State! It is a sign of the times'. Sir Henry, of course, was 'hopeless'. Yet he won the coveted medal.

Over a long career, Anderson, the professional philosopher, was to take his revenge on Jones and repudiate many of the central tenets of Absolute Idealism—monism, the doctrine of ultimate or higher truths, and constitutive relations. However, certain pervasive influences could not be so easily shaken off. Professor Jones, the knighted philosopher and popular teacher, demonstrated the public role that philosophers should perform in society: he was a stirring controversialist in religious and educational matters, a seasoned political fighter for the Liberals, and friend and mentor of Lloyd George. Professor John Burnet's forceful advocacy of general culture and classicism at the same time also impressed this public role on the young undergraduate.

As to Jones' philosophical influence on Anderson, there are some fundamental assumptions they share, notwithstanding all the later differences. First is the belief that 'there is, in the end, only one way of knowing', which applies to all the sciences and philosophy alike: 'The sciences, philosophy, even ordinary thought, are engaged in forming and testing conceptions or hypotheses in the light of which facts are disclosed and become intelligible'.[5] From Burnet, too, he learnt the importance of general culture and 'the folly of any estrangement between Science and Humanism':

> It is therefore no time for futile bickerings between Science and the Humanities. There is no real quarrel between them, and their interests are identical. The common enemies they have to contend with are Nationalism and Vocationalism, which are quite as inconsistent with Science as they are with the Humanities.[6]

For Anderson and the idealists, reality is rational, and while Anderson's logic is of the traditional kind rather than the dialectic, it occupies a central place in his philosophy, for 'reality is propositional'. In an unpublished textbook on logic of 1922, Anderson elaborated his view of logic as 'the fundamental measure of things':

> Logic, then, as truly expounded by Socrates, starts with the rejection of the dogmatic appeal to 'facts', as something inaccessible to argument. It insists on the actual occurrence of agreements and disagreements and attempts to persuade; and maintains that this involves, in place of isolated facts, a certain connectedness in the objects of argument and belief, an objective order which makes communication possible and from which the criteria of significance and validity are to be derived. For we cannot agree unless there is something to agree about; and we cannot even understand one another, whether we agree or disagree, unless there is a common denominator of discourse.[7]

Anderson's emphasis on 'togetherness and plurality as conditions of significance' clearly distinguishes him from the English school of Locke, Berkeley and Hume, and gives to his empiricism an unmistakable doctrinal character. It also leads Anderson to share with the idealists an opposition to utilitarianism and relativism.

Jones and Anderson also shared the Scottish 'common sense' view of society as integral to human individuality. According to Jones, the individualist '*is* his society individualized, its impersonal forces focussed. There is in him no content whatsoever, whether intellectual or moral, which he has not borrowed from it. His personality . . . would show nothing rational that is not social'.[8] Anderson also held that 'there is no such thing as the pure individual apart from society, any more than society apart from the individuals who compose it'.[9] Finally, teacher and student held the conviction that philosophy is 'at every step, a way of life', and a strenuous one at that.[10] As Jones delivered the Gifford lectures during 1921 while fighting the throat cancer that killed him, Anderson became a reluctant admirer. It was Jones not Anderson who said:

> The fundamental vice of 'Hegelians' and 'Neo-Hegelians' is confusion. They have confused many things. They have mistaken a theory of knowledge for a theory of being, the facts of their own consciousness for the real things which they represent; they have identified their own ego with a logical category, and themselves with God.[11]

There can be little doubt, however, that the philosopher who exercised most influence on the young Anderson was not a Scot, a Welshman or even an Englishman, but the Australian-born Samuel Alexander from Manchester. During 1918 he lived at the university while he prepared and delivered the Gifford lectures, later published as *Space, Time and Deity*. In these lectures Alexander sought to provide a realist account of the universe and mind in the grand manner, and no less wide-ranging, evolutionary and architectonic than the rival idealist system. There was much stimulating discussion of space, time and the categories, and Anderson found the visiting professor 'a most genial man'. He wrote to Jenny, 'Alexander's course is finished now. I had to miss the last three lectures, but in compensation I was present at a discussion at No. 1, The College, on Saturday morning, when Alexander expounded his views to and met criticism from Russell [a tutor], Scott, Willie and myself'.[12] At one meeting of the Philosophical Society Alexander read a paper on the American new realists, which greatly interested Anderson. 'I find myself more and more in agreement with him', he wrote, but shrewdly noted, 'I'll have to be careful how I hand out Alexander's ideas to Jones and Latta'. He had just finished an essay on 'Space, Time and Consciousness' and was embarking on a study of William James for his M.A. thesis. The latter he found 'much more convincing than the Idealists'. When Alexander returned to Manchester, he began a correspondence with him.

In February 1918 Anderson gave a talk on 'the fallacy of optimism', in which he developed a realist criticism of normative notions of the 'good' and 'progress': 'Optimistic theories are based on the view that the "ultimate nature of reality" is good or that good is more real than evil. But reality as such can be neither good nor bad'.[13] On another occasion a speaker gave a critical account of the views of Bertrand Russell, comparing his pluralism, realism and atomism with the idealist position. The back-to-Kant movement associated with Kemp Smith at Edinburgh also signified a retreat from Hegelian metaphysics to problems of epistemology, from idealism to realism. As Kemp Smith summed up the situation:

> If some such realist view . . . proves to be, on the whole, the most satisfactory interpretation of the cognitive situation, need we be driven out of it by those objections which we have been considering? In view of the present infant stage of psychology, of our very imperfect knowledge of the brain, and of the very incomplete analysis yet made of our fundamental categories, and perhaps not least of the baffling character of time and space, which have not yet yielded all their secrets even to the mathematician, any theory of knowledge is bound to be highly conjectural and tentative. Every type of philosophy has to be allowed some freedom in the choice of its difficulties as well as of its strong points.[14]

Such a conclusion was too tepid for Anderson, who tersely noted some of the contradictions in the argument. Kemp Smith was a 'convinced idealist' and declared philosophy 'is a more precarious enterprise than science. The personal factors cannot be eliminated in the same complete degree'.[15] All the same, Anderson commented, 'idealist philosophy aims at guessing the form of the stellar universe!' Clearly, these were brave days for philosophy and young irreverent philosophers. That Anderson was one of the ablest of them is shown by his winning the Ferguson Scholarship in 1917 and the Shaw Fellowship in 1919, the 'blue ribbon' all-Scottish scholarship in philosophy awarded every four years.

Late in 1918 Anderson took up an appointment as acting assistant lecturer in the Department of Logic and Philosophy at the University College of South Wales at Cardiff. Philosophically, it was an outpost of Glasgow and the professor, Hector Hetherington, was a close disciple of Jones. Anderson spent a year in Wales, much of it clouded by the war's end, demobilisation, and the influenza epidemic. Because the Workers' Educational Association (W.E.A.) paid most of his salary, Anderson taught several workers' classes at Cardiff, Bridgend and Swansea. He was enthusiastic about the cause: 'it is among the workers, the producers, that we really come nearest things themselves: because even in this system they are not entirely divorced from the common spirit'.[16]

In 1919 his prospects improved considerably when he was appointed assistant lecturer in Logic at the University of Glasgow at a salary of £200 p.a. Next year he was appointed a grade A lecturer in the Department of Logic and Metaphysics at Edinburgh on a salary that enabled him at last to marry. In December 1920 his brother William resigned from his lectureship at Glasgow to take up the chair of Mental and Moral Philosophy at Auckland University College, the University of New Zealand. At about the same time John's eldest sister Kate also left home to emigrate to the U.S.A. after her marriage to George Murdoch. Emigration abroad in the pursuit of a male career was the choice of a large number of Scots—'about 50 per cent of the natural increase of the population in the first two decades of the twentieth century'[17]—and Jenny already anticipated that it might be her fate when she married John.

'Kirky' Edinburgh did not appeal to Anderson, who commented unfavourably on its political 'quietism' during a miners' strike. Unlike Glasgow, most of his students were training for the kirk. 'It brings out the necessity of keeping in constant touch with the working-classes themselves', he wrote to Jenny; 'It makes me more than thankful to have my W.E.A. class, and to have the chance of making issues clear for those who really have the revolutionary impulse'.[18]

If the philosophy students did not inspire him, Anderson gained more from his association with Professor Norman Kemp Smith. The latter had spent ten years at Princeton before his appointment in 1919 to the chair of Logic and Metaphysics at Edinburgh, and his American experience introduced him to wider currents in philosophy and psychology. On his return to Edinburgh, he found much Scottish philosophical disputation narrow and petty and, seeking to raise the level of argument and debate, he reorganised the teaching of philosophy in his department. He introduced an honours course on Kant and a first-year course on Fundamental Problems in Philosophy, in which the rival claims of realism, scepticism and idealism were critically considered. With his tolerance, urbanity and tact, Kemp Smith built up a varied team and encouraged independence in his staff. John Anderson became the principal exponent of realism in the department and assisted Kemp Smith with the first-year course and the honours class, where he benefited from the professor's labours on the *Critique of Pure*

Reason. Kemp Smith, in turn, valued Anderson's judgement and learnt from his 'very searching criticisms' of the *Prolegomena to an Idealist Theory of Knowledge*. Anderson hoped Kemp Smith would reciprocate when his own book on logic neared completion. In addition to teaching and scholarship, Kemp Smith supported the work of the W.E.A., and himself taught philosophy to groups of workers in the dangerous year of 1919. Anderson found him a more congenial colleague than Professor A. E. Taylor, whose 'Christian' interpretation of Socrates irritated him. Nor did he much like Mrs Kemp Smith's social airs and 'conventionalism'.

Concerning the industrial disputes of 1920, he wrote about his colleagues, 'they all regard the strike as something to be got safely over'. In a further letter to Jenny, he pointed to some of these differences:

> At least I think, Jenny, that you and I had a better idea of what we were learning because we had the emotional impulse of Socialism—or of proletarianism. It was at least a criterion of *significance*, enabling us to recognise the trend of things as well as their immediate presentation.[19]

His choice of a house at Eskbank, a miners' town twelve miles south-east of Edinburgh, underlined his radical political commitment since miners became increasingly militant during the 1920s and regularly voted for the new Communist Party. In 1926 Anderson boldly sided with the militants during the general strike and criticised student volunteers and colleagues who enlisted as special constables for their 'servility', the vice he most detested. It seems likely that one of the factors behind his decision to apply for the chair at Sydney was his growing political isolation in the department and university, and disappointment with his career prospects. The refusal of A. R. Orage to publish his logic book because of its apparent eccentricity was a severe blow to his ego and reputation. Would his unpopular public stance during the general strike also be held against him and impede his academic advancement in Edinburgh and canny Scotland? Was he reliable? Did he uphold the right standards? Was he a gentleman? Perhaps his eminent referees were more than a little relieved to learn of his successful application for the Sydney chair. Kemp Smith and A. E. Taylor had certainly encouraged the fiery particle on his way to the antipodes, and by this time Anderson had developed the essentials of his realist position.

Anderson worked out his philosophy in reaction to the Absolute Idealism of Sir Henry Jones, which he was later to condemn as 'woolly-minded' literary philosophy, a kind of secular religion, or no philosophy at all. Of course, Anderson's revolt against idealism was part of a wider movement in the English-speaking world at the turn of the century, and he was to profit from the earlier work of G. E. Moore, Bertrand Russell, William James and Samuel Alexander. To what extent Anderson's own attack was driven by purely philosophical concerns or by personal experiences, beliefs and commitments, such as his opposition to all forms of religion, is a moot point and a subject which we will need to consider and return to. 'I have no use for religion—and very little for morality', he wrote to Jenny in 1917. Yet he also claimed, 'my opposition to Idealism in philosophy is bound up with my opposition to Capitalism'.[20] Questions of motivation aside, what is surely remarkable is the rapidity and scale of his philosophical achievement: within a few years of graduation Anderson had assembled the framework and materials for his system of realism, and this great burst of creative activity coincided with his wooing and winning of Jenny.

At his most radical, Anderson attacked the idealist view of truth and knowledge—that 'there is no break or division whatsoever between the stuff of thought and thought itself, between fact and its meaning'[21]—and replaced it with 'realism' or the doctrine that objects do exist in space and time independently of mind:

> The general conclusion is that all the objects of science, including minds and goods, are things occurring in space and time . . . and that we can study them by virtue of the fact that we come into spatial and temporal relations with them. And therefore all ideals, ultimates, symbols, agencies and the like are to be rejected, and no such distinction as that of facts and principles, or facts and values, can be maintained. There are only facts, i.e., occurrences in space and time.[22]

In particular, Anderson rejected the idealist belief in 'constitutive relations', or the view that things are constituted by their relations with other things, especially the mind:

> Arguing then, as realists, that no thing or quality of a thing is constituted by the thing's relations, we have to assert that nothing is constituted by knowing and nothing by being known. The notion of 'that whose nature it is to know' is expressed in the term 'consciousness'; the notion of 'that whose nature it is to be known' in the term 'idea'. Realism is therefore concerned to reject these terms, as involving the attempt to take relations as qualities.[23]

For Anderson, logic, meaning traditional propositional logic, was the key to his understanding of reality. That 'reality is propositional' was his most distinctive doctrine:

> The empiricist, like Socrates, adopts the attitude of considering things in terms of what can be said about them, i.e., in propositions. And he regards this not as a 'second-best', but as the only method of speaking or thinking at all, since every statement that we make, every belief that we hold, is a proposition. Since, then, the supposed higher and lower objects of experience both take the propositional form, we are concerned with a single way of being; that, namely, which is conveyed when we say that a proposition is *true* . . . But in order to indicate data or ideals, we have to make statements. If there were anything either above or below the proposition, it would be beyond speech or understanding.[24]

So, for Anderson, 'a realist can only be an empiricist' and he must oppose rationalism (of which idealism is a variant), dualism, monism and relativism. In his understanding of reality, Anderson always emphasised complexity both in things themselves and in the minds that perceive them: 'We deal always with complex states of affairs and never with "simple entities" '.[25] This view diverged sharply from the early Russell's logical atomism. Similarly, Anderson's rejection of the coherence theory of truth did not lead him to espouse a sense-datum correspondence theory of knowledge, as Russell did. Anderson stood for the Greek directness of things.

Above all, Anderson wished to dethrone 'mind' from its privileged position in the idealist universe, and he drew extensively on Freud's work to demonstrate mental conflict, the role of the unconscious and repression in mental processes, and to undermine any 'unitary' view of mind. For Anderson, the mind was not passive but an active field of drives, feelings and conflicts; and, as early as 1922, he was developing a connection between the work of psychoanalysis and his own logic in clarifying problems and dispelling 'illusions'. Psychoanalysis, he wrote,

> in effect, presents to the mind affected a wider conspectus of things, by giving it access to the observations and beliefs of another mind, by enabling it to treat that other mind as part of itself. But on this showing it is simply an advanced degree of that communication which occurs in all discourse and which is especially noticeable in education.[26]

He took from William James, pragmatism and the American new realists the idea that truth entails certain regular ways of 'working' in the world, and that the pursuit of knowledge is always a provisional, risk-taking activity that can never produce absolute certainty. The latter is for 'incurably sick souls'. Healthy people accept their fallibility and the mistakes they make as part of 'the common character of things':

> For Realism, then, as against all the 'ultimates', facts are good enough. It does away with the philosophy of good intentions, of 'service' to the idol of social utility or any other, and establishes philosophy as logic, the logic of events . . . And, rid of 'meanings' and 'purposes' and other products of 'vicious intellectualism', it proposes as the formal solution of any problem *the interaction of complex things.*[27]

Not that Anderson always took risks, his respect for William James notwithstanding. There is one significant example of risk-averse behaviour that warrants some scrutiny. In 1922 or 1923 he wrote a textbook on logic, which for Anderson was a very important thing to do. After Kemp Smith studied the manuscript and made his suggestions, Anderson submitted it with high hopes to a man whom he greatly admired as a liberator of minds, Alfred Richard Orage, the editor of the *New Age.*

Orage declined to publish it, either because there was a glut of logic books on the post-war market or because of the perceived 'eccentricity' of Anderson's view of logic and Freudian psychoanalysis. Whatever the reason, Orage's rejection was traumatic for the young man on the verge of a brilliant career. Does not this painful fact help to explain why John Anderson never published a major coherent study of his philosophical system, despite all his undertakings and promises to do so? That most of his philosophical writings were published in the *Australasian Journal of Psychology and Philosophy* while he was the editor may also be related to this formative experience. When in retirement, many years later, he came to write his *magnum opus* it seemed to Jenny that he could not bear to open the drawer of his desk containing the old rejected manuscript. She told a student that she thought his taking it out killed him in the end.

If he did not always live dangerously or 'send his ships out into uncharted seas' neither did Nietzsche, in spite of his many strident injunctions to do so. The latter was a general cultural influence on Anderson and his generation. Much of the impact came through Orage and the *New Age* and it included Nietzsche's celebration of the artist as Dionysian rebel, his attack on bourgeois society and conventional Christian morality, and the exaltation of the 'strong and healthy' individual. There is certainly a Nietzschean ring to Anderson's injunction to 'carefree and forceful activity':

> Seize hold of things, hammer out the issues, abjure dilettantism in any shape. This is the true attitude of the artist, whose mind . . . permits no ideals or taboos to come between him and a direct handling of things themselves. No sentimental attachments, no higher meanings, no irrelevant antecedents or consequences, are allowed to affect the positive treatment of things, their presentation as a balance of forces or sequence of phases.[28]

Anderson's non-naturalist, positive ethics, his view that 'goodness' is some positive content that resides in 'the nature of the activities themselves', owed much to G. E. Moore, and, as we have seen, he developed the outline of his aesthetic theory in close association with Jenny. At the same time he was hugely enjoying *Ulysses*, another forbidden pleasure.

In developing his 'realist' philosophy, Anderson found a striking affinity with the sixth century philosopher, Heraclitus of Ephesus: 'We have to reject the distinction between being and becoming, and recognise, with Heraclitus, that whatever is, is in process and whatever is in process, is'.[29] John Anderson's study of Greek philosophy and his view of classicism—'to see life steadily, and to see it whole'—owed most to the pioneering work of John Burnet, the Professor of Greek at St Andrews from 1891 to 1926. 'Owing especially to the work of the late Professor John Burnet', Anderson was later to write, 'it is now possible for us not only to recognise the Greek philosophers as the founders of modern science, but to distinguish and appreciate the contributions of Socrates and Plato to science and general culture'.[30] In one of those periodical rediscoveries of the ancient world, Burnet studied the thought of the pre-Socratics to find much exciting and original speculation about the nature of the universe and metaphysics. That his researches into Greek science coincided with the contemporary revolution in physics added to his high appreciation of the pre-Socratic philosophers:

> My aim has been to show that a new thing came into the world with the early Ionian teachers—the thing we call science, and that they first pointed the way which Europe has followed ever since, so that . . . it is an adequate description of science to say that it is 'thinking about the world in the Greek way'. That is why science has never existed except among peoples who have come under the influence of Greece.[31]

According to Burnet, this period of fertile curiosity and scientific discovery culminated in the work of Socrates and Plato, after which there was a steady decline in independence and originality. Burnet was himself a Platonist and devoted much of his life to editing and dating the dialogues and to disentangling the historical Socrates from the Socrates of Plato, Xenophon and Hegel. Anderson greatly admired Burnet's work and accepted his main conclusions.

Paradoxically, at the end of his life Anderson testified to the great influence that Hegel had exercised on his development as a philosopher—he 'did aim at completeness, at a comprehensive treatment of the totality of things'. Hegel also did 'much to stimulate interest in Greek philosophy; and this, along with his attention to logic, has helped to discredit the pragmatic or utilitarian attitude'.[32] There was a certain irony in Anderson's tribute, for as a young man he had rebelled against Hegel's British disciples:

> For an answer to Hegel, then, we have to drop epistemology—the intrusion of mind into logic and of a false logic into psychology—and return to the Greek consideration of *things*, as Burnet, no less than the English realists, assists us to do; we have to develop a positive theory of mind as feeling and as multiple, on the lines suggested by Freud; we have to be empirical, like James, and to recognise Space and Time as the conditions of existence, as is done by Alexander, largely under the influence of Kant. Doing this we can reject significance and purpose and any single 'stuff' of reality, whether matter or spirit.[33]

Nevertheless, Anderson claimed always to have admired certain features of Hegel's philosophy, above all its systematic character: 'Hegel is right, then, in maintaining, in opposition to eclecticism or pragmatism, that philosophy should be systematic. But its systematic character should appear in the form of a single logic, not in the form of 'totality', of a pretended *solution of all problems*'.[34] Was Anderson at heart a heretical Hegelian?

This question may suggest some strong parallels with the intellectual development of the young Marx and the 'left Hegelians', who, while rejecting Hegel's absolute idealism and religious views, were still moulded by the master's system and love of coherence. Marxism, in conjunction with the General Strike of 1926, turned Anderson into a young comrade (or fellow-traveller) in a hurry. Were there certain tensions between his emergent 'realism' and his new Communist belief? If there were, he would not be the last Scot to embark for Australia with great hopes and a divided mind.

A RED ATHENS IN THE SOUTH, 1927–1940

The philosophers have only *interpreted* the world, in various ways; the point, however, is to *change* it.

Karl Marx

6

Sea City—Provincial Mind

SYDNEY grew lustily as a Moreton Bay fig from its first European toehold around the Tank Stream and Circular Quay. To the west of Sydney Cove, where the ground rose to sandstone outcrops, convicts lived in tents and barracks and gave a raw earthy vitality to the 'Rocks' that continued long after the convict era in the life of crowded tenements, pubs and sailors' dives. To the east, the governor and his officials set up their residences and later the 'exclusives' and colonial gentry built villas with views along the coves and inlets of the beautiful harbour. To the south, beyond the long rectangle of George and Elizabeth Streets, the settlement straggled following the dusty main road to Parramatta. It was here, about two miles south of the Post Office, that in 1853 the New South Wales Legislative Council chose the site for Australia's first university. William Charles Wentworth was one of the chief founders of an institution intended 'to enlighten the mind, to refine the understanding and to elevate their fellow men'. His considerable efforts ensured that the university would be secular—in that it would 'belong to no religious denomination and require no religious test', be 'accessible to all classes' through a system of bursaries, and housed in splendid buildings.[1]

Within less than a decade Edmund Blacket's Gothic masterpiece rose on Petersham Hill to contemplate the commercial city serenely from broad-banked lawns. The massed sandstone façade of gables, gargoyles, griffins, and oriel windows, with its central tower and flanking Great Hall, was softer and more English than the craggy black baronial of Glasgow's Kelvinside. From the lofty timber ceiling of the hall, angels bearing the names of the seven liberal arts peered down. Oxford and Cambridge were the traditions to be cultivated under Sydney's southern skies. The more serviceable Scottish influences would come later. Two of the university's three foundation professors were scholars from Oxford and Cambridge. The Rev. Dr John Woolley, the first Principal, was a distinguished classicist who believed the university was first 'a school of *liberal* and *general* knowledge, and secondly a collection of *special schools*, devoted to the learned professions'.[2] His successor, the Rev. Charles Badham, a fine Greek scholar, was in the same Oxford mould. Despite the grand beginnings and buildings, however, the institution languished for a generation and its narrowly classical curriculum rarely attracted more than a handful of students.

The university's rebirth in the 1880s can be attributed to the leadership of Sir William Manning, Chancellor from 1878 to his death in 1895, and to the philanthropy of John Henry Challis. The latter was a prosperous merchant and landowner whose generous bequests made possible the development of professional schools and the establishment of several new chairs, including one in mental and moral philosophy. The occupant of that chair from its foundation in 1890 until 1921 was Francis Anderson, a product of Glasgow and an exponent of Absolute Idealism. Many Scots joined the university in these years: Mungo MacCallum became the Professor of Modern Literature in 1886, Alexander Mackie the first Principal of Sydney Teachers' College in 1906 and Professor of Education in 1910, and there were a regiment of Scottish 'medicals' led by the redoubtable Anderson Stuart, Professor of Physiology, and J. T. Wilson, Professor of Anatomy, both from Edinburgh. Another Scot, Sir Normand MacLaurin, presided over the university as Chancellor from 1896 to 1914. When Professor Henry Jones visited Sydney in 1908, MacCallum and numerous graduates from Glasgow gave him a dinner. 'In my speech', Jones wrote home, 'I referred to old Caird, feelingly, and MacCallum moved that we should cable to him: "Glasgow graduates dining Jones send affectionate greetings" '.[3] In time MacCallum was to become Dean of the Faculty of Arts and in 1924, after a knighthood, the university's first full-time Vice-Chancellor. His successor in 1927 was Robert S. Wallace, a tall spare Aberdonian who had held the chair of English in the University of Melbourne. When young John Anderson arrived at Sydney in 1927 Scottish influences were at their zenith. He soon made friends with Alexander Mackie and visited Francis Anderson at Hunters Hill.

Francis Anderson was born in Glasgow in 1858 and at the age of fourteen became a pupil-teacher. He next completed a degree at Glasgow University under Edward Caird, gaining firsts in the two philosophy classes, and for some years assisted in the teaching of the department. He also studied theology under Caird's brother John, who was the Principal and a disciple of Hegel. Anderson first went to Australia in 1886 as a theological student to assist the controversial Rev. Charles Strong in his Australian Church, a modernist breakaway from the Presbyterian Church. After completing his engagement with Strong in Melbourne, he went to Sydney to give some university extension lectures on modern philosophy and in December 1886 was appointed a lecturer in logic and mental philosophy. He was a popular lecturer and the students strongly supported his application for the new chair, which he was successful in obtaining in 1890.

As a 'preacher professor' Anderson was attractive, eloquent and inspirational but too thinly spread and literary in his interests to become an authority in any one field. He wrote no serious works of philosophy and saw himself as one of 'the great working army of middlemen, through whose labour the thoughts and achievements of the few become the common and permanent possession of the many'.[4] Henry Laurie at Melbourne was a more serious practitioner of Scottish idealism and intuitive realism, 'grafting a quasi-Kantian idealism onto a Scottish common-sense stem'.[5] Together with William Mitchell at Adelaide, these three Scottish professors ensured the triumph of idealism in Australian universities by the turn of the century. As Passmore sums up, 'Philosophy was allied to literature and theology rather than to science, was committed to the defense of a liberal Christianity and to orthodox *mores*, and was Idealist in its metaphysical presumptions'.[6] Idealism was nothing if not a colonising creed and the visit of Henry Jones in 1908 was a great success. His farewell lecture to the University of Sydney, 'The answer of Idealism', concluded grandiloquently:

> It is easy for me in closing to wish you well. I cannot forget the greatness, and the difficulties of your enterprise—a new people amidst the lonely silence of a vast continent. Material prosperity you will attain, I have no doubt; and it is worth attaining. Perhaps power amongst the nations of the world awaits you, which is also worth attaining. But a kingdom founded upon righteousness, a life amongst yourselves sanctified in all its ways by this faith in man, in the world and in God, is greater far than all these things. I can form no higher wish for you than that it may be your destiny to try by actual experiment how far this faith of the Idealists will stand the strain of a nation's practice.[7]

Francis Anderson, like Jones, was keenly interested in social, religious and ethical questions. Following Caird and T. H. Green, he criticised the old liberalism for being too narrow and individualistic and he sought to inspire his students with a wider sense of social responsibility to the poor about them. He became involved in the Workers' Educational Association, advanced the cause of women's education, and supported the work of the university settlement at Woolloomooloo. Because he regarded Australia as a new country and an advanced social laboratory, he advocated the serious study of sociology and the social sciences in the university, appealing to American rather than British precedents. Although he failed to establish a chair of Sociology, his efforts were more successful in the fields of Psychology and Education, and chairs were established. He regarded the prevailing pupil-teacher system as a form of bondage and fought for more liberal conditions of training for schoolteachers at the Teachers' College and the university. With Alexander Mackie, he achieved some success after the royal commission of 1902 and the appointment of Peter Board as Director of Education in 1905. Anderson endorsed the 'new education', which emphasised pupil initiative, imagination and free inquiry rather than memorising, rote learning and drill. His own practice of encouraging questions during lectures was an appealing demonstration of the theory. According to one of his students:

> Anderson's was the first and only lecture room that I found in my undergraduate days at Sydney where questions were asked and discussion was encouraged . . . Anderson would dictate a few sentences to us slowly, and then begin to walk about, elaborating his points, popping questions to us, encouraging our replies, and trying to get as many of us as he could to join in the discussion . . . To how many generations of students was that lecture room of his, right up in the Tower, a refreshment after arid mornings of note-taking in other lectures?[8]

Anderson, who was a Christian non-conformist, eschewed all religious denominations. During the First World War he became an ardent supporter of the League of Nations, and in 1936 he was knighted for his services to education.

His successor to the chair in 1922 was Bernard Muscio, a local product who had gone to England after completing his degree at Sydney. At Cambridge Muscio encountered the work of Bertrand Russell and G. E. Moore and seriously began to question aspects of idealism. Muscio was also a friend of Wittgenstein, when he was first in Cambridge, and wrote a perceptive review of the *Tractatus Logico-Philosophicus* in an early issue of the *Australasian Journal of Psychology and Philosophy*. Returning to Sydney, he became a lecturer in Anderson's department and published a pioneering book on industrial psychology. Had he lived, he would have led the department in new directions and brought it into greater contact with the 'new realism' but in 1926 he died of heart disease at the age of thirty-nine. It was on the generous testimonials of Kemp Smith and A. E. Taylor and the recommendation of Francis Anderson that the Senate appointed John Anderson to the Challis Chair of Philosophy on 6 December 1926. There was only one other applicant.

The university that John Anderson joined as a professor in Lent Term 1927 was a small, close-knit and fairly conservative institution. The student body numbered about 3000 and the academic staff about 120. Arts and Medicine were the largest faculties, followed by Science, Law and Economics. Most of the ten professional faculties were quite small. Medicine and Law wielded great power on the university governing bodies, the Senate and the Professorial Board, and the Chancellor was usually a judge or some eminent medical personage. There was certainly no tradition of dissent at the university; only Arnold Wood, the historian, had been roused to speak out about the injustices of the Anglo-Boer War and he had been trounced by the patriotic MacCallum and censured by the Senate for his pains. MacCallum's appointment as the first full-time Vice-Chancellor in 1924 further enhanced the university's loyalist and conservative image, for the diminutive professor and famous Shakespearean scholar was a 'king's man' who had strongly supported the war effort and conscription—as had all the professors of the university. Some 1700 members of the university had enlisted for service during the war and in the year that John Anderson arrived MacCallum launched an appeal for a war memorial fund.

Departments were small, teachers were versatile generalists rather than specialists, and professors were god-like in their authority. Lectures were the principal means of instruction for pass students and there were no tutorial classes, though honours students and the minority of College residents might receive more specialised and individual attention. In general, its members would have agreed with John Henry Newman's view that the university was essentially a teaching institution for 'the diffusion and extension of knowledge' rather than its advancement, and research was accorded far less importance than teaching. Almost half the Arts students were part-timers attending lectures at night, and this was a pattern that went back to the turn of the century. Fees were still substantial and a bar to many from the working class. For the talented élite there were one hundred bursaries and five hundred exhibitions, which exempted students from fees, but for the many much depended on winning an Education Department studentship. Unlike most other faculties, Arts had an unusually high proportion of female students, more than half the total enrolment in 1927, and most of them were headed for a teaching career. Fisher Library and the cloisters had been recently completed, making the handsome Arts quad a favourite meeting-place for students. Union nights were an exclusively male affair and fostered a strong debating tradition. Commemoration or Commem Day was the principal town and gown event to celebrate the university's foundation. Decorated floats and student revellers left the university grounds to parade and riot through the streets of a great commercial city. The festivities became so boisterous and unruly during the 1920s that the conservative Senate banned the procession for several years.

In 1927 Sydney's population was over a million, almost half of the state's total. A sea city, Sydney was Australia's oldest and, after the depression of the 1890s, largest city. Its prosperity had always been associated with overseas trade and the export staples of its vast rural hinterland—wool, wheat and minerals—and its merchant princes and squatter legislators dominated the city in the nineteenth century. Manufacturing developed slowly, piecemeal and late, so that the labour force from the Rocks and other working-class suburbs was mainly engaged in unskilled work on the docks or in small plant and factories. Suburbanisation occurred in the 1880s and again in the 1920s with the development of water transport, a tramways system and railways. Speculative building and rapid subdivision in the western and south-western suburbs created serious housing problems in Sydney's testing climate. Poor drainage and lack of sewerage resulted in much ill health, a high infantile mortality, and regular outbreaks of typhoid fever, sometimes even the plague. The class boundary remained the city's east–west divide and it met at the university, which was surrounded by the working-class suburbs of Redfern, Newtown, Glebe and Chippendale:

> Visually, the social differences between east and west were unmistakable. Well-heeled people who worked in the shops and business houses along George and York Streets probably seldom ventured further westward, but if they did, they would soon have found themselves, if not in a different world, at least in one considerably meaner and dirtier than their own . . . The visual impact was greater if west Sydney was approached from Darling Harbour, as it was every

> morning by commuters on the Balmain and Hunter's Hill ferries. Behind the squalid structures and fevered bustle of the wharves of the coastal shipping companies, rows of cramped terraces and crooked streets came into view, jammed between factories, flour mills and the gasometers of the Australian Gas Light Company.[9]

The loss of independence and erosion of skills associated with the 'industrial revolution' in Sydney's inner city suburbs, contributed to serious worker alienation and to the great maritime strike of 1890. The strikes, industrial struggles and depression of the 1890s exposed the hollow claim that Australia was the working man's country. Out of these conditions and the defeat of the unions, the Australian Labor Party rose to represent the working man in politics. Its early electoral successes drew on the support of Sydney's large Irish-Australian population as well as a vigorous local tradition of radical journalism.

Labor won office in New South Wales in 1910 and at the federal level briefly in 1904 and then, in its own right, in 1910, making it one of the two principal parties in the Australian political system. Many of its leaders were Sydneysiders, including J. C. Watson, W. M. Hughes and W. A. Holman, and its greatest hold was on Sydney's working-class suburbs. Strong links with the trade union movement helped to give the Labor Party an incremental and meliorist outlook, and most of its members were reformists rather than revolutionaries. However, there were small groups of socialists, influenced by a range of ideas from Bellamy and George to Marx, and in 1905 they persuaded a party conference to accept a version of the socialisation objective.

During the First World War, conscription and the Irish Easter rising of 1916 split the Labor Party, which was in government, and ousted the militants from power. Sydney's socialists exercised their greatest influence on the party at this time, which coincided with the Russian Revolution and Red Clydeside. Led by a Scottish socialist and union leader, Jock Garden, in 1920 they formed the Communist Party of Australia, 'which followed a policy of working within the Labor Party with the aim of converting it to socialism and even toyed with the idea that socialism could be introduced by parliamentary means'.[10] While linked with the Comintern, the Communists were willing to co-operate with the Labor Party and welcomed writers and intellectuals to their ranks. The party impressed John Anderson when he sought to become its 'theoretical adviser' in 1927 and when its membership was less than 250.

Why did Anderson seek to become associated as a Communist at this moment? He had, of course, a deep commitment to socialism that went back to his radical father, Stonehouse days, Red Clydeside and Jenny, but it had been difficult to translate his theoretical interests into political action. The 1926 General Strike changed all that. Anderson was greatly impressed with the militancy and enterprise of the ordinary rank and file during the ten-day strike, but also deeply disappointed by the timidity and moderation of the trade union and parliamentary leadership:

> The General Strike was called off just when it was at its strongest. It was not just a question of numbers. Day by day the organisation of the strike had improved—bulletins, pickets, security, control of transport and goods distribution. Day by day organisation developed more and more in the localities around the strike committees, trades councils and Councils of Action. The weaker and more hesitant the General Council became, the stronger, tougher and more united became the *local* leadership or, at least, the best of them. The gap had widened between the effective forces of struggle in the localities and an ineffective reluctant national leadership. Mass political understanding of the issues was becoming ever clearer. And all over Britain thousands of men and women, whose factory, pit, depot or unemployed committee had been their university, who drew their strength from their class, from their experience of struggle, were becoming acknowledged leaders of the strike.[11]

Only the Communists supported the miners after 12 May and urged a continuation of the struggle, in spite of the arrest of their leaders. There were many like John Anderson who admired their stand, and party membership doubled during the strike, from 5000 to 10 000. But he was not one of those to join. What almost certainly resolved the issue in 1927 was his decision to emigrate and leave behind the unduly cautious ways of the Scottish academic establishment. A new life in a new country—perhaps even the workers' country—provided him with the chance to be himself at last. One of his first acts in Sydney after installing himself in his room at the university was to go to the Communist Party headquarters in Sussex Street, introduce himself, and seek membership. It was a bold step.

Yet, as if to qualify his action, Anderson did not choose to live near the university in a crowded workers' suburb; instead, like any other professor, he chose the salubrious Turramurra on the north shore, an area disproportionately settled by prosperous Scots and Protestants. The proximity of Alexander Mackie's home at Wahroonga may have influenced his decision. A large roomy house in a garden setting on a spacious block was certainly a more attractive proposition than cramped inner-city living with the proletariat. It was also a shrewd investment as Dr Bradfield's Harbour Bridge gradually took shape above Sydney's skyline. But did the isolation and alien bushland appeal as much to the shy and reticent Jenny or to the boisterous Sandy? There were few neighbours or children in easy walking distance of 'Levenshulme' in Turramurra Avenue. Not to worry, the professor had his rural retreat to rest, contemplate and read and, at weekends to entertain his admiring students. His salary even permitted a maid and a gardener. As Marx said, it is from the bourgeois intelligentsia that good Communists are made.

7

Founding a School

IN A REVEALING ADMISSION to Jenny at the time of the Russian Revolution, John Anderson wrote that he had 'the feelings of a romantic, with the thoughts of a classicist'.[1] Such a confession helps shed light on Anderson's most romantic phase—his complex and passionate involvement with Marx and Marxism during the 1920s and 1930s: 'There is, indeed, no solid social theory except the Marxist', he confidently asserted in 1932, and one of the major attractions of Marxism for Anderson was its marriage of theory and practice—'true theory is that in the light of which we *transform* things, and which we arrive at only by being active'.[2] It was, of course, to be a Marxism largely mediated through the great revolutionary Lenin and the historical materialist Engels; and John Anderson's political and social commitment also entangled his wife in the long drawn-out affair with Russia and all things Russian. Dostoevsky in the Constance Garnett translations became and remained her favourite novelist and a rack of his novels was never far from her bedside.

That a Scottish philosopher and his wife from Red Clydeside should become, in the decade after the Russian Revolution, converts to the 'science' of Marxism and believers in the imminence of a proletarian revolution should cause no surprise. It was to become the secular faith of a whole generation of Scottish intellectuals, many of the Andersons and Baillies among them. However, the shifts and turns in Anderson's relations with Communism and the Party over the decade are unusual and striking; and they manifest some of the tensions between his romantic temperament and critical intellect, individual ego and group loyalties, and between liberal and collectivist values. After some years spent with, though not in, the Communist Party as 'theoretical adviser', Anderson fell out with the leadership in 1932 and left to help form a breakaway Workers' Party. Trotsky replaced Stalin as the true heir of the revolution and the correct expounder of Marxism-Leninism. Though Anderson had begun seriously to question the philosophical underpinnings of 'scientific' Marxism, it was only in 1937 with the Moscow trials that he broke decisively with the practice of Communism and left the Trotskyites for good, causing much contention among his Scottish family and relatives, whom he visited on his sabbatical in 1938. The waning fascination with Marxism as social theory lasted for another decade. Then one of the great positive influences on his social and political thought soured. The realist critic had triumphed over the romantic, the professor over the comrade, experience over youth.

Anderson's close association with the Communist Party began in 1928 during the period of Jack Kavanagh's leadership. He supported Kavanagh's policy of 'propaganda' and infiltration through trade unions, the labour movement and the working class, a policy of 'boring from within' familiar to many an old socialist. As professor, philosopher and 'theoretical adviser', Anderson was a real 'catch' for the party, but he soon posed problems about the role of the disinterested intellectual. In several articles in *The Workers' Weekly* and in more extended pieces in *The Communist*, he and Jenny attempted to raise the level of theoretical discussion above mere agitation and propaganda; and, for a time, they found supporters in Kavanagh and H. Moxon. He attended the first session of the plenum of the party at Easter 1930, 'his status unknown to most comrades present'.[3]

For the young comrade professor, 'class' was an objective reality and the major division in society. The 'working class' or proletariat was the class of producers and 'the *best* class in society' because of its beau role—its members were 'nearest to social realities, most "socially necessary", and forming the material and the motive-force for a new society'.[4] Their emancipation, Anderson believed, would lead to complete freedom and 'the final disappearance of the exploitation of man by man'. Anderson defined freedom as 'not mere unhampered activity' but a particular kind of activity 'which is marked by initiative and responsibility, and which is of a productive character'.[5] Class struggle and revolution were both necessary to achieve the new society, and Anderson attacked 'reformism' and 'philanthropy' as 'a mere tinkering with social problems, as against a radical treatment of them'.[6] He strongly opposed arbitration, social work and all attempts to ameliorate the workers' lot on the grounds that:

> . . . the individual elector cannot make his claims good within the limits of the parliamentary system . . . Merely as an elector he has no political education; censorship and the press keep him, by general consent of the parties of capitalist government, ignorant of foreign affairs and confused about home affairs . . . There is nothing in these devices to justify the application of the term 'democratic' to the form of government. Democracy can only mean general participation in the framing and carrying out of policies, and this does not exist in capitalist communities.[7]

He accepted Lenin's analysis of parliament as an instrument of class rule—the state 'is an organ of exploiters against exploited'.[8] Indeed, he contrasted the passivity and 'undemocratic character of the parliamentary system' with the Soviet Union, the best example of 'a thoroughly planned economy, to replace competitive anarchy and brigandage . . . The Soviet system is truly democratic in that policies determined by the higher elected organs are returned to the lower organs for carrying out, and not handed over to a class of bureaucratic officials'.[9]

In lauding the Soviet achievement and attacking fascist movements in Australia, like the New Guard, Anderson did not spare the Labor Party, which advocated 'the realisation of socialism within capitalism':

> Orthodox 'Labour', then, whether it is showing how it can govern or inventing Utopian schemes of 'socialisation', is diverting the workers' movement and concealing the true

> character of the proletarian revolution, which arises from the position of the workers *as a productive force* in relation to the disintegrating capitalist form of production. Only working-class organisation, preparation to take over industry, to form a workers' State with real political activity for all workers, can prevent Fascism and war, and lead on to a classless society, exhibiting real solidarity. Such a society cannot exist until after the conquest of power and dictatorship of the proletariat. Thus the working class *is* the coming society, and must, like the Sinn Fein movement, form its own organisations and regard the capitalists as invaders of its industry, exploiters of its production. And in the formation of a productive, and necessarily international, society, it is for the educated, the thinkers, the active investigators, to be on the side of the producers.[10]

The alliance between intellectuals and 'heroic' workers, imbued with Sorel's ethic of the producer, was a theme he would elaborate and return to many times in this decade. One of his most dedicated students explained the necessary link between intellectual activity and the working class:

> The intellectual movement is a *productive* movement. Production, investigation and artistic activity are *good* and cooperate. They support one another. In present-day civilization industrial production, organised from a consumptive point of view dominates investigation and art to a great extent. But investigation when carried on in the pure intellectual spirit (not as a means for producing better employees or making more money) is independent of the commercial forces and in fact opposes them by exposing their nefarious ways of working. Commercial forces are very largely obscurantist so the investigator finds himself in the position of opposing commercialism or capitalism or the acquisitive or consumptive spirit. But this is what the working class movement is also doing, though it may start from a different point. It is concerned to expose the errors commonly imposed upon the proletariat and to organise against the censorious forces and the forces which enforce censorship i.e. capitalist forces.[11]

An emphasis on 'social culture', co-operation and experiment was also a marked feature of his educational writings at this time: 'Education properly understood, then, is liberal; it implies the most thorough-going democracy, the rejection alike of privileged ideas and of privileged persons'.[12]

Such views were highly provocative in the conservative political climate of the late 1920s, especially from a professor and Scottish outsider interested in major university reform. The Nationalist government of S. M. Bruce had used its emergency powers in 1927 to restrict the import of 'seditious' literature, a term interpreted to cover *The Communist Manifesto* and all the works of Lenin and Stalin. Anderson took a leading part in the struggle against growing political censorship and press control, seeing the two evils as 'features of capitalist disorganisation and oppression' that 'hang together'. He helped organise petitions at the university, and in Communist and Sydney newspapers widely publicised his opposition to all forms of censorship. Any voter, he wrote, who has not read some Communist books 'is condemning himself as unfit to vote either for or against Communism':

> In short, are we, Communists and non-Communists alike, to be allowed to discuss Communism? Or are we to regard ourselves as political infants, and to assume (a) that public opinion consists of the opinions of newspaper proprietors, (b) that political discussion is politically dangerous, (c) that the only thing that prevents us all from becoming Communists is our ignorance of what Communism is? Surely not.[13]

Anderson compared public censorship by governments and press owners to the work of Freud's 'private censor' on the individual mind: both activities were repressive and hindrances to freedom and spontaneity—'the theory of Freud, then, strengthens the case for the recognition, instead of the prohibition, of human motives and likewise of social movements'.[14] The banning of Joyce's *Ulysses* in 1930 was clearly an instance of the two processes at work—'it appears as a political expedient whereby a governing class secures the elimination . . . for the lower orders of anything which would make them reflect on their condition'.[15] Naturally, Anderson expected that in his efforts to fight censorship and promote 'the disinterested pursuit of knowledge by methods of free inquiry' he would enjoy the complete support of fellow Communists, since they were also dedicated to 'cultural, national and social emancipation'.

When in August 1932, however, the party leadership prevented the publication of an article by Anderson in the third issue of *Proletariat*, the journal of the Melbourne University Labour Club, because of its critical nature, he was outraged. This action precipitated a crisis in Anderson's relations with the party that led him to distinguish between the working class and a party executive increasingly identified with the Comintern and its policy of 'democratic centralism'. He accused fellow Scot J. B. Miles, the general secretary, of being sectarian, ignorant, authoritarian and bureaucratic:

> Whatever, then, be the exact relation between leadership and spontaneity, it is obvious that a *fear* of spontaneity is a sign not of leadership, but of bureaucracy. It is this which gives rise to personal abuse . . . and to the guarding of members from contamination by having any contact with those who have been expelled.[16]

Anderson also charged the party leadership of Lance Sharkey with neglecting 'independent social movements', local circumstances, and failing to think for itself because of the bogey of 'revisionism'. Above all, they neglected to study the works of Marx:

> The grotesque errors made by Marxists regarding the history of philosophy would be an interesting subject of discussion, although difficult to present in non-technical language. It may simply be pointed out here that Marxists in general do not even go to Marx's sources, but study only Marxist literature—and this applies in economics as much as in philosophy. Here we have another example of fear of contamination; but those who confine their attention to what is 'correct' *are not studying*.[17]

One particular philosophical error he castigated was the putative distinction between objective and subjective factors in history. 'Recent realist philosophy', he claimed, 'has shown that mental facts are as objective as anything else. But, while the distinction between subjective and objective does not hold, the fact of independence remains'. It was this criticism that caused the leadership to suppress his article, for they saw in his remarks a defence of idealism. 'In 1929 I had an argument with him over this question, in 395 Sussex Street', Kavanagh dutifully reported to the Central Committee:

> He denied that his ideas of things were the result of sense impressions. I asked him if a table that was in the hall was on the floor or in his mind. He said that the table was in his mind and not an impression of it. I pointed out that if that was the case there must be two tables because it was also in my mind.[18]

Kavanagh had crudely misrepresented Anderson's doctrine of 'realism', which denied both the representative theory of truth and the distinction between mind and matter. For Anderson, 'minds' were as factual and objective as any other thing, and so the distinction between objective and subjective facts broke down and could not be sustained. But such were the proletarian mentors of Anderson that they attacked him as a bourgeois renegade and a 'professorial lackey'.

Already Anderson was pointing to some of the philosophical confusions and shortcomings of 'dialectical materialism' that he would adumbrate over the next decade. In a talk given in the university to the Literary Society in 1932, he exposed certain relativist confusions in the Marxist view of art, especially the confusion between class origin and ideological correctness on the one hand, and the quality or character of the work of art on the other. 'The view that "art is always a social servant and historically utilitarian" is simply false', he maintained and, championing the cause of *Ulysses*, he began to advance 'an independent aesthetic'.[19] Anderson's ethical doctrine of goods working together through the vehicle of spontaneous social movements accorded well with his own political practice:

> We do not, in fact, step out of the movement of things, ask 'What am I to do?' and, having obtained an answer, step in again. All our actions, all our questionings and answerings, are part of the movement of things; and if we can work on things, things can work on us—if they can be our 'vehicles', we also can be vehicles; social and other forces can work through us.[20]

Anderson's first realist manifesto appeared in 1927 in the *Australasian Journal of Psychology and Philosophy*. If the journal's editor, Francis Anderson, sought to encourage the idealist virtue of 'conciliation', John Anderson introduced a denunciatory tone and an uncompromising professionalism from the start. In a spare but devastating review he demolished the 'false doctrine' of Canon Streeter's book *Reality*. 'On this issue there can be no compromise; the realist and the idealist simply cannot recognise each other's competence. Speaking as a realist, I find myself bound to assert that Idealism, so far from being competent philosophy, is not philosophy at all', he declared to his Australian audience.[21] It was to be war to the knife with idealism. In a major article of 1927 entitled 'Empiricism', Anderson distinguished his general philosophical position from rationalism and idealism, and commenced to lay the foundations of a philosophical logic: 'To get rid of idealism we have to go back upon all sophisticated "modern" views and recapture the Greek directness. We have to banish mind from philosophy, and in so doing make incidentally possible a positive account of mind itself'.[22]

An early skirmish with the Australian idealists, W. A. Merrylees and A. C. Fox, occurred over some issues in logic, including the question of universals. For Merrylees, the Melbourne idealist, 'the universal is necessarily and essentially an ideal, and ideals are essential to thought or discourse'. Anderson denied that universals were 'any sort of ultimate' and regarded universality as a characteristic of the proposition—'there are no "higher" entities but everything that concerns particulars is on their own level of existence'. A. C. Fox, a former student of Francis Anderson, took up the issue of mind and its active role in knowing, and asserted the idealist position that 'what we know, we know in relation; and what relates and recognises relations can only be the mind'.[23] Anderson returned to the defence of independence and pressed his attack on relativism and constitutive relations—'nothing is constituted by knowing and nothing by being known'.

> Thus the recognition of the 'subject-object' relation, or relation between knower and known, implies that each of these is an independent thing, or thing with an existence and characters of its own, and that it cannot be properly described in terms of the other thing or of the relation between them. This point I expressed by saying that the thing which is known, or the 'object', is not *constituted* by the knower or by being known, nor is the thing which knows, or 'subject', constituted by knowing or by the known. In other words, we cannot define the nature or character or constitution or 'what is it' of a thing by saying what relations it has or what it is related to. Hence I concluded that we must reject the notions of 'that whose nature it is to know', or *consciousness*, and 'that whose nature it is to be known', or *idea*.[24]

Anderson also repudiated the idealist assertion that motives, or passions, and objectives, or ends, were 'essentially correlative terms'. Rejecting evolutionism and all teleologies, Anderson asserted that realism 'does away with the philosophy of good intentions, of "service" to the idol of social utility or any other, and establishes philosophy as logic, the logic of events'.[25] His study of Marx helped to deflate idealist and 'solidarist' notions of the common good, of 'all (exploiter and exploited alike) standing together for mutual aid'; on the contrary, 'all activities or proposals of a solidarist character, all schemes of "class-collaboration" or social unity, are for the benefit of the ruling class and for the deception of the workers'.[26] Likewise, Anderson exposed 'moralism' as compulsive behaviour rather than free and spontaneous activity: '*Good* motives may be said . . . to arise through sympathetic induction, or through the spontaneous development of a person's natural capacities'.[27] In further important essays on utilitarianism (1932), ethics (1933), and mind as feeling (1934), Anderson elaborated his realist position. His attack on utilitarianism and relativism in ethics disconcerted the idealists because, as Passmore shrewdly observes, 'he did not fit into the picture which Australian idealists had constructed of their opponents—as in the fortress at Singapore, their guns were pointing in the wrong direction'.[28]

During these years the young professor's zeal went into founding and building a strong school of philosophy at Sydney that would embody the prized qualities of system, coherence and rigour. For the first six years he did most of the teaching in the department and his own ideas necessarily moulded the curriculum. In Greek philosophy there was a new emphasis on the pre-Socratics and the Platonic dialogues. His 'journeyman phase' at Edinburgh influenced his teaching of modern philosophy, and 'the theories of Space and Time' and 'the distinction between the rationalist and the empiricist standpoints' featured prominently in the syllabus and his lectures. Within another few years Anderson added substantial new courses on logic, ethics, eighteenth century thought and political philosophy. During the depression, the university experienced serious problems with funding, and for some years Anderson had only one lecturer to assist him. In time, he came to believe that the Senate was hostile to his educational aims and had even frustrated the appointment of two personal nominees. 'I have no doubt whatever that it is because of my political views that these obstructive tactics have been adopted', he protested to the Vice-Chancellor in September 1933.[29] That was after his famous confrontation with the University Senate over the issue of free speech and war memorials.

During 1933 Anderson took a leading part in the move to liberalise the faculty regulations concerning choice of subjects and degree structure. His strong opposition to the compulsory language requirements in an overburdened Arts curriculum threatened the interests of the 'old guard' and angered Professors Woodhouse and Todd of Classics and Nicholson of Modern Languages, among others. Anderson's reform proposals caused considerable acrimony but in the end they were carried, with the support of Mackie, Mills and others of like mind.[30]

In teaching philosophy, Anderson held to his Scottish ways and a conservative style of pedagogy. 'Lectures', he believed, 'will always remain the central feature of any course of higher study'. Accordingly, the daily lecture was all-important—Anderson dictated his lectures slowly and deliberately, while pacing before the famous murals of the philosophy lecture room, or promenading up and down the aisle. He expected students to take good notes and go away to wrestle with the problems, and did not encourage questions during the lecture: 'If students think over the lecture-material for themselves and discuss it with one another, they will make more progress than if they are continually running to the staff for further explanation', he wrote.[31] There were no tutorials, so Anderson's genial manner and accessibility to students outside formal classes in the quad was a real stimulus and help, and rare among staff of his day. There was much in the lectures that was original and exciting but nothing superficial or showy, for, as Anderson affirmed, 'the question is of the gradual unfolding of a position and the growing understanding of it on the part of students'; it was all part of a seamless whole and students needed to do more than a year's philosophy to appreciate the sweep and complexity of Anderson's system. Logic was central to the experience. Most students felt the compelling presence of the tall gowned professor with the deep brown eyes and the distinctive Scots burr, but only the élite of honours students 'could observe at first hand what intellectual creation is like'. As one of his best students recollected:

> From Anderson, then, we got a sense . . . of the relatedness of the different branches of culture; the idea of a common theoretical or 'critical' approach to the different fields of intellectual creation and discovery. Anderson's philosophy was, from one point of view, a criticism of culture. For that reason, it provided an education of an unusually broad and fundamental kind. It was not merely that he introduced one, as any other cultivated and perceptive teacher might have done, to the important things that were being said and thought in the contemporary world and linked them to the history of thought. Anderson was, of course, no mere expositor, not even merely a critic. He was still very young

> when he came to Sydney: between 1927 and 1937, he was thinking strenuously, still developing his 'position'. And consequently those of us who studied with him (or later worked with him) had the experience of being associated with a thinker engaged in the work of creating a very impressive intellectual construction.[32]

Throughout his career at Sydney, Anderson held a liberal view of the university and strongly emphasised the role of criticism in the 'cultivation of free inquiry': 'in the absence of an organisation devoted to the prosecution of inquiry, there will be nothing decisively to combat the routine which accompanies a personal or provincial outlook in any department of life'.[33] A liberal education was fundamentally opposed to censorship because 'the drift of all that kind of thing is narrow, unimaginative, mischievous, stupid'. In his discussion of censorship in 1928 he deplored the increase in political and moralistic censorship since the war, comparing its stultifying effect on ideas and social movements with the repression inflicted on the mind by the Freudian 'censor':

> Repression may prevent motives from operating in certain ways, but it cannot put them out of existence. It can force them to adapt themselves to it, but this only means that they find some clandestine and insidious mode of operation, while they remain ready to break out in the original direction at the first favourable moment. This theory receives verification from dreams, 'accidents', obsessions and a whole range of cognate phenomena.[34]

Such frankness and courage, when applied to sexual matters and their open and public discussion, were unusual in a professor in the 1920s and 1930s. Some of Anderson's senior colleagues had been official censors during the war, and one of them had played a leading part in the dismissal of Chris Brennan for adultery. They can hardly have welcomed Anderson's blunt assertion that 'man is a sexual animal, and in this as in other activities can only learn by "trial and error" '.[35] Why had they not been told of his opinions before his appointment?

8

Socratic Gadfly

WHEN IN SEPTEMBER 1930 some radical students formed the Society for Free Thought, Anderson became its first president. Many of his principal concerns found expression in the aims of the society—anti-clericalism, his view of science and knowledge as experimental, and his opposition to all forms of censorship. According to the basis adopted in March 1931, 'This Society (a) recognises the primacy of science, holding that in every subject without exception knowledge is to be gained only by observation and experiment; (b) supports the widest possible extension of knowledge of all subjects; and (c) is therefore opposed to every form of censorship and restriction of inquiry'.[1]

On 9 July 1931 Anderson gave his first presidential address, a bold fighting speech in defence of free thought in politics. Deploring the widespread association of religion and politics in patriotic ceremonies, he attacked all '*political* superstitions or idols':

> An idol is any object treated in such a way as to prevent or hamper discussion and criticism. Thus a superstitious regard for or loyalty to 'the State' or 'the Country' is a noteworthy feature of modern political life. But such sayings as 'your King and Country need you' appeal to prejudice and superstition and will be criticised by freethinkers. War memorials too are political idols and the keeping up of religious ceremonies connected with them

> are merely fetishes for the purpose of blocking discussion. They prevent critical thinking about the character and conditions of the last war and thus about war and social relations in general.[2]

Anderson's stern comments provoked much student discussion and when accounts of the address were published in the Sydney press, a storm of protest. As a well-known Communist sympathiser, Anderson attracted the hostility of many in the Nationalist and Country Parties, ex-servicemen's organisations and the churches. The Returned Soldiers and Sailors Imperial League of Australia condemned 'the recently reported utterances of Professor John Anderson', and on 14 July the Nationalist–Country Party opposition in the New South Wales Parliament launched their attack against the red professor. Mr Sanders, the member for Willoughby, urged that Professor Anderson 'is anti-Christian and non-patriotic; that he is a curse to the country; and that the sooner the Senate of the University takes steps to put him out of his job and send him back to Glasgow . . . or make him abide by the laws of the country, the better it will be for the country'.[3] The Country Party Deputy Leader, Colonel Bruxner, declared that Anderson's views were 'against the best interests of the community' and were 'not in accord with the national sentiment of the people of this State'. He also called on the university Senate to take drastic disciplinary action. 'Our concern is to get him out', he bluntly stated. Premier Jack Lang was philosophical and did nothing except to reflect on the slaughtered redcoats in *Sartor Resartus* and quote Dr Johnson, 'patriotism is the last refuge of the scoundrel'.

The University Senate met on 20 July to consider its course of action. Already, Anderson had received many letters of support from individuals and groups all over the country and, although alone and 'misrepresented' by the press, he determined to take his stand on the issue of academic freedom. In a submission to the Senate before the meeting he defended his use of the terms 'idols' and 'fetishes' in connection with war memorials and patriotic ceremonies:

> My first point was that here we have something set above discussion and criticism: and this is borne out by the very

> reception of my statements, and particularly by my being accused of deriding the dead. This shows that it has become an absolute dogma that an attitude to these emblems is an attitude to persons who have died. And that bears out my further point that such dogmas prevent discussion of matters of the utmost social importance.[4]

Provocatively, Anderson stated his opposition to patriotism or 'state religion', saying that 'to attempt . . . to give a religious sanction to national sentiment, even assuming such sentiment to be defensible, is to sink to the level of tribal superstition'. He also stated his general objection to war memorials because of 'the ritualistic and militaristic elements involved', and maintained that the recently dedicated university war memorial was 'prejudicial to academic life'. While he did not accept 'the official British theory of the war', he was careful to point out that his views did 'not imply any attitude of disrespect or derision towards the University men who died in the war'.

In the late mid-winter afternoon he appeared briefly before the 76-year-old Chancellor, Sir William Cullen, and the Senate. To the Chancellor's many uncomprehending questions, Anderson remained impervious and refused to give an inch:

> *Chancellor*: Loyalty to the King. Do you consider this a possible subject for discussion?
> *Anderson*: Yes.
> *Chancellor*: Revolution or a rising, as in Russia. Do you think this a matter for discussion?
> *Anderson*: Yes.
> *Chancellor*: Do you think such subjects as murder, marriage, rape etc. should be discussed?
> *Anderson*: I think so.
> *Chancellor*: What about assassination?
> *Anderson*: I think all political questions should be discussed. There should be no limit to discussion in any matter.
> *Chancellor*: Are there no matters sufficiently sacred to be outside the scope of discussion?
> *Anderson*: I consider that good must come from criticism. The spreading of information in accordance with intellectuality is within the functions of an academic man. A philosophical person should be prepared to discuss any matter.[5]

No compromise was possible. For Anderson academic freedom was simply incompatible with loyalty or 'an uncritical adherence to any object or standpoint'. Professor Todd, 'the Metternich of the University' and a war censor to boot, raised the matter of Anderson's persistent refusal to stand and doff his hat during the national anthem when it was played on the carillon. Todd was the composer of the war memorial hymn, *Campanarum Canticum*. 'My act was not due to inadvertence', Anderson calmly replied; 'The custom involves some elements of ritualism and militarism'. MacCallum intervened to suggest 'that there may be such a thing as reasoned loyalty', but Anderson remained adamant: 'No. I am bound to oppose that view'. 'Loyalism', he submitted, was a false theory 'of the nature of actual social and political forces. It mistakes the basis of social co-operation, which lies, not in any common adherence or common emblem, but in common interests, in the actual work that people care to perform'. Then he left 'the scribes and Pharisees'.

His extremism and intransigence alarmed most of the Senate. The Chancellor and the Chief Justice, Sir Philip Street, believed Anderson was 'wholly unfit to occupy his chair' and called for a strong vote of censure at the very least. The octogenarian member, Judge Backhouse, thought his views were 'fantastic and idiotic', and Professor Sir John Peden, the punctilious Dean of the Law Faculty and President of the Legislative Council, found him 'lacking in common sense and decent feeling'. Eventually MacCallum moved the resolution that was carried by eleven votes to eight:

> The Senate, while asserting the principle of free speech in Universities, and assured that Professor John Anderson in his class lectures has maintained due impartiality in treating the various topics with which he has to deal, finds that when discussing the questions of patriotism, loyalty, war memorials, religious observances, and unconstitutional methods in his address delivered at the University on 9th instant, to a society of University students, he used expressions that transgress all proper limits, and for so doing severely censures him, and requires him to abstain from such utterances in future.

Anderson was incensed by the motion and challenged the authority of the Senate for taking 'insufficient account of the importance of the staff, of their quite fundamental function in our academic society'. He felt it absurd that he, 'as an educationist, should be censured by a body which has no educational competence whatever', and he attempted without success to persuade the Professorial Board to bring pressure on the Senate to rescind the motion.[6]

But he had made his mark on the university and wider community, outraged the conservatives and contributed to the making of a legend among students. 'I will not insult the intelligence of this class by asking it to put the Senate's resolution into logical form', he is reputed to have said, followed by the reflection that Socrates was also attacked as a 'corruptor of youth'. Apocryphal or not, there was substance in the myth, for Anderson, like Socrates, 'gloried in the fact, that he had striven by example and precept to inculcate the spirit of criticism'.

At the heart of Anderson's view of the university was the activity of criticism, 'the questioning of received opinions and traditions', a conception which derived in large measure from the life and death of Socrates. To illustrate the controversial and disturbing nature of Socratic criticism, Anderson drew an analogy between Athenian 'piety' of Socrates' day and Australian nationalism in the 1930s:

> Now the position of Socrates is simply that this uncritical acceptance of tradition, this acquiring of Athenian virtue, is no education at all. There is no virtue in being an Athenian, no peculiar and superior Athenian brand of goodness, but goodness is the same wherever it occurs, and what passes as good at Athens may not be really good at all. It requires the most careful scrutiny, and until this process of examination has begun, education has not begun. To see the full force of this criticism, we may substitute Australia for Athens, and imagine Socrates saying, 'You think there is some virtue in being Australian, and that a good Australian is better than a good Greek or Italian, but what you call goodness is just your own ignorance'. Clearly such talk would be infuriating, clearly also it would be very hard to answer.[7]

When Anderson denounced war memorials and patriotic ceremonies as 'fetishes' and 'idols' it certainly was infuriating to many Australians. But what did he mean? Anderson's ideas were more influenced by Marx than by Freud on this issue. According to Marx, a commodity becomes a fetish when people treat it as an object external to themselves and falsely invest it with independent power and reality, even semi-magical powers and properties; in this way, it becomes a source of mystification and confusion. 'To find an analogy', Marx wrote in *Capital*,

> we must have recourse to the mist-enveloped regions of the religious world. In that world the productions of the human brain appear as independent beings endowed with life, and entering into relation both with one another and the human race. So it is in the world of commodities with the products of men's hands.[8]

War memorials were, therefore, expressions of a spurious state religion of 'unthinking adherence' to one's country and as such were hindrances to critical thought about war, peace and reality in general. 'It is part of my business as a philosopher to remove symbols and get down to realities', he asserted:

> And the same conditions apply when I am trying to get down to political realities. Whatever is used to cloak political realities I am prepared to call an idol. And I contend that war-memorials are so used, even if other sentiments are also attached to them. Indeed it is just this mixture of sentiments which makes cloaking possible. And the solution is to think of the realities—the actual persons in their lives and deaths, and the actual issues of the combat. When all this is thought of, there is no need to think of the symbol, and great possible harm in doing so.[9]

Like Marx, he maintained that 'the criticism of heaven is transformed into a criticism of earth' as the exposure of such quasi-religious illusions as patriotism led to a consideration of the social and economic conditions that produced them. Imperial rivalries for markets, profits and scarce resources as well as the international conflicts they generated should be at the core of any 'realist' consideration of war and its causes.

That the philosophical creed of Sir Henry Jones should provide as much justification as Christianity for the 'symbols' of patriotism, duty and service to the nation, was sheer provocation to the realist professor. Absolute Idealism regarded the nation-state as the moral embodiment of the 'common good'. If that was not enough, there was the sore point of the university carillon, which Anderson had strongly opposed, regarding it in the circumstances of depression and high unemployment as a pretentious folly. He had unsuccessfully advocated a system of bursaries to commemorate the war dead.

War, nationalism and bravery—these were highly charged issues in the over-heated political climate of mid-1931, and it is worth recalling that they remained sensitive issues for Anderson himself, who was still something of an outsider in the university and community. According to one opposition speaker in parliament:

> This man never felt the privations of war; he never exposed his body upon the battlefield in defence of the principles of liberty for which the soldiers fought. Because he never felt these things and has never been touched by the war, he can take up this attitude of high aloofness.[10]

Anderson had been exempt from military service for medical reasons in 1917 and there is no evidence to suggest that he was either a pacifist or conscientious objector then or later. In fact, he had refused to put on sackcloth and assume a penitential air at Glasgow; there he had boldly championed the causes of academic autonomy and disinterested inquiry in the university magazine, seeing the university itself as a battleground of opposing forces. Did he also sense that the University of Sydney and its traditions were threatened in the early 1930s, as the forces of 'commercialism' and reaction marshalled their strength for a showdown with 'Bolshevism' and the socialist Lang? It is evident from his contributions to *The Communist* and *The Workers' Weekly* that he subscribed to a Leninist interpretation of war as the result of secret diplomacy, capitalist profiteering and imperial rivalries. Like many Communists, he daily expected news of another 'imperialist' invasion of the workers' republic of the Soviet Union. One can only speculate on his reactions when the tsarist national anthem was played on the university carillon. Whatever the provocation, Anderson gave handsome demonstration to the public, the university authorities and students of a certain splendid recklessness, fierce opposition and a refusal to yield. He had no shortage of the warrior virtues. Few of his enemies forgot it.

Did he seriously risk losing his chair in 1931? Within the university, there were some senior professors who wanted him to go, but they hardly comprised a majority of the Professorial Board or even the Senate. A commitment to liberal values was strong enough among academics to have made it almost impossible to dismiss a member of staff for opinions sincerely held and expressed, no matter how unusual or eccentric. The Vice-Chancellor thought that dismissal or a public reproof 'would be taken outside as an attack on free speech within the University. A public reprimand would be dangerous to academic discipline'. Sexual misconduct was another matter, of course, and the university took its moral responsibilities towards the students—'*in loco parentis*'—very seriously indeed. This had been the real reason behind the forced resignation of R. F. Irvine in 1922 and the dismissal of Chris Brennan in 1924. They had caused offence by their open adulteries. Political and religious opinions of an unconventional and provocative character might shock the older 'war' generation of dons but they were unprepared to go beyond a strong censure and an undertaking to desist, unless the state intervened. Might they, then, seek to impose a political test on staff? This was Anderson's real fear.

As to that possibility, it was very fortunate that Jack Lang was Premier and Will Davies Minister of Education in 1931. By mid-1931 depression, deflation and high unemployment were rapidly polarising society and politics in New South Wales. The Right believed Communists had infiltrated the state Labor government, which wanted to repudiate interest payments to British bondholders and ignore the federal government's deflationary policies. A zealous few, like Anderson's neighbour in Turramurra, Eric Campbell, even thought the Communists were preparing to seize power by force and 'must be stamped out ruthlessly and without mercy'. The real drive to sack and deport the red professor came from the Nationalist and Country Parties, which were in opposition, from some churchmen and the returned servicemen's organisations. Had Thomas Bavin or, more remotely, Colonel Bruxner been premier, there would have been a great deal more pressure on the university to take severe disciplinary action, pressure which the Senate would have found hard to resist.

As it was, Lang declined to do anything until the Senate censure and the storm blew over, while Will Davies warmly supported Anderson's action and his right to free speech. In retrospect, Anderson's cause had been helped by the internal divisions created in Australian society by the war itself and the conscription referenda. After those traumatic events, no party could wrap itself in the flag. The widespread support Anderson attracted throughout the community confirmed his faith in the good sense of the people and his contempt for the reactionary élite. It was a moment to savour:

> Dear Professor Anderson,
>
> I want to thank you for your courageous action in speaking against war. What a mockery it all is! Religious services and monuments for the dead—while the living are left to starve. There are plenty of hungry and disillusioned Diggers who will serve as living war memorials. If the patriotic gentleman [*sic*] who condemn you—would back their noble sentiments with deeds one could admire them but all they have to offer is a twenty per cent cut in war pensions—their brand of patriotism pays good dividends.
>
> Margaret Larsen.[11]

In a grey institution in a grey decade, Anderson's public stand stood out like the splash of crimson rosellas against the drab wintry bush. It was the stuff of colour, charisma and legend, and helped to make Anderson into one of the most influential and popular professors in the university, with a notoriety extending well beyond its ivy-clad walls. As a student wrote in *Honi Soit*:

> We are not concerned with what John Anderson has to say about Communism or patriotism, but we are concerned that he be allowed to say it. There are working in this community

> forces which are continually gaining strength and which serve their various purposes by a constant and progressive stifling of the public mind, by artificial selection of the public information, and by careful biassing of the minds of the country's youth. Against this constant tyranny we must welcome John Anderson's revolt and we must support him.[12]

Anderson's bold stand epitomised philosophy as a way of life 'as contrasted with the mere acquisition of a number of arts or accomplishments'. His role as Socratic gadfly stinging the comfortable and complacent was costly of time and energy and would eventually take a heavy toll on his life and work. But was there any choice for a man of Anderson's moral and intellectual stature in the 1930s? Could he have acted otherwise in that dismal decade of censorship, depression and xenophobia? Fortunately for Australian cultural and intellectual life, he never relented. His action convinced the university authorities that he was not a man to be trifled with, and, in time, greatly strengthened his hand in shaping the department into a 'school', making his own appointments to the staff, and raising the standing of philosophy in the university and community.

9

A Realist 'Til it Hurts

IN 1932 Anderson broke with the leadership of the Communist Party over the issue of censorship. Disenchanted with the bureaucratic methods and increasingly authoritarian nature of the party, he helped to found the Workers' Party (Left Opposition) in 1933 in the depths of the depression when unemployment reached 30 per cent of the male work force. Anderson still retained his belief in the Soviet Union as a 'workers' republic' but he now subscribed to Trotsky's theory of 'permanent revolution' rather than Stalin's doctrine of 'socialism in one country'. With the rapid rise of Nazism in Germany, he realised the tactical necessity of a common front on the left and deplored the fratricidal strife between German Communists and Social Democrats (or 'social fascists' as they were labelled) that allowed Hitler to seize power. For all that, however, he still maintained his opposition to 'reformism' and working within the parliamentary system. The Comintern's attacks on Trotsky as the betrayer of the revolution revealed the self-serving nature of the Russian leadership, 'the intellectual degradation and the unscrupulousness of the Stalinists' with their 'almost incredible falsification of documents', and Anderson asked in a radio broadcast:

> How can culture spread without independence of thought, without open criticism of governmental policies, with the freedom to denounce Trotsky but not to read his works? How, in general, can culture flourish in a regime of

> denunciation (where informing passes as a virtue)? And how is culture compatible with the prevailing servile adulation of Stalin?[1]

Jenny also contributed to the work of disseminating Marxism. During the 1930s she organised and led a women's reading group at Turramurra, a quiet assertion of independence and initiative that was to have major effects on the intellectual development of its members. In discussions on a wide range of books, the group came to appreciate Jenny's skills as a teacher, her alert curiosity and high critical standards, if not always her forthright views on religion and the classless society to come.

In the depression years Anderson produced two dense major essays, 'Marxist Philosophy' and 'Marxist Ethics'. The first, published in 1935, was a brave attempt to rescue Marx from the Marxians—his disciples, expositors and devotees; it directly challenged the philosophical theories of 'secondary figures like Engels, Lenin and Stalin' because Marx 'made no consecutive statement of his philosophic views and . . . it was left to men of inferior intelligence like Engels, or men like Lenin for whom philosophy was of merely incidental interest, to supply the missing doctrines'.[2] Anderson's words remind us of how little was known in the 1930s, especially in the English-speaking world, of the young Marx's left-Hegelianism, his theory of alienation, the Paris Manuscripts of 1844 and the *Grundrisse.* In 'Marxist Philosophy' Anderson singled out some major philosophical errors for exposure and criticism: Engels' relativist view of 'class truth' and ethics, Lenin's representationist theory of knowledge and materialism, and Engels' monistic and teleological conception of society and 'universal history' borrowed from Hegel. His arguments deserve more detailed consideration.

Anderson had a short way with relativism and, in his characteristic manner, showed that any claim to relative truth involved one in self-contradiction. 'The only relevant distinction is that between absolute truth and absolute falsity' and not between absolute and relative truth. As for the copy theory of knowledge, Berkeley had convincingly refuted it when he argued 'that, in order to show that "an idea" is a good or bad copy of "an external thing", we should have to know them both and compare them—but, of course, if we can know external things directly, then the whole picture-theory collapses'.[3] Accepting that there was 'a direct knowledge of actual things', Anderson wielded his propositional view of truth and his pluralist critique to attack and discredit the monism implicit in Lenin's materialism. He also made short work of the 'dialectic' as logic. Contradiction was a feature of propositions and not of historical processes, so the law of contradiction—the negation of negation—was a 'mystification', involving the believer in something suspiciously like religious faith or 'fideism':

> 'Dialectic', like any other theory postulating an ultimate reality, is necessarily authoritarian or 'fideist', to use Lenin's term; and it is already sufficiently obvious that the conception of 'contradictions', of something which can both be and not be, is admirably adapted to the purposes of an unscrupulous and corrupt leadership. The struggle against the corruption of the movement for social revolution, for the establishment of a society of producers, is thus, in my view, linked with the struggle against 'dialectic'.[4]

It is significant that, in spite of the thorough-going nature of his criticisms and the pointed references to 'the cult of Stalin' and 'the fetishism of "Socialism in one country" ', Anderson claimed only to be clearing away the philosophical undergrowth for a better understanding of Marx and Marxism: 'I am convinced that Marxist philosophy has been an obstacle to the acceptance of Marx's main social views, and that a refutation of the philosophy can only advance the most typically Marxist contributions to science'.[5] Among these permanent insights of value that Anderson never repudiated were Marx's atheism, secularism and determinism, his emphasis on economic motivation, and his view of class struggle, of 'irreconcilable antagonisms in society'. Marxism stressed the social, co-operative and participatory character of philosophising and 'a philosophic tradition', and the realist philosopher, by virtue of his participation in a producers' movement, would 'see his intellectual levelling as an integral part of social levelling'.[6] * Anderson still believed that, once capitalist exploitation was removed, the workers were capable of the virtues of production, initiative and enterprise. But he also questioned essential aspects of Marx's labour theory of value and proposed an independent role for enterprise and technology in production.[7] Already, he was reading Marx in a realist and pluralist way.

That position was much more difficult to maintain as 'fundamentally Marxist' after the publication of 'Marxist Ethics' in 1937. It began with the bold assertion 'that Marxism is a *metaphysic*, a doctrine of guiding principles, a mingling of logic and ethics to the detriment of both', and Anderson proceeded to scourge the common errors of rationalism and relativism in Marxism and Hegelianism.[8] ' "Scientific Socialism" reveals itself as Hegelian metaphysics, with the substitution of Society for the Idea'. Was Marxism only 'spilt religion' after all? Throughout the essay, he subjected Marx's relativist and utilitarian ethics to the sort of devastating critique he had formerly reserved for Absolute Idealism. He contrasted the Marxists' 'unscientific ethics of an evolutionist and rationalist character' with his own pluralist theory of organisations and positive 'goods', and called for 'a complete recasting of Socialist theory'. Marxism denied the goods of 'enterprise' and 'independence', and was contrary to Sorel's 'ethics of the producer': 'Until the metaphysical rubbish with which it is encrusted is removed, Marxism will fail to develop as the science of social movement, and social movement will have a much reduced chance of going forward'.[9] The 'reactionary and disintegrating influence of Stalinism' now left little credibility for the Soviet Union as a workers' state, in spite of Trotsky's pronouncements, and Anderson sought to trace these fundamental errors back beyond Trotsky and Stalin to Lenin and Marx.

In February 1937 Anderson delivered a forceful attack on Stalin *and* Marx at the Workers' Party Conference:

* Eugene Kamenka saw a strong resemblance between Anderson's position and Feuerbach's empiricist attack on idealism.

> . . . the crudities which are the whole stock-in-trade of the Stalinists, have their basis in the theories of Marx. His 'reflection' theory, his denial of the independence of social movements, is based on his MONISM, his conception of reality as developing along a single track—a position most appropriate to the fanatical sectarian. With this goes the theological conception of the inevitability of Socialism as rooted in 'the nature of things'.[10]

A few months later he denounced 'the bankruptcy of Trotskyism' and 'the present Russian tyranny' in a paper on 'the present position of the Workers' Party'. Increasingly disenchanted with its 'lack of theoretical clarity' and 'policy of drift', he called for 'a reconstruction of the party on a broader basis':

> . . . we require to broaden the party by making the basis of membership not Trotskyism or Marxism but a belief in militant struggle and a desire to work out the conditions of the Australian revolution. No doubt such a reconstituted party would contain Marxists and Trotskyists . . . but it will not be a purely Trotskyist affair and many have already disowned Trotsky. Failing such a change, the party, I am certain, will dwindle and will lose even such influence as it has at present.[11]

In June 1937 Anderson had proposed 'the overthrow of capitalism and the setting up of workers' democracy' to be an objective of the Workers' Party.

Not unexpectedly, Anderson was keenly interested in the waning fortunes of the Republican cause in Spain at this time and, like Orwell, was most impressed by the 'heroic' resistance of the anarchists and Trotskyist P.O.U.M. of Catalonia. Their struggle was as much against Stalin and the Communists as the Falangists, and stirred Anderson's interest in anarchism and Sorel's doctrine of 'permanent opposition'. Spain, however, appealed to the Nietzschean romantic in Anderson more than the democratic liberal.

Such then was Anderson's position on the eve of the Bukharin trials and his first sabbatical leave in 1938. In the decade since his arrival in Australia he had sought in various ways to realise 'the overthrow of capitalism and the setting up of workers' democracy'. If he had become bitterly disillusioned with the party apparatus, its authoritarian leadership and Stalinist dogmas, he still retained faith in the proletariat and the class struggle. But would that survive his searching philosophical scrutiny and iconoclasm? He was well aware of the work being done in the U.S.A. by Max Eastman and Sidney Hook and on his leave he visited Hook in New York. After his return to Sydney he did not renew his association with the Workers' Party and came to question even Lenin's 'heroic' role in the Bolshevik Revolution. He now saw the state not as the executive arm of the ruling class but, akin to Marx's doctrine of Bonapartism, as a mediator between conflicts, interests and institutions—'as machinery for maintaining a certain distribution of powers, for preventing upheavals or a straightout war between opposing factions'.[12]

In the early years of the Second World War Anderson finally jettisoned Lenin's view of the democratic state 'as a democracy only for the bourgeoisie'. Gradually, albeit reluctantly, Anderson came to develop a grudging respect for parliamentary democracy, though he maintained his objection to 'mere voting' as a sign of democracy:

> It should be understood of course that mere voting gives people little if any power, that if mere voting were the distinguishing mark of democracy, then democracy would certainly not be the rule of the people. If, on the other hand, we understand by democracy political activity and responsibility on the part of all members of the community, then it would be clear that no community had ever been completely democratic but that some communities were more democratic than others, and the parliamentary system might be indicative of a certain progress in democracy.[13]

The individual citizen, by virtue of his social character and membership of groups and movements, was able to exert a collective influence on the system and assist the public discussion of issues. Accordingly, 'there *are* rights of organisation and agitation and thus possibilities of political activity on the part of workers, and these are parts of the democratic system (such as it is) of which parliamentarism is an outstanding expression'.[14] The extent to which Anderson's reassessment of liberalism and parliamentary democracy was influenced by the arrival of Alan Stout from Oxford to take up the new chair of moral philosophy is a nice subject for speculation. Stout was appointed in 1938 to temper some of Anderson's more extreme views on politics and religion, but in time the latter's powerful critique of 'solidarism' and the 'common good' was to have a considerable impact on Stout's own teaching. Yet if parliamentary democracy could raise one small cheer from Anderson during 'the great patriotic war against fascism', little good could be said for the Labor Party. 'The producer's mentality was never characteristic of the Labour movement, or even the Socialist movement, as a whole', was his doleful conclusion to 'The Servile State' of 1943.[15]

Lenin's massive contempt for bourgeois democracy and dissent only showed his utopian and monistic view of society, and Anderson renounced the absurd simplicity and 'childlike optimism' of such views, especially the naive faith in the 'withering away' of the state. In fact, Lenin's doctrine of liberation was a 'servile doctrine' and its practitioners

> have no notion of goods as ways of living, as causes to which people are devoted . . . they seem never to have encountered the view that such activities can go on only by wrestling with difficulties, that goods can exist only in the struggle with evils, so that to abolish evil would be to abolish good—or if they have heard of such a view, they would dismiss it as theological.[16]

Like Milton's 'true wayfaring Christian', Anderson had tasted the fruit of knowledge and had known good and evil, 'that is to say of knowing good by evil'. The bleak conclusion to the most radical and forward-looking phase of his life was that the bourgeoisie and capitalism were as necessary for 'progress' and democracy as the proletariat itself: 'If we could remove the clash, the opposition (of social tendencies) the result would be a lowering of culture, a tyranny'. It was a condition of the existence of freedom that it should always fight against obstacles and 'that such freedom as there is exists through the clash of interests, so that if the working class movement attacks capitalist democracy it may be said to be undermining itself (as it has done), if it destroys capitalism it may be destroying its own freedom'.[17] The break with Marxism as a political creed was complete.

To explain this fundamental break is no easy task. Intellectual reasons jostle with political developments in the decisive decade of the 1930s, in Australia, Europe and the Soviet Union, and with all the personal circumstances and complex philosophical development of Anderson's life. Anderson's view of independent objective reality and propositional truth was bound sooner or later to clash with the Marxist notion of ideology and relative 'class' truth: 'Thus the Marxists, just like Berkeley, neglect the proposition (the statement of fact) as the object of any knowledge whatever, and, in taking their departure from "ideas", are unable logically to *arrive at* propositions and thus to have any coherent theory'.[18] Like Gide and other intellectuals, he placed truth above the party. The great terror and the Moscow trials shattered any faith he once had in the Soviet Union as a workers' state. The purges merely demonstrated the rise of a new centralised tyranny out of the practice of conspiratorial, secretive and élitist politics. For Anderson, then, the failure of the Russian Revolution was not a contingent failure—a product of Russian backwardness or even of Lenin's misinterpretation of Marx—but a necessary outcome of Marxism as philosophy. In 1937 he wrote:

> The lesson we have to learn to-day is that Bolshevism is dead, that a chapter in working-class history is closed. We have still much to learn from it, but we have above all to learn the errors it contained. It was not that by some misfortune the Bolshevik party took the wrong turning, but that it was *always* deficient on certain points, unversed in certain features of social life, and so, while it could succeed up to a point, it was bound to become bankrupt unless some other movement came to its assistance—a possibility which its doctrines of dictatorship, of the relation of the party to the class, and its misunderstanding of culture, did much to

> prevent . . . The situation is sufficiently illuminated by the fact that Lenin preferred as co-workers crooks who were Bolsheviks to honest men who were not.[19]

Marxism, according to this analysis, contained the seeds of its own destruction in its monism, its teleological view of history and its utopianism. The Stalinist 'theocracy' showed that, as in Dostoevsky's legend of the Grand Inquisitor, the masses were not imbued with the revolutionary spirit of enterprise but preferred 'happiness' and material security to the risks and dangers of strenuous liberty. 'Man was created a rebel', declared the Grand Inquisitor, 'and how can rebels be happy?' It became Anderson's question as he pondered whether the workers had forfeited their claim to be the heroic class of producers. Such a disparaging view of the masses was, paradoxically, pure Leninism but Anderson was past caring:

> In fact, the notion of true society or true humanity which is essential to Marxism, the whole humanitarian ideology, leads on to a despotism which professes to be benevolent but which as suppressing independent movements is benevolent in no important sense. What we have here is a peculiar kind of solidarism, the doctrine of a unitary society after certain evils have been removed and for the sake of which any oppressive action can be justified; and if the idealists lack the sense of economic realities, it might be said the Marxists are deficient in *political* sense, in the sense of freedom.[20]

Anderson's rejection of 'solidarism', 'the view that there is a total social interest, which can never conflict with individual interests',[21] was a product of his earlier attack on Absolute Idealism and monism. Idealism and solidarism denied the 'necessity or naturalness of conflict' in the individual and society, and promoted a spurious 'harmony' and 'social quietism':

> [They were] not prepared to recognise a definite conflict, an irreconcilability of tendencies both in the person and in society, whereas it is only if we recognise fundamental

> conflicts in both of these that we can find any real connection between them, that we can see how the social affects the personal and the personal the social.[22]

Anderson's logic had always emphasised plurality as much as togetherness; and in his refutation of 'solidarism', which he detected in Marx as much as Hegel, he developed a new emphasis on opposition, complexity and variety as social goods. Pluralism, or the view 'that there are quite different forms of activity or ways of life or "interests" ', was a progressive sign in society whereas solidarism was a state of degeneration and reaction:

> . . . there are in any society, as a necessary feature of society, quite irreconcilable interests—there are tendencies we can call progressive and tendencies we can call reactionary, there are periods of *progress* (pluralism) . . . and periods of *reaction* (solidarism) . . . and there is no plan of the whole . . . there are in any case different interests which cannot be brought to a common denominator.[23]

In rejecting Marx's meta-history of leaps and stages, Anderson came to have a greater appreciation of Heraclitus' view of ceaseless struggle, flux and of 'irreconcilable antagonisms in society'. According to Heraclitus, 'This world, which is the same for all, no one of gods or men has made; but it was ever, is now, and ever shall be an ever-living Fire, with measures kindling, and measures going out'.[24] Anderson also came to reject the planning and 'social engineering based on conscious directions' (associated with Stalin's five-year plans) because of the Heraclitean and Freudian insights into unconscious motives—'that men are not conscious at all of a great deal that they are doing; and even in regard to policies themselves, we may find them to be determined by forces of which the framers of policies are unconscious'.[25] As Heraclitus counselled, expect the unexpected.

Diversity was, therefore, an essential mark of a healthy society and 'the freest possible interplay of movements and institutions is the condition of a vigorous social life'.[26] Such movements and ways of living manifested in their social activities the 'goods' of co-operation, communication and vigorous enterprise. Anderson's rejection of Marxism and 'solidarism' did not lead him, simply on the rebound, to espouse possessive individualism, the market-place and liberty; rather, he came to appreciate anew the complex interplay between the individual and society: 'the individual is not an exclusive unit' but 'can be understood only as a participant in activities going beyond himself and . . . it is only under these conditions that he himself has a complex and varied life'.[27] Indeed, Anderson criticised Freud for his individualism or social atomism and for 'reducing the social to the psychical' as Marx had reduced 'the psychical to the social'.[28] At this time Anderson's attention turned increasingly to the relationship between his social philosophy and ethical theory. There was a certain irony in the university's decision at this point to establish a separate chair of Political and Moral Philosophy and appoint Alan Stout to it.

On this showing, then, the break with Marxism led Anderson to re-assess his ethical and aesthetic theory, 'to distinguish aesthetic from ethical valuation and either from economic valuation'. He renewed his attack on 'moralism', relativism and utilitarianism with its calculus of happiness. Happiness could never be a final end—'there will always be some degree of discontent (say, some degree of *tension*, of opposition of tendencies) in any state in which we could possibly be and certainly in any state in which we are said to be "happy" '.[29] He cited Nietzsche with relish: 'A man does *not* strive after "happiness"; one must be an Englishman to be able to believe that a man is always seeking his own advantage'.[30] Anderson eliminated any element of teleology from his ethics because valuable activities or ways of living were such that they continued to operate in regular ways through time, regardless of ends. In his definition of 'goods', relations were as objective as qualities:

> It may be that what leads us to consider them (activities) in a special way, or apart from other things, is not merely the characteristic we started with but their relations to one another, and not merely their relations to one another as

> forms of mental activity but their relations to one another in society, the way they hang together—in the working of institutions—and give us a continuous tradition which may be what is referred to as *culture* or *civilisation.*[31]

Anderson found 'the subject matter of ethics in what is permanent in social life' and among the chief goods were love, inquiry or scientific and artistic investigation, communication and co-operation: 'Goods, we may say, are those mental activities, or those social activities, which are "free" or enterprising, which exhibit the spirit of enterprise. It might be better to come down on the mental side. The main point is that ethics penetrates both the psychological and the sociological field, but is nevertheless a distinct and positive inquiry'.[32] Goods entered in and worked through individuals and movements—'a way of life is not something that we adopt, by a voluntary decision, but something that adopts us, takes us as a vehicle, kindles a certain "spirit" in us'.[33] Goods assisted one another and 'have the real permanence and continuity, while evils have not', being divided among themselves. Goodness 'exists and develops in struggle with evils'.[34] Institutions in a pluralist society embody particular goods in a continuous tradition so that the university supremely embodied the good of inquiry.

Was beauty also a good? Because 'the only goods are human activities', Anderson thought the activity of artistic production was the good rather than the product itself.[35] Criticising current theories of expressionism, which confused the artist's mentality with the character of the work of art, Anderson proposed three objective criteria for testing a work of art—coherence, structure and thematic development. Aesthetic appreciation was 'substantially the same as disinterested inquiry' because its interest was 'in the working of things themselves as contrasted with interest in their uses, in the ways in which they can serve our special purposes'.[36] Anderson maintained not only that 'the artist is supremely productive or creative' and 'has much of the scientist in him', but that great art embodied the morality of freedom and initiative, unlike the 'preceptual morality' of servility, utility and repression. Society was itself a battlefield of rival moralities, ways of life and movements, and Anderson exposed the 'low morality' and covert 'solidarism' of the official censors and public protectors of the young and 'immature'. Joyce's *Ulysses*, by contrast, epitomised the morality of freedom and enterprise, particularly in the sexual arena, where the forces of 'moralism' and repression fought it out with the 'goods' of love, enterprise and equality. Anderson even asserted that there was a close association between sexual emancipation and cultural and political freedom:

> Feuerbach, in fact, treats love (natural love) as the core of humanity, the central good; and it may be argued, along these lines, that freedom in love is the condition of other freedoms, that while in itself it does not constitute culture, there can be no culture without it, that it continually enriches and is enriched by the various forms of productive (enterprising) activity—Science, Art, Industry.[37]

Did Anderson's rift with Marxism also have implications for his metaphysics? In one sense, of course, Anderson's critique of Marxism was a by-product of his rejection of Absolute Idealism. Social totalism or solidarism was no more acceptable than the Absolute of Hegel or Bradley, for both doctrines denied the reality of conflict and pluralism. But in rejecting Hegelianism and its brawling offspring, Marxism, Anderson was forced to reconsider his own 'pluralism without ultimates'. This exercise was greatly assisted and stimulated by the philosophy of Samuel Alexander, whose Gifford lectures 'Space, Time and Deity' he had attended as an undergraduate and which now became a regular feature of the senior honours course. The arrival in Sydney of the distinguished philosopher and psychologist G. F. Stout, the father of Alan Stout, provided Anderson with a subtle and knowledgeable critic, for the elder Stout had been a friend of Alexander and knew his philosophy well.

In the honours lectures, Anderson tackled major issues of metaphysics and epistemology in the history of European philosophy, beginning with Kant's critical philosophy. The latter's achievement had been to answer the scepticism of Hume by showing that experience was ordered in terms of space, time and the categories. However, Kant regarded the categories as 'forms of understanding' or modes of cognition; and he also distinguished between the objects of experience or phenomena and things-in-themselves, which alone were real. Alexander was a more thorough-going empiricist than Kant and treated empirical sense-data as objectively real. Moreover, he argued that the categories, far from being mental properties, were objectively real and existed in space-time as features of things or forms of existence. In an intellectual *tour de force*, Anderson expounded and criticised Alexander's ideas, transmuting and transforming them into a system of great philosophical daring and courage. He welcomed Alexander's objectivism but criticised his rambling treatment of space, time and the categories; he also repudiated his evolutionism and his mystical view of deity. Anderson understood space and time as the medium in which all things existed rather than the stuff of existence. The most exciting part of the course was Anderson's treatment of space, time and the categories in terms of the proposition and its form. With all his intellectual force and virtuosity, Anderson proceeded to unfold the categories beginning with identity as the first and primary category, much as Hegel had done with the category of being. But Anderson, unlike Hegel, clearly distinguished between logic and history:

> Working on Alexander's basis we can give a spatio-temporal interpretation of the proposition, describing the subject as a region and the predicate as an activity, or as something going on within the region. And from that interpretation we can see not only how there can be many intersecting activities—conjunction—but also disjunction and juxtaposition, the subject not only having distinct qualities but distinct parts.[38]

The first group of categories—identity, difference, existence, relation and universality—were categories of the situation and embraced both quantity and quality. The second group—particularity, number, order, quantity with universality as a link category—'are ways in which we give an account of things *as* spatio-temporal' and they located the subject. The third group—intensity, substance, causality, individuality and quantity as a link category—'are ways in which we give an account of things as *distinct* from space and time—in other words, as qualitative' and they characterised the predicate. In refuting the Hegelian dialectic of reason he declared:

> There is for us no question of trying to think the whole in terms of this or that conception or allowing each conception to generate its own world; but from the very beginning we have recognised propositions, recognised a variety of facts, and our later procedure at no time calls that starting-point in question, at no time tries to do away with the proposition or with the variety of propositions trying to run them all together or make them all signify one fact—the totality of things; it merely elucidates that starting point, bringing out characteristics and relations of propositions which remain as distinct (i.e. as *different* from one another) as ever they were.[39]

Alexander profoundly stirred Anderson's philosophical imagination, reflected one of Anderson's students, and 'those who heard his lectures on Alexander felt that they were being led into the very heart of Anderson's philosophy'.[40] In the end, his students were to be liberated from all conventionalism—even Marxism—and enabled to view everything objectively, in its own terms. For some, it was an exhilarating moment of freedom and boldness, of intellectual mastery and power, indeed a Faustian moment. For others, it was an acutely disturbing time when all moral props and religious defences were systematically destroyed and battered away. Alone, without refuge, security or comfort of any sort, one had to be strong to confront a bleak indifferent universe, where death spelt total extinction. In Anderson's austere world, some survived, some flourished and some went under.

10

Love and Strife

ALICE RUTH WALKER was barely seventeen when she won a bursary to the university and began an Arts degree in 1934. She had grown up at Lismore but, after the failure of her father's printing business, the family moved to North Sydney, where Ruth attended the Girls' High School. Her mother, the driving force in the family, was a seeker after the 'truth' and her religious quest led her, after a Catholic upbringing and education in Adelaide, to become successively a Methodist, Presbyterian and a theosophist before finally converting to Christian Science. She often took Ruth and her brothers along to the religious services. Ruth was the youngest child and had four older brothers, none of whom went to the university, although her favourite brother had gone to Sydney Teachers' College some years before Ruth matriculated in 1933. She commuted most days to the university from her home in North Sydney and, with many young men and women, studied English, history and, on the recommendation of the headmistress, philosophy. A lively and spirited girl, she was soon impressed by the reputation and awesome presence of Professor Anderson. A girlfriend quipped that he was the local deity.

In August 1935, when she was in her second year, Anderson approached her in the quad and invited her to his study for a 'small talk about her essay'. The conversation soon widened, and as he discussed religion and her mother in his 'soft Scotch voice', she felt both fascinated and terrified. Did he find the young girl's questioning of religious and maternal authority too tempting to resist? Many young women and men studying his philosophy passed through some sort of a religious crisis as they struggled to reconcile Anderson's secular logic with belief in the supernatural or in special revelation. Few retained their religious faith if they went on with the subject.

In Ruth's case, however, Anderson was dealing with a 'rare *puella*' and a small religious sect whose tenets accorded with his view of the 'religious illusion'. Christian Science taught that God was spirit, being all, while matter and sin did not exist. Pain, suffering and disease were illusions that must be banished from the mind. Happiness was a state of harmony with the Divine Mind, and she went on to record her dilemma:

> . . . having explained Christian Science beliefs for some time I explained how mother had devoted herself to them etc. Then he asked me why I did not try to convert Mother. Squirm! he pulled my attitude to pieces and has made me feel most uncomfortable. My attitude being that my mother is an essentially religious nature and would be desperately unhappy if she didn't have religion to turn to always. To which John replied what was this happiness anyhow? Did I think he was unhappy? and so on . . .
>
> This happiness, he told me that I was so fond of, was merely a state of satisfaction—a blind refusal to meet facts. He pointed out that my mother was at present a blockage in the social system, so to speak, preventing me from progressing and disseminating a false doctrine which leads to stultifying of the intellect.[1]

Ruth's intellectual and emotional encounter with the philosophy professor over the next year was to cause great distress and division in the Walker family, particularly between mother and daughter. She recorded and reflected on every detail of the relationship and her vivid responses to it in a closeted private diary. Ruth could not help admiring and revering Anderson as a 'mental prodigy' and half-acknowledged to herself the advantage of having a powerful patron in high places. A tall slim girl with a pleasant smile, she was conscious of the power of her sex and the professor's amorousness. While Ruth was studying English and philosophy, she participated in the activities of the Literary and Freethought Societies, affecting some of John's Scotticisms, as many students did, and, for a brief time, even sucked on a pipe. Anderson often spoke to the Literary Society, which he had inaugurated in 1931, on his realist aesthetics and provoked lively discussion with students and members of the English staff, among them 'Johnny' Waldock and Guy Howarth. Occasionally, he intervened on Ruth's behalf because she had difficulty in speaking in public and fulfilling her duties on the executive of the Freethought Society, being shy, often ill and diffident about her abilities.

Over several months Ruth radically revised her ideas about religion, Communism and free love, which magnified the conflicts with her mother at home:

> I see I shall have to set to work and reform my mother. She is altogether too illogical. Having got into a comfortable groove, she wants to stick there and kick at anyone who says anything that disturbs her equanimity. Belief in God can certainly do tremendous amount of harm.

In further reflections, she developed the argument:

> All Christian Scientists I think must have a kink—they are logical so far and no further. Accepting the old religious beliefs that
>
> God is good
> God is all powerful
> God created man
>
> they infer, quite consequently that all things were created by God, and that, therefore, all things are good, therefore, there is no evil.[2]

Ruth found that their 'premises were incorrect', and so she decided that 'Religion is finally a shutting of the eyes to facts and an escape into a means of delusion into a world of ideal happiness i.e. ultimate stagnation'.[3]

Anderson's 'realist' logic was central to her experience of his philosophy, and for Ruth it took on an almost sexual quality. She interpreted his exposition of relational arguments as a personal reference to their relationship and was acutely embarrassed during a lecture, blushing and suppressing a strong urge to flee—'if that was more psychological experimenting it was altogether too cruel', she wrote. Like other students who became devotees, she was converted to Anderson's own position after an intense religious and psychological crisis, but this placed her in a vulnerable position both as a woman and student, for, as she confessed, 'I do love the man—he affects me physically in a way I cannot understand, worst of all I cannot understand the *fear* he inspires me with'.[4] When the professor conveyed his sexual interest to her, it is clear from her diary that she found it impossible to resist his advances, even had she wanted to. The 43-year-old Anderson was bemused and excited with the role of sexual adventurer and awakener, a part he may well have rehearsed with one or two women students at Sydney. She accused him of cruelty and of showing 'sardonic amusement' at her predicament, without any lasting commitment or responsibility—she felt sometimes like 'an insect on a microscope slab, being prodded to see how it will react'—but in spite of the 'anger and repulsion' she remained infatuated with him. He advised her to 'take things lightly', and invited her to the visiting French art exhibition at Anthony Hordern's Gallery—their first public outing together—and three weeks later to afternoon tea at a nearby restaurant, where they were interrupted by some of Anderson's male students. An unaccompanied visit to Turramurra followed when Ruth met Jenny and Sandy, and in January 1936, on the invitation of the professor, she also spent a few days with the Andersons at Narrabeen on holiday. There could be no doubt about her intellectual ability and Anderson was delighted to award her the G. S. Caird scholarship for philosophy. Then he persuaded her to read his favourite Hardy novel, *Jude the Obscure*, and when she had finished its savage indictment of the marriage vow she felt 'somehow loose, disintegrated, aimless. Can see not much sense anywhere'.[5] The furtive affair, for so it must be, bloomed in the hothouse atmosphere of national crisis and popular hysteria as the uncrowned king, no less, abdicated his throne for the woman he loved. Ruth succumbed at last to 'the quivering fingers', 'the slightly uneasy grin' and the unrelenting logic of her master and *alter ego*, and then completed her degree to win the University Medal and first-class honours in philosophy. On 1 April

1937 she was appointed to the staff as a part-time 'correcting assistant' in the Philosophy Department. It was the first humble rung on the academic ladder.

The department that she joined was dominated and moulded by the personality and ideas of Anderson. After one or two short-term assistants, Anderson appointed P. H. Partridge to a lectureship in 1934 and John Passmore in 1935. Both were former students and both taught within the philosophical system of Anderson's realism. The professor justified this policy, insofar as he ever did, in terms of the intellectual coherence and rigour of his 'school' and the dangers of eclecticism and 'piecemeal' philosophy. His department was to embody a distinct system of thought and be the bearer of a cultural tradition. In practice, it meant that the staff knew one another's teaching areas very well, and all were encouraged and expected to teach the central parts of the course. This helped to create much co-operation and discussion in the department and a vigorous social life, involving staff and students, outside of it. This powerful sense of identity as a school under the presiding genius of Anderson also developed in reaction to the 'sodden ecstasies of rectitude' at Melbourne, whether of the Idealist or Stalinist kind; and the annual conferences of the philosophers took on the aspect of a gladiatorial contest between Sydney 'realism' and Melbourne 'idealism'.

There are striking parallels between Anderson's affair with Ruth Walker and his wooing of Jenny Baillie twenty years before. The two women were young intelligent students undergoing a religious and intellectual crisis, which was closely associated with their relationship with Anderson and partly caused by it; and both were plunged into deep irreconcilable conflicts with their families over the controversial philosopher and his ideas. The intense conflicts with the two mothers over religion, sexuality and marriage are especially noteworthy, as was Anderson's flinty opposition to the two of them. Insofar as there was any resolution of these conflicts it had to be on Anderson's terms or not at all—namely, renunciation of religion and family for him and philosophy. Anderson consciously set out to mould them in his own image, playing Pygmalion in each case to their Galatea. He even advised Ruth on her use of cosmetics and dress. The role of Ruth as lover-disciple, philosophical muse and working companion bears a close resemblance to Jenny's role before the marriage. Jenny and Ruth were intimately involved in the two most fruitful and enterprising periods of Anderson's philosophical development, and Ruth's detailed correspondence during the late 1930s and the 1940s parallels Jenny's almost daily letters to Anderson during the First World War. Ruth also tendered several of her dreams to him for comment and analysis. His letters during the sabbatical year of 1938 chronicle some of the important discoveries of these years. In one of them, he wrote:

> You know, of course, that I put forward the view that love 'communicates' with other goods—I certainly admit that I haven't worked it out very far. Beyond that, I suppose I've been more or less in agreement with Socrates that the virtue of a woman and that of a man are identical—or, more in my own terms, that it makes no ethical difference whether a woman or a man makes scientific discoveries or produces works of art; though I've still believed that women generally had less capacity for these things than men generally . . . It is possible that men and women should both contribute to science—and both be 'scientists' in the same sense—and yet that their contributions should be of distinct sorts . . . there may still be something in such popular distinctions as that between woman's 'intuition' and man's 'intellect'—though, even then, it may be a question of what is found more commonly, but not exclusively, in one and in the other.[6]

Anderson found Ruth a rare girl, attractive, impressionable, imaginative and lively. There was an element of amusement and opportunism in his dalliance, of playing with her affections and intellectual ambitions, that revealed the 'double standard' of the Edwardian Glasgow of his youth and the Sydney Bohemia of the 1930s. To be sure, he welcomed the devotion of a female acolyte and, doubtless, he relished the thrill and risk of seducing a student in his study within earshot of the 'old guard', and then appointing her to his staff. But there was a rather more desperate note as the relationship developed, compounded of his approaching middle years, her insecurities, and the personal crisis as he shed his Marxist persona and beliefs. At one desperate moment, he wrote:

> Sweetheart,
>
> I'll have to get back to the simple seriousness which first drew you to me. I think I can, Ruth; I think I can manage always to be there when you want me, so that you won't feel it a privation if you should have noone else to turn to but will rather turn joyfully and hopefully to your lover and friend and comrade.
>
> John.

Underneath he scribbled, 'Oh God, Ruthie, I need you. Come soon, soon, soon'.[7]

Boredom and restiveness with marriage showed in thoughtless, even malicious remarks to Jenny about his muffed marriage lines, and his re-reading of Hardy's *Jude* suggests a detestation of the 'common funk' of matrimony. But if in the best of all possible worlds he would have liked to leave Jenny for the younger Ruth, clearly that was impossible in Sydney for an outwardly respectable professor with a wife and son. And so he resigned himself to the 'sexual entanglements, cross-purposes, dissatisfactions' and hypocrisies of bourgeois existence, tolerating Jenny as housewife, domestic drudge and cook, and enjoying the comradeship of Ruth at the university. Such was the home life of a master spirit, a liberator of minds from illusion, but did he have any inkling of the suffering he inflicted on the women who loved and served him? What was the wound that poisoned his love for men and women in the most intimate relationships?

Once, seemingly alone, her son saw Jenny weep over the basin in the kitchen; sometimes she quietly sang to herself the old Scotch lament,

> O little knew my mother,
> The day she cradled me,
> The lands that I should wander o'er,
> The death that I should dee.

After Ruth's unaccompanied visits to Turramurra and Narrabeen she suspected the truth and was bitterly hurt by it, confiding her great unhappiness to her sister in Scotland during the sabbatical of 1938. Any thought of divorce was immediately suppressed in the interests of their 15-year-old son and, paradoxically, the professor. For, like Ruth, she passionately believed in the genius of Anderson and considered it essential to protect and nurture him for his life-task. Ruth shared this urge to mother and protect John. In time, Jenny came reluctantly to accept Ruth as John's philosophical 'comrade'. When Ruth visited Turramurra, Jenny would only serve her corned beef. The hint was palpable, but Ruth and John chose to ignore it. In the longer term, there was a period of estrangement between John and Jenny, as they played out the conventional roles of husband and wife at Turramurra. They began to sleep in separate beds. John often stayed back at the university until late at night, and in the morning barely had time for a rushed breakfast before leaving. He showed little interest in Jenny's reading group and discouraged its meeting while he was at home marking exam papers. At night Jenny's sleep was sometimes disturbed by nightmares. She had to be woken and soothed back to sleep.

The young Sandy Anderson began to suspect the nature of the relationship between his father and Ruth in 1938. He bitterly resented the betrayal of his mother and, although only a few years younger than Ruth, never accepted her as a friend or a close member of the family. In fact, unhappy as a day-boy at Knox Grammar School, Sandy was critical of Ruth's 'pretentious' accent and manners, and found fault with her too exclusive attachment to his father. He was torn between pride in his father and loyalty to Jenny.

Ruth soon learnt that it was no paradise she had entered. Several months after her appointment, Anderson left Australia on his first sabbatical. He tried to comfort her:

> Ruth, dear, I've been thinking a lot about you and me, but nothing very coherent, except that I miss you very much. I think we should find ourselves a lot more assured when we're together again; a sort of purgative period, as it were, only a year is such a confoundedly long time. The kind of thing that creates occasional uncertainties between us is a difference of 'idiom', due largely to the difference of our

> histories, but partly to my folie de doute—and that, I think, will be very much improved by my getting away from Sydney for a bit and seeing my job in a proper perspective.[8]

Barely twenty years old, she felt apprehensive, guilty and abandoned, and her insecurity and lack of confidence began to show in nervous mannerisms before students. How could she ever feel secure? Had her brains earned her the position in a fair and open field, or was it a case of *his* patronage and her body, about which she felt increasingly inadequate as the prospects of marriage or even a love child by the prodigy receded into fantasy and dreams. While he was away in England, Scotland and North America she corresponded regularly with Anderson, grateful for the least crumb, but before classes of students she felt nervous and strained. She appeared 'a pitiable character' to one of her students in 1940, who thought she was seriously ill. She taught a course on ancient Greek philosophy and among the pre-Socratics she developed a special affinity for Heraclitus, Anderson's favourite classical philosopher. In her lectures, which she slowly dictated in the professor's manner, she expounded the Heraclitean doctrines of 'becoming' and ceaseless change, of conflict and opposition at the heart of things, of the necessary inter-connectedness of love and strife. The great themes resonated in an Australia torn by vast global conflicts:

> The all is finite and the world is one. It arises from fire, and is consumed again by fire alternately through all eternity in certain cycles. This happens according to fate. Of the opposites, that which leads to the becoming of the world is called War and Strife; that which leads to the final conflagration is Concord and Peace.[9]

In 1941 Ruth became a full-time assistant lecturer and could afford a flat in Neutral Bay and there, at night, surrounded by the iridescent harbour, she entertained the professor and their friends. The wartime atmosphere of crisis and danger drew out the courage of the lovers. Anderson was inspired to write her a series of love poems that summed up his view of the affair.

My ardent girl, with ardent mouth on mine
Forget the furtiveness, forget the pain
Of halfway love, of love that feared and shrank—
Embolden me to hold you to my heart.

My ardent girl, my tender, lovely girl,
Breathe your sweet breath on me, enfold me in the warmth
Of your divine embrace—forgive me, sweet,
And love me, love me, even as I love you.[10]

Ruth's perspective was rather more serious and troubled:

> My last words on the subject? One thing I feel sure of is that I would use any written matter, perhaps anything, to serve my loves. Make what you like of it. I have felt beaten, chastened, heroic and what now, and I'd still say to the world what does it matter?
>
> Yours,
> Ruth.
>
> I have also felt afraid to know the truth.[11]

AGAINST SERVILITY, 1940–1962

To hell wi' happiness!
I sing the terrifyin' discipline
O' the free mind that gars a man
Make his joys kill his joys,
The weakest by the strongest,
The temporal by the fundamental
(Or hope o' the fundamental)
And prolong wi'in himself
Threids o' thocht sae fragile
It needs the help and continuance
O' a' his vital power
To haud them frae brakin'

Hugh MacDiarmid

11

Sydney's Wars

WHEN ON 3 September 1939 Prime Minister R. G. Menzies declared war on Germany, it seemed the logical outcome of dominion status and Britain's decision at last to stand up to Hitler over Poland. Many Australians still regarded themselves as 'British to the boot heels' and were proud of the empire and their place in it. More realistically, the British navy shielded them from unknown dangers to the north, and the seemingly impregnable base of Singapore was the strategic pivot of that defence. Menzies led a minority United Australia Party government and believed that the fascist aggressor must be resisted in Europe. For the next two years Europe remained the major focus of Australia's attention and war effort. After the first winter of 'phoney war', Hitler launched his *blitzkrieg* and in a matter of weeks overwhelmed the allied armies to occupy Paris and overrun France. The Battle of Britain followed in the air, and Australians anxiously awaited the outcome. The Australian Navy became a part of the Royal Navy outside Australian waters, Australian airmen were absorbed into the Royal Air Force, but the army fought in its own right in North Africa, the Middle East and Greece.

Until the German invasion of Russia in June 1941, the Communist Party opposed the war as another 'imperialist' scramble for profits, trade and colonies, and was made an illegal organisation. From mid-1941 the ban was lifted and Communists enthusiastically supported the people's war against fascism and advocated a 'second front' to relieve the Soviet Union. In spite of tensions between Churchill and Menzies over the seriousness of the threat from Hitler's ally in the Far East, Japan, the two of them agreed to sink their differences in the common task. However, there remained serious misgivings about the effectiveness of the Singapore naval base and the strategic priorities of the British War Cabinet. Would Churchill honour his undertaking to 'cut our losses in the Mediterranean and sacrifice every interest, except only the defence and feeding of this Island' to prevent a Japanese attack on Australia?

Menzies resigned in August 1941 to be succeeded briefly by Fadden until John Curtin became Labor Prime Minister on 7 October 1941. Within a few months the war situation had been completely transformed and Australia faced 'her gravest hour' alone. Japan's surprise attack on Pearl Harbor on 7 December 1941 and her rapid occupation of French Indo-China and *rapprochement* with Thailand opened the way for an assault on British Malaya and Singapore. Suddenly white Australia, a European outpost in an alien world, was in danger and the climate of fear grew steadily with the sinking of the *Prince of Wales* and *Repulse*, the speedy loss of Malaya, and the capture of Singapore on 15 February 1942. Darwin was bombed on 19 February, followed by Broome and Townsville. During March the Japanese occupied the entire Dutch East Indies and New Guinea up to Port Moresby. 'In these three months', writes a historian of the war, 'Australia had lost one of her four AIF divisions (the 8th), and two of her few warships had been sunk, while her airmen, flying obsolescent planes, were easily outfought by the Japanese'.[1]

Sydney's crowds continued to rush to work from Circular Quay up Pitt Street to city offices, factories and workshops. Shoppers paid high prices for food and clothes in short supply as rumours of economic blockades and rationing circulated. Some of the wealthy left their mansions at Darling Point or around the harbour for the safety of the country, while women and children were temporarily evacuated to the Blue Mountains. The most noticeable sign of the war occurred at night when black-outs or brown-outs left the harbour city in sepia or shrouded in gloom. The tall clock-tower of the G.P.O. in Martin

Father and son

John, Jenny and young Sandy, with John's sister Nellie and her fiancé, Robert Dick, farewell his sister Katie and husband George Murdoch (centre), *soon to leave for the United States,* c. *1925.*

'Old Trotsky', the benign 'dominie' in the garden at Lesmahagow, and his wife with a grandchild

The photograph submitted by John with his application for the Challis chair at Sydney, 1926

The Philosophy Department at 'kirky' Edinburgh. John is seated, third from right; in the centre are Professor N. Kemp Smith (left) *and Professor A. E. Taylor*

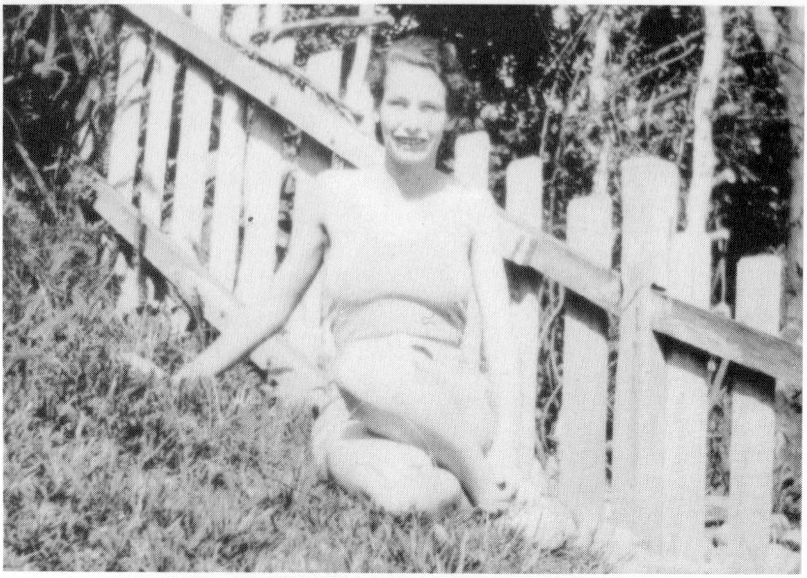

Ruth Walker in bathing costume, and with her father, 1938

Place was dismantled and removed to avoid becoming a target or reference point for aerial bombing or naval raiders. The continental and raffish life of Kings Cross was extinguished. But the black-out also revealed another timeless city beneath the full moon:

> A black and silver city rose resculptured by light and shadow. Black mysterious doorways, lanes like dark primeval canyons, smooth buildings one had never noticed before, whole districts that looked as if they had been gutted by fire long ago, and elsewhere, masses of still and tranquil beauty. The trams were stationary, dark and empty where they stood on their faintly gleaming lines . . . The Anzac Memorial, the Archibald Fountain looked as unreal as stage settings.[2]

Young conscripts in khaki waited for invasion. Everywhere uniforms, men and women, air force, navy, A.I.F., militia and volunteers. Up at the university, professors, staff and students dug slit trenches around the Gothic buildings and manned them during air-raid precautions. On the night of 31 May two Japanese midget submarines passed through the barrage net and entered the harbour in pursuit of the American ship *Chicago*. There was a fiery hour, the submarines were destroyed, several Australian service men lost their lives when an old ferry was torpedoed near Garden Island, a broadside from *Chicago* carried away a few stones of Fort Denison.

The country was heartened by the arrival of General Douglas MacArthur, followed by thousands of American troops, who were welcomed as saviours. 'Without any inhibitions of any kind', exhorted the Prime Minister, 'I make it quite clear that Australia looks to America, free of any pangs as to our traditional links or kinship with the United Kingdom'. Sydney's young women did their patriotic best at work during the week in factories, industry or munitions production, or in their time off pleasure-bent on a good weekend. On the lawns of the Domain or in the shadows of shrubs and bushes lovers sought and found one another. In the crisis of war and imminent invasion, Sydney was reverting to its anarchic and turbulent past.

Soon society doctors with a secretive clientele were in demand among those with introductions and means.

In a world on fire, where all things lived by conflict and destruction, and where 'war is the father and king of all', Heraclitus was a fitting and realist source for Anderson's brooding on the war. There was no permanence or stability in the world, nor should we desire a stagnant system of peace and repose. Whatever lives, lives by the death of others. 'The world', said Heraclitus, 'is an ever-living fire, kindled in measures and in measures going out'. From Heraclitus' fiery visions Anderson took his most fundamental insight into reality, that there is 'no total or maximum system or minimum system' either.

Applying these most general principles, Anderson saw the present global conflict as a continuation of the Great War. Hitler's grasp at the mastery and domination of Europe was a result of the unsatisfactory Versailles settlement and a renewal of the German grand strategy of 1914. This time France had rapidly collapsed and the main theatre of operations had moved eastwards to Russia. Anderson's comparative lack of interest in Japan, the Far Fast and the Pacific theatres was characteristic of his age and generation. As at Glasgow in 1917, he managed to keep the war alarms and confusions at a distance. He was no simple patriot and regarded the war effort with some scepticism and mistrust, particularly after the universities were threatened with closure. His deepest loyalty remained to the university and the life of the mind, not to his adopted country. 'Australia is just a geographical expression', he jested and 'patriotism apart, there is such a thing as love of country'. Disillusionment with world Communism did not make him an admirer of 'Uncle Joe' and he had always suspected American leaders of superficiality, naivety and hypocrisy. Roosevelt's Atlantic Charter of 1941 did not impress him but seemed to be an exercise in sentimentality and wishful thinking. He also thought the American insistence on unconditional surrender premature and unwise.

John Dedman, the Scottish-born Minister for War Organisation of Industry, arranged a conference with the universities in January 1942. At a time when student numbers had dropped from 14 000 to 9000 and closure seemed likely, except for the 'strategic faculties' of Medicine and Engineering, Dedman encouraged the universities to continue teaching and by mid-1942 the Commonwealth government agreed to subsidise all students on reserve. Later that year the first Universities Commission was established to administer the scheme. But Anderson did not welcome it or other moves by educationists to 'reform' universities and make them more amenable to public opinion. His hostile reaction to Commonwealth intervention in university education during the war crisis of 1942 parallelled his earlier stance at Glasgow in support of academic values and autonomy in another war. His fear that Commonwealth entry quotas and subsidies foreshadowed government directives and an erosion of intellectual independence underlay his oppositional role and vividly recalled his defence of university values in 1917 and 1931. Equally, he proved to be a stern critic of the 'welfare state', Fabianism and philanthropy—they were cures for civilisation far more deadly than its diseases. Just as proud Scots in the nineteenth century had resisted the introduction of the English Poor Law lest they lose their thrifty independence and mutual sympathy for one another, so John Anderson now opposed the state's increased provision of social welfare, education and health because it would undermine self-reliance, independence and the 'producer ethic'. He was not the only one to express misgivings. In 1942 in a memorable broadcast to the 'forgotten people',* Menzies said 'that the greatest element in a strong people is a fierce independence of spirit. This is the only *real* freedom, and it has as its corollary a brave acceptance of unclouded individual responsibility'.[3] Dependency on the state was a great evil because it bred a mendicant and spineless spirit. Dour Scottish sentiments indeed.

As Anderson attacked the servile and consumerist values associated with the 'servile state' and all the 'sickly apparatus of welfare', he also challenged the assumptions on which much post-war reconstruction and centralised planning were based. Heraclitus' advice 'to expect the unexpected' became his slogan.

* Menzies' forgotten people were, of course, the middle class or 'those people who are constantly in danger of being ground between the upper and the nether millstones of the false class war'.

How could we plan for all contingencies when many of them were unknown and in the future? The spurious sense of control and security 'from the cradle to the grave' purveyed by the 'intellectual experts' and planners was simply a form of whistling in the dark. Even the assumption of widespread human rationality was questionable, for many of our own motives could not be known with any certainty. With social democrats, humanitarians and philanthropists he showed scant sympathy, and in matters of public policy he became increasingly conservative. Alf Conlon, one of Anderson's favourite students and a former intimate, became University Manpower Officer until he set up a research department for the army and moved on to post-war reconstruction. Advocating rational manpower planning and mobilising the intellectuals for 'total war', he acquired considerable influence over ministers, politicians and generals. No one was ever quite sure what he and his outfit were doing, since 'careless talk cost lives', but at least on one occasion he and Anderson were discovered together in the back room of a pub deep in beer, conspiracy and contemplation.

Anderson's oppositional and critical stance was not popular in Sydney. The heroic victories of Stalingrad and Kursk that helped to turn the war against the Axis won much local enthusiasm for Stalin, 'sheepskins for Russia' and centralised planning. Communist Party membership rose to an all-time high of 25 000. For all that, however, Anderson's misgivings did anticipate a later mood of general disenchantment with the grey mediocrity, bureaucratic controls and standardisation of total war that A. D. Hope captured in his famous lines from 'Australia',

> A nation of trees, drab green and desolate grey
> In the field uniform of modern wars.

Thoughtful people in Sydney began to fear the loss of individual freedom, choice and independence in a society marked by growing collectivism, cultural uniformity and centralisation. Anderson strongly opposed the 1944 referendum on post-war reconstruction because it would have conferred substantial new powers on the Commonwealth. Yet if Anderson was ceasing to be politically radical, he was not going to join the ranks of the bourgeoisie. In 1943 he shocked parliament and a pious public when he attacked the teaching of religion in schools; provocatively, he claimed that he could 'deal with this subject as briefly as with the subject of snakes in Iceland [*sic*]—"There is no religion in education" '.[4]

Opposition to Communism remained, however, his most enduring political commitment. It was based on his 'detestation' of Stalin and Stalin's methods—in his eyes, indistinguishable from those of Hitler and the Nazis—but it also entailed a philosophical critique of the 'totalist' and 'solidarist' claims of Marxism and, by implication, of all totalitarian systems. According to Anderson, 'there is no such thing as an absolute totality':

> . . . the empiricist, the critic of totality, will also be a critic of *social* totality, of solidarism, i.e. he will recognise that society too is pluralistic, is a field of divergent tendencies and, again, is no more self-sustaining than 'the individual' is, though he may naturally look upon it as a protection or support. And this is where we can criticise the Marxian development of Hegelianism—for while it may be quite proper to find the prototype of the Absolute in *society*, it is quite another matter to treat society as an Absolute, i.e. to give it the character of totality or self-subsistence.[5]

'Solidarism' or 'totalism' masked 'real conflicts and differences' in society for the sake of a supposed unity-in-difference. But its inevitable results were stagnation, tyranny and repression.

Across the Tasman in New Zealand, Karl Popper was doing his war work writing *The Open Society and Its Enemies*. The book was a more partisan and limited *pièce d'occasion* than anything Anderson wrote during the war and contains a withering attack on Hegel and Plato as architects of fascism and the 'closed society'. By contrast, Anderson had always appreciated the vital contribution of German philosophy to a criticism of English empiricism and he was not going to deny this debt in wartime; in fact, his major criticisms of Russell's logical atomism derived from his study of Kant and Hegel. Kant's important work on space, time and the categories constituted an answer to Hume's scepticism, and Anderson was impressed with Hegel's systematic working out of the categories. Nevertheless, Popper's account and criticisms of Marx and scientific 'historicism' closely resembled Anderson's attacks on 'totalism' and the Hegelian-Marxist confusion of logic and history.

Within the university, Anderson's influence was at its zenith. If in the philosophy lecture room he was an awesome gowned figure and in meetings with students in the quad a mixture of diffidence and consideration, at parties he was known to sing in a pleasant tenor a repertoire ranging from Mozart and Mussorgsky to the Hebridean songs of his youth, to jitterbug, and to listen to Duke Ellington. At weekend gatherings at Turramurra he wore a many-coloured waistcoat and smiled his carnivorous grin at Ruth and admiring students. Sometimes he played tennis in an ungainly way. At the Teachers' College one of Anderson's 'young lions' taught a course on his logic and empiricism. In Sydney's tepid and conventional religious climate, his bold atheist system won many open and covert followers among the war generation of students; for them the churches had ceased to count because they had ceased to think. They were refuges for the timid and compliant. Overall, Anderson's influence contributed to a sceptical, questioning strain and a distrust of the state that was quite missing from the more collectivist and monochrome political correctness of Melbourne student life. There the Labour Club dominated:

> Communists were seen in the glow of the Red Army's struggle against the Nazis. Few among those who believed the worst about Communism and the U.S.S.R. ventured to say anything; their criticism could so easily be construed as an attack on Allied unity or Australia's war effort, a fact which Communists frequently exploited, no doubt with all sincerity. Further, the war had brought about an unprecedented fervour for social change which was not confined to members of political parties. Out of the blood-bath a new and better world would be born . . . We were all socialists and in terms of practical co-operation there were few if any differences which could arise between Communist student leaders and those whose reforming zeal derived from the A.L.P. or Christianity.[6]

Melbourne intellectuals came to regard Anderson 'as the man who had betrayed the Left, a man who had gone over to the other side. Melburnians wanted Anderson to answer a simple question: was he or was he not interested in the fact that some were very rich and some very poor?' To this question Anderson replied that 'we were all bothered by different things. That finished him with the Melburnians'.[7] His wife and co-worker in Communism provided a somewhat different account of his transformation:

> He worked his way through Trotskyism, always quite publicly, so that anyone might see, if he cared to look, thought (or criticism) in action. His final political position is somewhat hard to define, but I have often thought of him as one who had gone full circle and ended up (now consciously and politically) as he began—one of Gilbert's 'little Liberals'.[8]

Was there anything left of a positive character in Anderson's philosophy after the rejection of Marxism as a form of 'solidarism'? By default, there was a less than enthusiastic acceptance of parliamentary democracy and liberalism, but much more telling was the corrosive critique of all forms of optimism, humanitarianism, philanthropy and social planning. The nihilism cut deep, giving to much that Anderson said a note of almost Russian despair and cynicism. Was there any purpose really worth defending? A certain weary pessimism and despair also affected his close followers to become more than just an undergraduate pose. One of them, James McAuley, would write:

> It's my own judgement day that I draw near,
> Descending in the past, without a clue,
> Down to that central deadness: the despair
> Older than any hope I ever knew.[9]

At least there was permanent opposition, a passion to oppose and doubt everything, and a tough-minded stoicism. Only the mature and strong could survive the loss of all illusions and attain a stoic fortitude and a sober, unflinching acceptance of reality. As Anderson turned away from Marx, he gained a new respect for Freud and the 'Freudian revolution'. Another thorough-going determinist and atheist, Freud was more attuned to Anderson's bitter disenchantment with politics and humanity, his growing pessimism and despair.

When P. H. Partridge gave a study course for the Workers' Educational Association containing a Trotskyist critique of the U.S.S.R., he incurred the wrath of the local Communist Party. 'This course is a wholesale attack on our Ally, the Union of Soviet Socialist Republics', denounced Lance Sharkey and, when attempts to get the course withdrawn failed, the party boycotted the W.E.A.[10] Later conflicts between W. H. C. Eddy, representing the pluralist position, and Lloyd Ross, a tutorial class lecturer and prominent in the Ministry of Post-War Reconstruction, made the W.E.A. and adult education a scene of fierce disputation between the disciples of Anderson and left-wing planners and fellow-travellers.

Similarly, the Communists were soon involved in a bitter union battle with the shop stewards and Trotskyists of old Balmain. Balmain was a hilly working-class suburb situated on a neck of land that jutted into the harbour west of the city and Darling Harbour. Dominated by its waterfront industries of shipbuilding, general engineering and repair work, it had been closely associated with the founding of trade unions and the Labor Party in the 1890s, and its residents, fierce as a nest of bull ants, possessed a strong sense of community. Balmain shared with isolated mining and industrial towns 'a long tradition of industrial militancy and proud independence in which the men struck first and reported to the union later. They were not good material for centralised control'.[11]

In 1942 the Communist leadership of the Federated Ironworkers' Association decided to take control of the Balmain branch. They were soon opposed by the old local executive and a Trotskyist faction led by N. Origlass at Mort's Dock and L. Short at Cockatoo Island Dockyard. The Trotskyists questioned the Communists' total identification with Stalin and the war effort, and argued that the workers should still pursue their own class interests against local capitalists and the state. Throughout 1943 and 1944 savage infighting occurred between local leaders and the Communist executive led by Ernest

Thornton. Eventually, the silencing and removal of Origlass as shop delegate at Mort's Dock led to a six-week strike, which began late in April 1945 and involved 3000 men. As Robin Gollan sums up:

> The battle of Balmain is significant in more than one respect. It is clearly a case of a communist trade union bureaucracy, convinced of the verity of its own policy and arrogant with power, attempting to impose its policy and its authority on a reluctant rank and file. It is a case of a principled militant minority emerging as the leadership of relatively unpolitical workers driven to revolt by what they saw as the oppression of employers, government, and their own union officials. Finally, it is the case of the anti-communist impetus leading to common action by the anti-communist militant left and the militant right.[12]

Balmain's brave struggle against the central executive was the prelude to a much wider battle in the union and labour movement of the late 1940s and 1950s between hard-line Stalinists and their opponents on the left and right. Communists were committed to 'democratic centralism', the Soviet line and an imminent proletarian revolution, while their opponents spanned the spectrum from Trotskyists and anarcho-syndicalists on the left, to moderates and Catholic Industrial Groups on the right. Sydney's cold war, with its narrow horizons and unforgiving witch hunts, had begun.

The end of the Second World War and the surrender of Japan on 15 August 1945 brought sudden violent release of long-pent emotion in Sydney's streets:

> Factories, shops, offices emptied. As the streets filled the traffic stopped, the crowd became a procession, all the scattered particles fused . . . the procession converged upon the heart of the city. Martin Place became a vortex, a cauldron. A vast crowd filled it, never still, turning on its own axis, continuing in the restricted space to be a procession, dancing, singing . . . The song that dominated the crowd was *Waltzing Matilda* . . . The streets were drifted with paper.[13]

At the end of a long and exhausting war, two of its unexpected outcomes raised fundamental doubts about the application of science to society and the conduct of war. The first was the discovery of the concentration camps and the evidence of the holocaust as the allied armies invaded Germany and Poland. Such gruesome facts demonstrated the Nazis' unrelenting determination to apply their biological doctrines of race and eugenics to the Jews and whole populations of 'subject peoples' in the Third Reich. That a highly civilised and cultured European nation was capable of perpetrating mass murder and genocide in the interests of a 'perverted science' and *lebensraum* outraged the canons of human decency and civilisation. The other discovery was rather less flattering to the allies' own sense of moral worth and superior virtue. It occurred with the dropping of the atomic bombs on Hiroshima on 6 August and Nagasaki on 9 August 1945. The instantaneous and massive destruction of life and property in a quasi-apocalyptic holocaust was one of the most spectacular and sustained 'triumphs' of science during the war. It had taken teams of American, British and other scientists and a large investment of two billion dollars over three years to make the bomb. In the end it had to be used, ostensibly, to avoid much greater bloodshed, to impress the Russians, and because it was there. 'I have become Death, Destroyer of worlds', reflected Robert Oppenheimer as he saw a film of the explosion. Science had known sin, he confessed, and the nature of 'total war' was transformed for all time by these events. The bomb was to have profound effects on the 'cold war' once it began in Eastern Europe in 1946.

It is against the backdrop of these universal and tragic events that Anderson's increasing disillusionment with science and social engineering should be seen. Recollecting the moral effect of the war on intellectuals and universities, Dr H. C. Coombs later deplored 'the cultivation of hatred of those against whom they fought: the subordination of moral, intellectual and spiritual values to the material needs of the war effort'.[14] For Anderson, science had lost its philosophical and ethical bearings and had become increasingly narrow, specialised and utilitarian in character. Like Wittgenstein, much of his later career and life was to be devoted to exposing and attacking the narrowness, eclecticism and 'practicalism' of science.

At the philosophical level, he became hostile to the influence of A. J. Ayer and logical positivism. Among the members of the Vienna Circle, who in the 1920s introduced logical positivism, only Moritz Schlick had a serious training in philosophy. The others were scientists who had become interested in philosophy and they thought that what the discipline needed was an infusion of scientific techniques and mathematical logic. Most had a drastic remedy for the traditional problems of ethics, metaphysics, theology and aesthetics. They dismissed them all as meaningless non-sense because they were not amenable to empirical methods of verification. Once philosophy had been purified of all unscientific elements only the 'logic of science' would remain. By 'the logic of science', Rudolf Carnap meant 'the logical analysis of the concepts and sentences of the sciences, for *the logic of science is nothing other than the logical syntax of the language of science*'.[15]

The outlook and methods of logical positivism were introduced to the English-speaking world by A. J. Ayer in his book, *Language, Truth and Logic*, published in 1936. Ayer presented and argued for a thesis of great generality. Unless a proposition could be verified by observation and experience, the statement could have no literal meaning. To have meaning a statement must be either analytic or empirically verifiable. Analytic propositions are tautologies and cannot be verified or falsified by experience; they 'simply record our determination to use symbols in a certain fashion'. A non-analytic statement has meaning only if it can be verified or falsified, at least in principle. All other thinking is literally meaningless. Religion, astrology, ethics, the metaphysics of Hegel lacked truth value and were therefore meaningless.

Wittgenstein's later work and influence at Cambridge, where he was Professor of Philosophy from 1939 to 1947, also encouraged the movement in English philosophy to linguistic analysis. By the 1930s Wittgenstein had turned from his earlier interest in mathematical logic and the structure of the proposition and reality to a study and therapeutic of language, linguistic puzzles and language games. 'Philosophy is a battle against the bewitchment of our understanding through the means of language', he said, and the *Philosophical Investigations* were the posthumous outcome of his endeavours. While it was the philosopher's task to analyse language, Wittgenstein said that 'philosophy may in no way interfere with the actual use of language'. What we have to do in philosophy is 'to bring words *back* from their metaphysical to their everyday usage'. Wittgenstein's influence was greater at Melbourne than at Sydney, and by the early 1940s George Paul and A. C. Jackson, both men of the left, were practising linguistic analysis.

Anderson, like the good idealists, was dismayed by the rise of 'ordinary language philosophy' at post-war Oxford as practised by John Austin and Gilbert Ryle. His response was complex. In one way it resembled Wittgenstein's lofty dismissal of Oxford as a 'philosophical desert' just as the older Anderson uncannily took on some of Wittgenstein's characteristic mannerisms: the latter, according to Ryle, 'gave the impressions, first, that he himself was proud not to have studied other philosophers—which he had done, though not much—and second, that he thought that people who did study them were academic and therefore unauthentic philosophers, which was often but not always true'.[16] Anderson's deteriorating eyesight and his refusal to wear glasses did not help:

> He was fond of saying, 'I am like Berkeley—a non-reading philosopher' (pretty hard on Berkeley, and even hard on himself); and I remember his once rejecting my praise of an historian with—'but he's a bloody bookworm!' There was a serious weakness here. Not only in his own work, but even more in the training of students he was preposterously indifferent to the techniques and craftsmanship of scholarship.[17]

In all this cantankerous eccentricity there were elements of vanity, egoism and whimsy, as Partridge perceived, and it was not always a healthy influence on students or an attractive sight to behold.

In responding to the challenge of logical positivism, mathematical logic and linguistic analysis, the mature Anderson came to a new appreciation of Hegel's achievement. Hegel's insistence on coherence and system was correct, but the systematic character of philosophy should appear not in the form of a 'totality', a monistic doctrine of the oneness of all things, but in the form of a single propositional logic, which applies in the same way to all things:

> If we reject the ultimate interconnection, the 'unity' of things, what can this contrast amount to? In the first place, there is the question of *logic*; a person has a 'position' when he has a logic, i.e. a theory of the characters of things in general, which will have a regulative or guiding influence in his special inquiries . . . His special views, then, seem to hang together, seem all to be derived from the same source; but all that is actually the case is that they are connected with the same logic. Secondly, a man is said to have a position when he has views on questions that are, at the time, socially important, views that he can link up with some sort of programme or policy, not something merely in the air but with a certain practical force. He has a position in that he has connected views on the leading questions of the day.[18]

Hegel was also right in his insistence on the Greek spirit of objectivity, the ruthless rejection of subjectivism, the insistence on disinterested inquiry. For Anderson, 'classicism' was to become synonymous with objectivity, disinterested criticism and total opposition to utility. 'As I now put it', he wrote some years later to Ruth Walker, 'if we reject the ethic of ends, we're left with the ethics of *rejecting ends* i.e. of disinterestedness and detachment, and the sole question for positive ethics (for the detailed science) is to find *species* of disinterested activity—and, of course, how they proceed'.[19]

The parallel with Hegel is worth exploring a little further. As a student at Tübingen, Hegel had welcomed the French Revolution as the actualisation of reason in the modern world. The Revolution exercised a formative influence on his development as a philosopher and, even though he repudiated the excesses of the Jacobins and the Terror, he continued to celebrate Bastille day as an event of world-historical significance. During the Jena period, when he developed his vast system, he carried out a radical critique of religion, economics, politics and all aspects of society. But in 1818 with his elevation to a chair at Berlin and the publication of the *Philosophy of Right*, Hegel became increasingly conservative, his sympathies contracted, and his social and political philosophy seemed to sanction the status quo. The resemblance to John Anderson is clear. At Glasgow the young Anderson espoused the Bolshevik Revolution as the emancipation of the working class, and much of his subsequent development as a realist philosopher occurred in the closest dialogue with Marx and Marxism. When at last he broke with Communism, he had become an influential figure in the university and wider community through a network of ex-students and close associates. Did his rejection of Marx also signify a narrowing of interests and vision, a hardening of the categories, and a loss of wider human sympathies? Had Anderson turned full circle? And did his stand epitomise what Hegel called 'the seriousness, the suffering, the patience and the labour of the negative'?

12

War, the University and the Servile State

BY THE YEAR that war broke out Anderson had acquired a powerful reputation among students as an atheist, rebel and free-thinker. His single-handed fight with parliament and the university Senate over war memorials had become a legend; and his striding across the quad without removing his hat while the carillon played 'God Save the King' and Professor Todd glowered from the Latin corner, endeared him to the students. One of them, an impressionable young man, wrote of his encounter with the myth and the man, appearance and reality:

> Anderson seemed the most important person at the University. I began to feel a yearning when he walked by; even if I saw him only out of the corner of my eye my skin might stiffen and my hair prickle at the roots. He was in his forties, very tall, stooped, gangling, striding loosely past in a brown suit and a green hat with an upturned brim, usually sombre, with his pipe jutting out from between his teeth. He seemed an embodiment of what was grave and constant in human suffering, but sometimes he would wave an arm at a student, loosely, as if it were a puppet's, and smile, strong teeth bursting out beneath his full black moustache. Recognition. Sunshine. His huge, sad brown eyes seemed to sag right down into his face, pulling the cheeks down with them, lost in wisdom. Sometimes he seemed very tired, both tough and fragile, bearing a great load, but still walking briskly. Then he would laugh, or wave his arm. I was gripped by the need to know him.[1]

During the war years Anderson was one of the most stimulating professors at the university, exercising a great influence over students and their intellectual development, especially through the student societies that he presided over. Donald Horne evokes the experience of many an undergraduate:

> Light came into the philosophy lecture theatre, where the Literary Society held its meetings, through leaded glass windows, and on either side of the blackboard there were murals of famous classical and modern philosophers. There was the sense of an inner temple about this room when early in term . . . I sat in it to hear Anderson give his annual address to the Literary Society, of which he was President. When he began speaking in an urgent Glaswegian sing-song the room seemed stilled by significance. Most of the time he spoke strongly, but occasionally his voice hovered and fluttered while he stuttered for words, by this hesitation building up a pressure that then burst through into a confident and sustained high note. The style of his address was intensely serious, but lightened now and again with a wisecrack, or with sarcasm. Most of the small audience took notes of what he said, and in the discussion that followed some of them stood up and elaborated parts of what they had just heard . . . Anderson sat silent, hunched over the rostrum as he wrote on a piece of paper, looking up from time to time, deep-eyed and intent. Then, when the discussion was over, he made a triumphant ending, flowing strongly again, correcting errors and confusions and bestowing agreement like a final blessing. It took only an hour, but we felt that we had just witnessed an important new contribution to the theory of aesthetics.[2]

Students were drawn to the mature Anderson not so much by teaching skills or lecturing technique but by the sheer intellectual strength of his position, the robustness of his personality, and his unwavering self-assurance. He had immediate rapport with students from his classes, and was able to talk confidently and knowledgeably about their essays and exam papers, even when the class was large. His influence was much greater on senior honours students and the 'inner circle' of longstanding

The Walker family, Christmas 1939

Ruth and small friend, 1977

A philosophy conference at Leura in the Blue Mountains, 1940: (above) *Ruth and John on the steps with little Helen Passmore between them;* (below) *Ruth is in the back row, second from the left, and John seated*

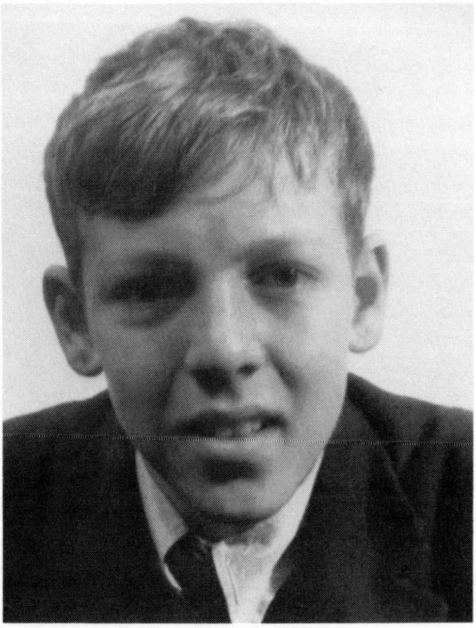

Sandy Anderson, schoolboy at Knox

His father, rugged up at Turramurra

John Anderson retired at home, c. *1960; and the site of his greatest labours, the philosophy corner of the Main Quad at Sydney University*

members of the Freethought* and Literary Societies, as Eugene Kamenka recalled:

> For many of us who were his students, the Philosophy Room in that splendid Main Quadrangle building of the University of Sydney became the site of a recurrent weekly drama in which Socrates faced his accusers and died for his beliefs, in which superstition, self-interest, sentimentalism, monism and solidarism were exposed in favour of the existence of conflict and complexity, in which thought triumphed over all, even if the thinking life, the life of protest and examination, was a life of permanent opposition, of unending struggle against powerful social forces that could never be ultimately and finally defeated.[3]

To outsiders, the Andersonians appeared to be initiates of an esoteric cult and practitioners of a local mystique, with their own language, rituals and favourite bogeymen. Anderson disdained to 'spoon-feed' his students and left the induction of new members to older proselytes like Oliver Somerville and F. W. Fowler, Anderson's 'young tiger' who lectured at the Teachers' College in the late 1930s. They were well versed in his teaching, logic and language. Apart from Anderson's psychological need for a close following, his technical vocabulary as a philosopher also promoted the development of an inner coterie. It was quicker and easier to expound a new idea to students who already knew his terminology and presuppositions, 'and the continuing influx of new recruits as the older ones streamed out relieved him of the necessity of re-translating his reflections into the common language. In that way, the phenomenon of Andersonianism has had a more lasting effect on Anderson than anyone else'.[4]

---

* Anderson was the first and continuing president of the Freethought Society, from its inception in 1930. 'Freethought' did not mean general 'freedom of thought' but certain characteristic doctrines: 'the primacy of science' as a way of knowledge; 'the widest possible extension of knowledge of all subjects'; and hence opposition to 'every form of censorship and restriction of inquiry'. Later 'freethought' came to embody Anderson's realism, his criticism of Marxism as 'superstition', and his opposition to 'the search for security' and the belief in 'constant human progress'. Anderson's followers were known as 'freethinkers', and so I have retained this usage in the text.

What was the key to Anderson's impact on so many students? His accessibility, charm and radicalism were important elements, of course, but so too was his provision of a corrosive critique, a set of powerful weapons that could be applied to psychology, religion and literature as much as to philosophy. 'Every icon was to be smashed: God, immortality, free will, moralism, the common good of society', and the young David Armstrong thought 'Anderson often seemed to go out of his way to be intellectually offensive'.[5] An air of intellectual menace pervaded the Philosophy Department as well as the whiff of taboo subjects and forbidden books. The banned *Ulysses* went the round of favoured students bound in the black and gilt of holy writ. Certainly, Anderson had his camp followers who, disregarding the master's subtleties and complexities, applied his teaching indiscriminately. These were the self-styled 'Andersonians' and 'to be an Andersonian was as self-sustaining as being a Marxist or a Freudian: it provided an answer to everything'.[6] The critique Anderson imparted, however, was not a simple rebellion against authority but a meta-iconoclasm, a rebellion against the rebels while still using the language of rebellion that had disconcerting results:

> The smasher of traditional icons is often quick to set up other icons in their place. Anderson was just as keen to smash the smashers of icons. The treatment of Freud and Marx was typical. Although their achievements were acknowledged, particularly their critical achievements, they in turn were subjected to trenchant criticism, often with the object of showing that they had fallen into the same errors as the ones which they had partially exposed. For pluralist empiricists, recognizing only a single level of being in a single space-time, the life of inquiry (a life which, in present days, was believed to go on only fitfully outside Sydney) was the life of 'thoroughgoing criticism'. No wonder we felt so superior to everybody else.[7]

Having broken with all political parties, Anderson retreated to the neo-Gothic citadel and cloisters of the university. His growing disillusionment with the workers as the 'producer class' led him to place his hopes in small groups of students and freethinkers imbued with the spirit of inquiry and aesthetic freedom. The intellectual and emotional relationships within his circle were extraordinarily close and took on the intensity of a large argumentative family. Among the favoured few, he encouraged discipleship and formed close relationships with young men that took on a strongly paternal character. Like Stephen Dedalus, some male students were in need of a surrogate father. Anderson had few doubts about his role as leader-mentor and insisted on his authority over the group. To the elect, he was simply 'John'. Anderson lived through his students vicariously, challenging them to do what he would or could not do himself in middle age, pushing some of them to the limit, and perhaps envying them their youth and the new freedoms they enjoyed. But his liberation proved a mixed blessing for the young women of the group. Jill Ker Conway later noted 'a stultifying conformity to what were considered "advanced" sexual mores' and wryly observed the 'asymmetrical results' of emancipation as men took advantage of the women.[8] Few were encouraged or guided to take up philosophy as a serious career and, for all their vaunted sexual emancipation, the rest ended as 'school teachers, lower echelon public servants, run-of-the-mill psychologists or journalists, and mostly, housewives'. As Anderson loftily said, they had found their level. Commenting on the hollow promise of Anderson's message for women, Elwyn Morris has written:

> . . . Andersonianism had seemed to be the perfect wave for which they [women] had been waiting, after years sitting scanning the flat, oppressive Australian horizon. That clear green wave had reared thrillingly above them, to sweep them up in its first exhilarating intellectual rush. Most of the men, gracefully riding the boards of male privilege, leapt to their feet and caught it, executing tricky personal variations as they rode it triumphantly to various golden shores . . . But the women, mere bodysurfers deprived of such streamlined support, flailed and floundered, dragged down by a sexist society. Some sank, and were never seen again, others . . . were ignominiously dumped in the shallows, suffering some concussion, even if not permanent brain damage.[9]

As freethinkers and Andersonians came perilously close to worshipping their master and guru in these years, had Anderson become the pope of his small sect? Some thought so. 'As to his "atheism", there is no doubt about this', reported Arthur Prior on seeing the philosopher in his prime:

> But when I first saw the man . . . another observer [Jack Smart] whispered as he was talking that he was exactly like a Presbyterian clergyman. And so, indeed, he is . . . though of a type which is now dying out. The leader of some fairly small dissenting Scottish sect, scorning mere 'conventional religion', reverencing nothing but his God, dominating his flock and yet honestly appealing for (and sometimes evoking) independence of mind and action.[10]

Because he demanded unconditional loyalty—'with me all or not at all'—Anderson experienced in his personal relationships many disappointments, and in time a growing sense of disillusionment, estrangement and even betrayal. The symbolic father had to be killed, Freud had said, and after great anguish and turmoil some of Anderson's best students had to break decisively with their teacher to achieve personal maturity and real independence of mind. It was an emotional and galling experience for them. As young Stephen felt the pangs of banishment, exile and remorse in *Ulysses*: 'agenbite of inwit. Inwit's agenbite. Misery! Misery!'

The group-mentality arising from such close-knit and intense relationships did not accord well with Anderson's frequent injunctions to freedom of thought and vigorous pluralism. At Sydney, his realist philosophy came to occupy a privileged position exempt from the savage critique applied to Christianity, Hegel and Marx. Little or no interest was taken in rival philosophies or contemporary developments like logical positivism or linguistic philosophy. 'Anderson's students', one of them admitted, 'were not encouraged to shop around among other philosophies and could find it easy enough to complete a full and lively undergraduate course specialising in Philosophy without having formed any but the very sketchiest idea of what was going on in the rest of the world in Philosophy'.[11] Partridge, too, was to lament the lack of intellectual challenge and competition at Sydney, and in these years observed both a hardening of Anderson's position as the university's 'no-man' and a contraction of his interests. 'As local as a magpie', he wrote of Anderson:

> It would be hard to think of a man of comparable ability who has lived so much immersed in the local scene, and so much enclosed in his own personal circle. The scene being so limited, provincial, remote from the world's intellectual centres, the personal circle so much below him in intellectual calibre, the original thinker in him has clearly been struggling against very heavy odds.[12]

During the first two years of the war, the university was not greatly affected except for the enlistment of considerable numbers of students, graduates and staff in the armed services. Total student enrolments remained about 4000. After the entry of Japan into the war and the capture of Singapore early in 1942, there was a greater sense of national crisis and compulsory military service was introduced for young men. Inevitably, the authorities made decisions about the value of particular university courses for the war effort. 'Generally students in the faculties of Medicine, Science, Engineering, Dentistry, Veterinary Science and Agriculture were "reserved"; students in the other four faculties of Arts, Law, Economics and Architecture were not so "reserved", although some mathematics and language students in Arts were'.[13] The proportion of women in the Arts Faculty rose from about half in 1939 to over two-thirds by 1942. Such was Anderson's fierce loyalty to the university as an institution and way of life that when a colleague left to take up an important war-time appointment, he remarked, 'Poor fellow, he believes in sacrificing the interests of his university to those of his country'.[14]

The war effort and 'planning the peace' greatly exercised Anderson's mind at this time. He distrusted the enthusiasm and 'moralism' of the planners, whether Marxists, Fabians or social democrats. For one thing, their patriotic rhetoric betrayed an uneasy conscience about the war and its causes as well as solidarist assumptions about the 'common good'. They showed an exaggerated faith in the conscious plans and policies of doctrinaire utilitarianism, and seriously underestimated 'unconscious' factors and the political context in which policies were made and carried out. History was not 'the product of a deliberate pursuit of ends'; and policy was not 'a *controlling* agency in social development'. Such 'rationalistic' and utilitarian ideas 'could only predominate in the thought of a political group which conceived of society as static, as a system in which all processes are predictable and political activity is purely a matter of routine'. More significantly, Anderson feared the 'rapidly increasing power of the state at the expense both of working-class organisations and of the property rights of the individual capitalist'.[15] As a student at Glasgow he had been influenced by Hilaire Belloc's writings in the *New Age*, especially *The Servile State*, and now in another war he revived some of these themes in an influential essay, 'The Servile State', published in 1943.

Anderson wasted little time in disposing of Belloc's historical myths about 'merrie England' and the baleful effects of the Reformation before turning to his main attack on socialism as the harbinger of a new slavery. Belloc had painted a depressing picture of workers sacrificing their legal rights and political independence for regular employment and material security in a 'servile state' and, while Anderson felt Belloc had exaggerated the danger in 1912, his analysis seemed much nearer the mark in 1943. State regimentation and 'socialist propaganda' had contributed to the decline of the sentiment of liberty, particularly in wartime. For Belloc the loss of liberty was a consequence of the loss of economic freedom and independence, but Anderson thought that the real cause of servility was 'the desire for security and sufficiency', and he cited the four freedoms of the Atlantic Charter as examples of a servile mentality. It was quite impossible to satisfy such universal desires as 'freedom from want' and 'freedom from fear': 'the expectation of such benefits is of course delusive; there is no system which can abolish insecurity and guarantee sufficiency. But, by the time that is realised, it will not be possible to have back for the asking the rights that have been surrendered in the name of solidarity'.[16] Those who promoted such nostrums were naive voluntarists or bureaucratic careerists, who themselves expected to benefit from the 'social service' state. Anderson drew on Burnham's *The Managerial Revolution* to illustrate his view 'that any break from capitalist democracy is a break into bureaucracy, autocracy or hierarchical socialism'.

'Solidarist' assumptions were implicit in the ideology of 'national service' and the sinking of differences, and the war had greatly accelerated the movement to regimentation by the 'protective' state. Anderson regarded such an ethic of 'protection' and security as a 'low aim', contrasting it with Croce's heroic view of liberty and Sorel's producer ethic. The producer ethic had never characterised the labour movement or even the socialist movement, and Stalin's attempt at collectivisation had produced all the conditions of a servile state: 'We may, I think, properly apply the term 'servile' to those States which are marked by the suppression of all political opposition and thus of all independent enterprise'.[17]

Anderson opposed all attempts at social engineering and planning as 'illiberal' and 'absurd'—'there is no one who is competent to make provision for all departments and aspects of social life'. The planners' appeal to principles of social utility suggested that they were fundamentally opposed to culture, which could never be planned for, and were really advancing commercial interests. Thus, planning for education would lead to the commercialisation of education and 'a growing acquiescence in bureaucracy and regimentation':

> The danger is especially great in the field of education where 'training for community service' and the fitting of people into their appropriate social pigeon-holes are taken very much as a matter of course. This is not surprising when social conditions are favourable as never before to careerism—however long or short a time that state of affairs may last. In the meantime there is only one thing that the lover of freedom and learning can do and that is to struggle 'against the stream', expounding political realities and exposing rampant mediocrity and vulgarity—realising as he does that liberty has untapped resources, that it is no less deeply rooted in human nature than the linked motives of dominance and submission.[18]

In further writings, Anderson developed his critique of educational reformers and planners, particularly as their 'advocacy' related to the university. They were misguided in their voluntarist and salvationist assumptions about the role of education in society, and failed to recognise the important part played by social movements, 'settled habits' and institutions in promoting a tradition of learning. 'As against this individualistic assumption it must be urged that institutions are prior to individuals, that they *form* individuals, determine the nature of their achievement and the heights they can rise to'.[19] Educational reformers like Melbourne's Vice-Chancellor J. D. G. Medley or Sydney's Professor Eric Ashby glossed over real conflicts in society or within educational institutions between cultural and utilitarian tendencies. 'In fact, the academic quality is largely developed in the struggle against utilitarian tendencies', Anderson maintained:

> If, then, we consider the history of educational institutions themselves, we shall find it largely taken up with the struggle between the development of inquiry (education in the strict sense) and opposing forces which regularly come in the guise of 'social utility' and frequently take the form of State interference. And any attempt to enforce a view of what education shall be, inevitably interferes with inquiry.[20]

For Anderson, education was critical or it was nothing, and certain fundamental studies, such as logic, were necessary for the cultivation of criticism and theory. Against an 'uncritical modernism', he defended classical studies as providing permanent standards of judgement, objectivity and culture: 'If critical inquiry is to go forward, then, it will be by *advancing* (not retreating) to "the classics and philosophy", which alone can provide that foundation".[21] Disinterested and objective inquiry must oppose 'social regimentation and cultural degeneration':

> The field of education, then, is a battlefield between liberality and illiberality—between cosmopolitanism and patriotism, between the treatment of the child as the 'heir of all the ages' and the treatment of him as job-fodder. And practicality, for the liberal, consists in keeping up this

> opposition, with the realisation that while he can never get control of the system, he also can never be ousted from it.[22]

Anderson's defence of education as aggressively secular and opposed to religion was a vivid demonstration of the work of criticism and opposition in society. In a provocative address to the New Education Fellowship on 1 April 1943, he maintained there was no place for religious dogma or authority in education; everything must be brought down to the level of inquiry, observation and experiment.[23] To Sydney's churchmen and churchwomen, whether evangelical Anglicans or pietist Catholics, the professor was next to Satan himself, although broader minds like Bishop Burgmann, Boyce Gibson and Professor Angus of St Andrews College welcomed his criticisms of a dull unthinking orthodoxy. For his pains, Anderson was once more condemned by the New South Wales parliament for presenting 'a travesty of the Christian religion', which was 'calculated to undermine the principles which constitute a Christian State'. On this occasion, the university Senate rebuffed Anderson's critics and, pointing to the secular clauses of the university's foundation charter, argued 'that nothing but harm would follow the stifling in a university of the spirit of free inquiry'. Was the Senate's courage on this occasion a measure of Anderson's success in converting his colleagues to 'the academic point of view'? 'In a developed university', he wrote in 1935, 'Marxist and anti-Marxist views, religious and anti-religious views, the theories of Freud and theories opposed to Freud, will be thoroughly gone into'.[24]

Behind the solidarist 'propaganda' of 'reconstruction' and the 'new order' Anderson feared the ugly realities of state regimentation, centralisation and bureaucracy—in short, 'the totalitarian line' and rule by experts. Already he detected signs of 'cultural degeneration' in the encroachments of utilitarian science, blinkered specialisation, and 'the whole mass of philanthropic ideas'. But if in these war years he became increasingly pessimistic about society, the state and the prospects for a free culture, his defence of 'intellectualism and opposition' did not abate one jot. He accepted Croce's view that liberty 'has lived and always will live . . . a perilous and fighting life'. Opposition was a permanent feature of society: 'For the measure of freedom in any community is the extent of opposition to the ruling order, of criticism of the ruling ideas; and belief in established freedom, or in State-guaranteed "benefits", is a mark of the abandonment of liberty. The servile State is the unopposed State'.[25]

'A certain irreconcilability' Anderson clearly displayed in his defence of culture and his thorough criticisms of educational reformers. But did he make any allowance for the popular audience Medley and Ashby were addressing? There was an animus in his attack that seemed hardly justified or wise, though in this he was following his brother's unrelenting crusade against the 'new education' in New Zealand. Anderson held the view that the new Commonwealth university scholarships were 'thoroughly detrimental' because the social effects of poverty they were intended to alleviate could not be eliminated without the elimination of poverty itself, and so he opposed them. The complacency of his belief that 'it is *desirable* that there should be obstacles to overcome, that "opportunity" should not take the form of a gift' contrasted strongly with his earlier views about bursaries and popular access to the university.[26] Did such views indicate a widening gap between the ageing professor and a new generation of students? Admittedly, he had no objection to the funds going to the university provided that it had complete freedom to allocate them as it chose. Likewise, his curt dismissal of Ashby's argument that more public servants should receive a university education after the war was neither graceful nor enlightened. On the expected increase in post-war students and the related issue of whether to increase the number of universities or not, Anderson favoured a consolidation of the existing metropolitan universities with perhaps some extension of the professional and technical schools to the country. He feared a lowering of standards.

With the end of the war and the influx of thousands of returned servicemen to the university, the student population almost doubled. The staff–student ratio rose to an all-time high of 1:32 in 1946, and this imposed 'grossly inordinate demands' on Anderson and his staff for the rest of the decade. There were large first-year classes of several hundred students and Anderson's conservative lecturing style and manner did not always appeal to mature men just back from the war. Unknown to him, a black market soon developed in his lecture notes. In spite of the heavy administrative burden of running a department and attending Faculty and Professorial Board meetings, which he did conscientiously, Anderson refused to have a secretary. His near-obsession with examinations and academic standards—and his insistence on reading all papers, even those of students taught by other members of his staff—did not help his working life or relations with colleagues. 'The unexamined life is not worth living' took on a special meaning in Anderson's educational practice. In 1947 he handed over the editorship of the philosophical journal to John Passmore, when it became the *Australasian Journal of Philosophy*. He published little thereafter; even when in 1950 Gilbert Ryle wrote a serious critical piece on Anderson's 'deflationist' empiricism and 'exiguous' logic, he did not respond but left John Mackie to reply. It was partly a reflection of age, weariness and the teaching load of these years when the university, crammed beyond its limits with students, was barely able to cope. But it was also a sign of the unbridgeable gulf between Anderson's great philosophical design and the technical detailed character of post-war Oxford linguistic philosophy, which he regarded as 'piecemeal and superficial, and a betrayal of the traditional responsibilities of philosophy'. Was the enemy within the gates? Increasingly he felt so, and it was a view he shared with his brother and conveyed to his students in a party song:

> I was sittin' on a hard bench
>   listenin' to Professor Ryle
> I was sittin' on a hard bench
>   gettin' nouns and verbs from Ryle
> And the thought came flashin' through my mind
>   'John's got him beat by a mile'.
>
> O those Sydney blues
> O those Sydney blues
> I'm stuck here in Magdalen
> Maudlin' with those Sydney blues.

13

Love and Freedom

JUST WHEN Anderson had survived the stresses of war on the university, the religious controversy in 1943, and the post-war crisis of student numbers, he was confronted by more serious conflicts at home. His only child Sandy, after a relatively unhappy time at Knox Grammar, matriculated in 1942 and embarked on a science degree. Ill health and chronic bronchitis prevented his successful completion of second year, and he had to spend long periods at home in bed, tendered by the solicitous Jenny and various doctors. Some years later he began an Arts degree, choosing to major in philosophy. It was to be a trying time for both father and son. John had always expected great things of his son, and was he now to be disappointed in his own academic domain? Once in Edinburgh many years before, he sent the small boy scrambling up a steep path to the castle rock above as a test; when Sandy stopped at an outcrop midway, unable or unwilling to climb further, the father urged him on, and only desisted when a park attendant intervened on the child's behalf. Significantly, Sandy blamed the attendant for his predicament. He so wanted to love and admire his famous father that he failed to see the hard taskmaster in him. John Anderson, on the other hand, was haunted by the oedipal myth. From Sandy's birth, there were unusual stresses in the family as the father, pondering Freud, speculated about this son who was bound to challenge and displace him. He already felt jealous.

Sandy grew up at Turramurra, in 'Levenshulme', the substantial brick home with its large leafy garden and tennis-court. Jenny did not allow him to attend the local primary school because of his bronchitis, poor health and a fear of persecution by the local children. Sceptical of Australian educational standards, she educated him at home, encouraging him to write and read widely. When he approached secondary-school age and began to show an interest in science, he was helped by some of John's students from the university. One of them, Alf Conlon, took a sympathetic interest in the lonely lad and supplied him with equipment for a chemistry laboratory at home. Then Sandy went to Knox Grammar as a day-boy. On the sabbatical of 1938 he accompanied John and Jenny on their visit to Scotland and the United States where, after an intense experience at the Grand Canyon, he became convinced of John's affair with Ruth. A sensitive if taciturn teenager, he keenly resented the betrayal of his mother.

As a Sydney undergraduate he experienced many of the wartime and post-war difficulties at the university, and they were not made any easier for being the son of a professor. If anything, he felt his way was made more difficult. At home, books were often unavailable, being used by his father for lectures. In 1949, his last year in philosophy, when he was twenty-six, he fell deeply in love with a young woman whose boyfriend was being unfaithful to her. The source of the attraction may well have been the resemblance he saw between her unhappy situation and his mother's plight. In resolving some of the psychological issues of the relationship, Sandy went through an emotional crisis and then briefly broke with his 'aged' and interfering parents to assert his freedom as a man and an adult. His love affair flourished, but it was not welcomed by Jenny, who disapproved of her son's wilful ways and new-found independence. Some weeks later, Sandy erupted in a rage against his parents, accusing his father, among other things, of calculated hypocrisy and dishonesty over his long affair with Ruth. John and Jenny were shocked and embarrassed, and shrank from the vehement attack and disclosure. John was acutely disconcerted and disturbed by his son's charge of deceit and duplicity.

The following day he told Ruth about Sandy's outburst, an action which revealed his love and need of her. But he sadly misjudged her capacities and resilience. Worn out by years of anxiety, deception and guilt, she was no longer able to cope with the family situation of the Andersons or the strains within the department. 'I can't stand it! I can't stand it', she screamed. She became physically and emotionally exhausted after a philosophy conference at Newport early in 1950, and was unable to lecture and take her classes. For a time Sandy and his grasp at freedom were forgotten. When Ruth became seriously ill, John, a non-driver, had Sandy bring her from her flat to Turramurra in the family car. There Jenny nursed her for some weeks. But it soon became apparent that Ruth was undergoing a nervous breakdown with serious loss of memory, delusions and an obsessive fear of betraying herself and others. Reluctantly, Anderson admitted defeat and handed her over to the Walker family, urging them not to have her confined to an institution. On medical advice, they placed her in the Woodleigh Private Hospital, Hurstville, and over three months she underwent the new electric shock and drug therapy for her acutely disturbed condition. 'Thoughts of turning into a flying saucer, of betraying Newport and all the rest of the highly-coloured "fates" have now evaporated', she wrote to Anderson; 'I am too concerned with getting decent meals and sleeps'.[1] At the height of the crisis, Ruth raved about a pregnancy, her guilt, the limitations of her body and reproductive organs, and 'shit on the brain'. There were also moments of lucidity, terror and great despair. In a letter to Anderson, she wrote:

> One of my horrors is just the feeling that perhaps I can only save myself by destroying you, that you are all the time wishing I wasn't so tense (abrupt), incapable of 'taking things lightly'—a phrase from an old letter of yours which I think has been haunting me for years . . . A rather similar horror is the feeling that you're leaving me too much to myself, more or less saying 'If she loves me enough, she'll come through, and if she doesn't well away with her'.
>
> I don't feel that there is anyone benign enough or wise enough, perhaps most of all tough enough, for me to take my troubles to.[2]

As Ruth suffered on the verge of insanity in hospital and John Anderson taught his classes at the university, did he recognise his responsibility for her torment and mental disintegration? If love and communication were 'goods' and the basis of a free culture, what had gone so radically wrong with their love? He had believed they were free and equal 'comrades'. 'It's just because we have both intimacy and intellectual companionship', he wrote to Ruth, 'that you mean so much to me—even if I have often muddled things and left you uncertain about one or other or both'.[3] But was that really true, or had 'extrinsic' ends of power and privilege perverted the expression of his love? Employing Marxist categories, he explained her condition as the superstructure out of joint with the substructure. Less condescendingly, he confessed to 'landing' Ruth among his own 'entanglements' and not helping her 'to any solid intellectual and *adult* outlet'; for once, he even accused himself 'of a certain "irresponsibility" and lack of objectivity'. Ruth was so upset by one of his visits to the hospital that her mother wrote to him:

> She has what the doctor calls a guilt conscience or complex, she has raved on these two occasions about her condition, calling on God to help her and to protect her unborn child. We are thankful to say that fear has been proved groundless, but no doubt she had cause to think otherwise . . .
>
> We do not hold you entirely responsible in the matter, we know Ruth is a woman of years and should be able to take care of herself, but she was very young and unsophisticated when she came under your influence at the university, and she had a great regard for you as a teacher, you should have been able to prevent things coming to their present pass. We realize we cannot harm you without harming Ruth more, but we appeal to you to keep out of her life in the future apart from your professional association.[4]

Anderson was greatly concerned about Ruth's condition and arranged her medical leave and for salary payments from the university. He told his staff that he wanted her illness kept quiet, discouraged them from visiting her, and expected everyone to help carry Ruth's teaching load while she rested from the shock treatment at a home in the Blue Mountains.

Such was his authority and the concern for Ruth that all accepted the obligation without question or complaint. When Ruth recovered sufficiently to return to the university in 1951, she resumed her work as a lecturer and a close associate of the professor. They were often seen together and, although never robust, she helped to bridge the gap between the stooped and greying Anderson and his staff and students. But she no longer visited Turramurra.

The gap between professor and students had widened considerably during the late 1940s. A dramatic event that emphasised the extent of the breach was the Chifley government's decision in August 1949 to send troops into the New South Wales coalfields during a bitter strike. Most students condemned the action as draconian and unwarranted, even though the Communist leadership of the Miners' Federation had largely engineered the strike for their own political ends. But so great was Anderson's detestation of Communism now that he supported the federal Labor government's action. His virulent anti-Communism also made him a less than enthusiastic opponent of Menzies' crusade to ban the Communist Party in 1950 and 1951, although an opponent of political banning he certainly remained. Within the university he declined to support the stand of the students' Anti-Conscription Committee, which had been formed by freethought sympathisers to oppose Menzies' conscription bill. According to one student:

> His line now (in 1950) was that we must not fight on all fronts at once, subsidiary issues must be subordinated to important issues; the important issue now was the encroachment of Russia, therefore, he argued in effect, we must not now oppose conscription for to do so would not be to oppose Russia. This was news to old freethinkers, who had always taken it to be a feature of freethought to fight on all fronts at once, not to look for allies, but to criticize superstitions, illusions and encroachments on liberty wherever they were found.[5]

Was Anderson becoming too reactionary? Many students felt so.

Important differences also developed between Anderson and the Freethought Society over Communism and sexual theory, and came to a head in 1951. Anderson criticised 'libertarian' freethinkers for their sexual radicalism, for the view that 'an active sexual life might help students to liberate themselves from their sexual illusions'. Opposition to superstition was the best general definition of freethought, he argued, and it included the rejection of religious, social and political superstitions: 'But there is no need to link views with activities or to say that the holder of certain views must practise certain things. This itself is superstitious and makes it another religion'.[6] Constant conflicts and disagreements between the student executive members of the society and the veteran president, who threatened to use his veto, rendered the Freethought Society ineffective and moribund. After 1951 a number of Andersonians left to found the Libertarian Society, which the master condemned for its 'naivety' and 'primitivism'.

Within his own realist 'school', Anderson encountered 'a barrier with the approaching 30 generation'. He had always enjoyed close emotional relations with an 'inner circle' of admiring male and female students but these relationships came under increasing strain during the bitter disputes over ethics and freethought in the early 1950s. 'I seem to be encompassed with opinionated young men and I can't be bothered with them', he wrote despondently of these 'malcontents'.[7] When the Libertarian Club was established, Anderson thought it would not 'come to much'. 'What annoys me about the "Libs" (apart from the stupidity of their position) is that they are (quite unconcernedly) *blocking* the kind of thing I could do for students—and did do in your time', he confided to Ruth.[8] In some cases he deliberately broke off communication with students.

Anderson's partial withdrawal from student life and controversy was not simply a result of age and these unhappy experiences. In a revealing letter to Ruth during her illness, he admitted to certain serious failings of his own. He had been 'too familiar with students' in the past and now resolved 'in the interests of objectivity' to 'stand farther off' from the Freethought Society:

> Even now I don't wholly repudiate the desire to stimulate students, to let them see, in a way they wouldn't otherwise get, some of the things that education can be—but still my orations have been too easy (and somewhat exhibitionistic) and if, for disciplined minds, they did on the whole open up lines of inquiry, they haven't made the general body of student hearers *think* very much. Anyway—and perhaps especially with the sort of students we have now—they've led to a lot of wrangling and bad blood, and the least I can do is to cut down on this side of my activities, with the reflection that it would have been a lot better for the department if I'd done it sooner.[9]

He also confessed that, while 'under any circumstances I would be attracted to students who have the *student's* attitude to the subject and aren't taken up with asserting their personalities or teaching *me*', he had courted 'discipleship' and he 'didn't look hard enough for the "spark" among my colleagues' because they refused to become his 'followers'. 'However', he went on, 'the thing that came home to me in connection with all this . . . is the extent of undergraduate mentality in me—which leads me into that sort of milieu and is expressed in the "vulgarity" we were speaking of'.

A dream that Anderson had at this time expresses some of the inner difficulties and uncertainties of his position:

> I wandered into an empty Church and thought I'ld [*sic*] like to mount the pulpit and read a 'lesson' of some sort, but there were no Bibles around. I wondered if, instead, I'ld recite the epilogue to 'Asolando' ('One who never turned his back but marched breast-forward' etc.) or Henley's 'unconquerable soul', but knew I wasn't letter-perfect in either. So I went outside and met P. Foulkes who said he had something suitable at his rooms not far away; he dashed off and came back with a volume of *Principia Mathematica*. So my pulpit-reading didn't come off.[10]

Anderson claimed not to have dreams and rarely, if ever, committed them to paper. This dream is therefore a significant source for the inner man and raises a number of questions about Anderson in mid-life. Why was it situated in a church? Atheism mattered to Anderson—he was no mere insipid agnostic—and can one be an atheist without some hidden debts to traditional theism? Whether the pervasive influence of the kirk in Scotland or the unhappy experience of his rebel father can account for his deep and abiding atheism is not certain, but there can be little doubt that he bore the unacknowledged imprint of a residual Scottish Calvinism throughout his life. He often assumed the public stance of the prophet and preacher-*manqué*, but where was the missing congregation? And where were the Bibles? The questions reveal serious insecurities about his university audience, role and personal authority. When he considered alternative gospels to preach he turned, significantly, to the 'heroic' verse of Browning and Henley of his youth, imbued with defiant *machismo* and egoism:

> Out of the night that covers me,
> Black as the Pit from pole to pole,
> I thank whatever gods may be
> For my unconquerable soul.
>
> In the fell clutch of circumstance,
> I have not winced nor cried aloud:
> Under the bludgeonings of chance
> My head is bloody, but unbowed.
>
> It matters not how strait the gate,
> How charged with punishment the scroll,
> I am the master of my fate:
> I am the captain of my soul.

Diffidence about knowing the lines word-perfect seems to betray some inner lack of confidence and reveal the excessive demands he placed upon himself. Help appeared to come from one of his student-acolytes, but it was really an insult. The last thing Anderson wanted was Russell's mathematical logic, against which he was fighting a somewhat quixotic battle. Hence the dream as a whole probably reflects Anderson's growing alienation from his students and staff, and his negative and critical stance as a philosopher. In this despairing and nihilist phase, had Anderson become the god of his own world and sect? If so, he was a god far more in the Calvinist mould than any other, an instrument of wrath and vengeance, scourging the conventional and complacent, shocking the bourgeoisie, admonishing and correcting his disciples, prophesying cultural doom.

Soon Anderson found other occasions to display his 'irresponsibility' and 'lack of objectivity' and again they involved his son. Sandy's bid for freedom and independence had been deflected by Ruth's sudden collapse and breakdown. In an effort to placate him, John and Jenny granted him some privileges at home and, seemingly appeased and reconciled to them, he continued his honours work in philosophy, specialising in logic for his dissertation. In the annual examinations he tied for first place with Alan Blum, an Austrian Jew who had arrived with his mother in Sydney just before the war. The two students gained first-class honours, but no medal was awarded in philosophy that year. In 1950 Sandy completed a dissertation on Herman Melville for the English Department and graduated with combined honours in Philosophy and English. When, early in 1951, his father recommended his appointment to a teaching fellowship in the Philosophy Department, the Vice-Chancellor demurred and set up a committee to consider the appointment. The committee decided that the position should be advertised, which was not the usual procedure for a teaching fellowship. Among the five candidates to apply were Sandy, Blum and David Stove, a first-class honours graduate in moral and political philosophy. The committee considered their merits and urged that Blum be appointed. The irascible Anderson appealed to the Senate against the decision, regarding the committee's recommendation as an encroachment on the professor's freehold. To the extent that he could ignore the committee and appoint Stove, though not his son, his appeal was successful. Some years later Blum committed suicide. Of course, there was no connection between these events except perhaps the observation made by Virginia Woolf 'that the public and the private worlds are inseparably connected; that the tyrannies and servilities of the one are the tyrannies and servilities of the other'.[11]

Behind 'the antics of some of our more nauseating young Sydneyers', Anderson saw a wholesale 'retrogression in contemporary philosophy':

> I suppose I have to class Peter among the malcontents; and I suppose, too, that his inability to understand that philosophy is just *anti*-eclecticism (and 'bitsa' views are anti-philosophical) is connected not merely with the environment he has been in but with his having a not quite philosophic mind—in fact, that he was badly infected with the disease of his century (the inability to take *large* views) before he ever saw Oxford. To-night at the Seminar David Stove gave us another exhibition of eclecticism . . . These people seem just to look at a problem by itself and put forward some bright idea that comes into their heads—and *then* that is their philosophy.[12]

Only Ruth remained his 'clue to quality' because she possessed a sense of wholeness and took the 'larger view'. 'This reminds me that I was thinking . . . that what distinguishes you from the rest of my (closer or more distant) crowd', he wrote to Ruth during 1952, 'is your *non-atomistic* mind. This may occasionally prompt charges of vagueness, but it's good to avoid the hammering on a single formula, the separation of the "issue" from all other issues, that these people go in for . . . And, in these times, it's certainly atomism that's the enemy'.[13]

Anderson's wide background in European philosophy enabled him to mount a radical challenge to Russell. In this endeavour, he was helped by his study of the Greeks and his assimilation of the main lessons of Kant and German critical philosophy. 'With minor modifications', he said, 'Russell falls into the English tradition of Berkeley, Hume and Mill, in not seeming to realise the force of the German critics of English empiricists'. Anderson contrasted his propositional theory of reality, that 'we are confronted with propositions and never with anything less than a proposition', with Russell's view of isolated logical atoms:

> . . . failing any such theory of initial complexity of experience Russell tries to build up experience as we have it from just simple entities and has to maintain that these entities are objects of experience and that a good deal of complexity involved in later belief is mere speculation or guesswork.[14]

For Anderson, a sound empiricism asserted universality and causality, and these categories were objective features of the world, and facts like any other. Moreover, Russell's atomism went along with individualism in society, and a representationist sense-datum theory of knowledge, both of which Anderson trenchantly condemned. The former failed to take society seriously and the latter contradicted the Greek directness of things. For Russell and Wittgenstein, the proposition expressed a fact; for Anderson 'the true proposition is the same as the fact'. Finally, Anderson resisted and repudiated Russell's mathematical logic on the grounds that a revised traditional logic could deal with all the new or 'modern' problems. Much of his later life was spent in a valiant (some would say foolhardy) attempt to rehabilitate traditional logic for these tasks.

Over the next decade Anderson was to spend much of his time and energy attacking the errors and shortcomings of Oxford linguistic philosophy, with its 'running together of questions of logic and questions of language, to the detriment of both'. His growing opposition to the eclecticism, instrumentalism and atomism of modern philosophy led him to rediscover the importance of history, classicism and Hegel: 'But now, when the question is of *reviving* philosophy, a different line is needed . . . If revival is to come, it will be from history of philosophy, as part of "history of ideas", from the alliance of philosophy with historical disciplines, and this is my job'.[15] History and classicism would counter the subjectivist, narrow and present-minded concerns of recent philosophy, while Hegel stood above all for the 'inter-relatedness of the different parts of culture'. These ideas would appear as major themes in his writings and lectures on education and classicism.

14

Education and Inquiry

DURING THE 1940s and 1950s Anderson doggedly fought a rear-guard action against utilitarian and pragmatic theories of education in the university and society. Such theories provided the staple of educational reformers like Medley and Ashby and received explicit formulation in the recommendations of the Murray committee in 1957. While deferring to the liberal and generalist ideal of the 'education of the whole man', the committee placed its main emphasis on the development of research, applied science and vocational courses to serve the needs of a varied and complex society:

> The great social sciences, industry, and the development of the resources of the land all require university graduates in very large numbers indeed. The problem is going to be to find enough of them and to educate them worthily to take advantage of the great possibilities of wealth and happiness which lie before the nation. It has frequently been said in recent years that what makes the strength of a nation to-day is its professional and scientific man-power.[1]

Only lip service was paid to the view of the university as the guardian of academic standards 'and of intellectual integrity in the community'. Anderson's implacable opposition to such 'practicalist' tendencies must be seen in the light of his growing fear of the centralised state and bureaucracy—a very different attitude to Matthew Arnold's faith in *étatisme*—and his sense of living through a period of cultural decline and degeneration, a relapse into 'a new barbarism'. By contrast with the 'democratic' educational views he had espoused in the 1920s and 1930s he had become a conservative élitist and some thought even a reactionary.

Fundamentally, however, Anderson's views had changed little. Like G. E. Moore, he was an objectivist in ethics, believing goodness to be an observable characteristic of certain activities. He removed these good activities from any idea of being commanded or required because a prescriptive ethics would have entailed relativism and subjectivism. Good is not good because God arbitrarily commands it, but simply because it is good. Anderson's own goods—inquiry, love, freedom, enterprise and courage—were intrinsic qualities that co-operated and flourished in certain traditions. The tradition which he zealously sought to foster was that of criticism and free inquiry, and the institution with which these goods were most closely associated was the university. A central feature of Anderson's position in ethics, education and political philosophy was the rejection of any common measure or touchstone of the good, any way of characterising the good which reduced it to some common stuff that could be quantified. Hence he was especially opposed to utilitarian theories based on 'the common good' or 'the greatest happiness of the greatest number'. Above all, Anderson wished to emphasise qualitative differences between various social activities and the traditions of which they were a part. Just as there could not be different degrees or levels of reality, so there could be no commensurability between conflicting traditions. It would be futile to try and reduce them to a common measure or market because 'there are definite social forces, which are not measurable as amounts of a common stuff but which differ qualitatively, and which fight out the social issues'.[2] For Anderson the elusive pursuit of quantitative increase—'spreading wide and thin' as he expressed it—would lead to the dilution of the good activities rather than their increase and development.

For his attack on utilitarian and pragmatic views of education, Anderson drew heavily on the Scottish tradition of generalist, inter-disciplinary studies. His incisive criticism of Herbert Spencer's utilitarian theory of education followed from his realism, ethics and aesthetics. 'Utility insists on conditions and consequences; its sharp distinction of means and ends is bound up with hierarchy, with the master-servant relationship', Anderson had written sixteen years before.[3] His criticisms of utilitarianism remained the same. As a theory, it was individualist, reductionist and only concerned with quantity; it promoted vocationalism and a spurious harmony of social interests or the 'common happiness'; and it was 'instrumentalist' and preoccupied with the local, the trivial and the contemporary. Utilitarianism discounted general ideas, distinction and culture in favour of the bread and butter issues of survival and 'living'. In taking a narrow and unreflective physical science as its model of knowledge, it ignored literature, criticism and judgement; and in promoting vocationalism and a present-minded 'relevance', it displaced the classics and the 'classical outlook'. 'Preparation for grappling with what is contemporary does not necessarily involve concentration on the *study* of what is contemporary', Anderson wrote, for 'the setting aside of tradition, of "the best that has been thought and said" on major human problems, may well be the way to miss their solution'.[4] Like Arnold, Anderson exposed the essentially philistine and commercial nature of these assaults on the university and the intellectual life. Like Arnold, too, he defended the classics as expressions of what was universal and permanent in human culture as opposed to the local and contemporary:

> The classics of philosophy, as of any other cultural subject, are those works which so fully expound and illustrate objective principles or expose subjective illusions that they have critical application in any age and do not depend on passing fashions. And this can be said particularly of the Greek classics, without which it would be impossible to see the foundation of the main departments of Western thought.[5]

But this was no mere restatement of Arnold's classicist and liberal position. Anderson stressed, as he always had done, the closest relationship between science, literature and philosophy. 'Science, if truly scientific, is literary', for its hypotheses were tentative and its conceptions were in need of critical scrutiny, while 'literature, if truly literary, is philosophical'.[6] For two decades at Sydney, Anderson contributed significantly to the development of a distinct school of literary criticism. His addresses to the Literary Society and the classes he gave for English honours students provided a vehicle to develop his aesthetics in relation to the study of literature, music and the plastic arts. In particular, his attack on 'moralism' and his distinction between the work of art and its context paved the way for a 'realist' consideration of structure, coherence and the development of a theme. Anderson also elevated the 'comic spirit' as the highest form of art because it was more objective and freer from illusions than tragedy and the epic. Above all, he raised the fundamental question of what is education. The classical answer involved intrinsic criteria, 'of considering education in its own character' and not as a means to some other end.

For Anderson, education was distinct from mere training and distinct from 'social organisation'; essentially, it was an intellectual activity that produced the qualities of disinterestedness and objectivity: 'This interest in things themselves, and how they work, I take to be characteristic of the educated man, the man who is not shackled by the assumptions current in his society or group'.[7] Anderson agreed with Orage:

> . . . all these exercises in culture are elementary, however, in comparison with the master-problem of 'disinterestedness'. No word in the English language is more difficult to define or better worth attempting to define . . . I venture to say that whoever has understood the meaning of 'disinterestedness' is not far off understanding the goal of human culture.[8]

Defining education as a 'training in judgement', Anderson placed the study of logic and criticism at the heart of this training. Logic involved 'the theory of the conditions of existence or of the characters of things as real', and a general apparatus of criticism provided 'an understanding of the main types of human confusion and illusion or of the kinds and conditions of human error, of the tendencies in human nature that lead to a neglect or distortion of logic'.[9] Socrates remained Anderson's beau ideal of an educator, even if he lacked the 'thorough-going objectivism'* of Heraclitus.[10] But to be complete, judgement required a study of culture or what was permanent in human affairs, 'the best that has been thought and said in the world', and also a knowledge of history or what was timely, 'of what are the issues of the moment'. Anderson's view of education as the development of 'a power of association or a sense of connection, that is, of the structure or build-up of things' was aesthetic and architectonic.[11] It involved a sequential study of logic, psychology, culture and history, and it entailed a repudiation of 'the whole ideology of utility and social service'. But was it democratic?

If in his brave days he had believed in the widest possible diffusion of culture throughout society, he now feared a wholesale degeneration as the masses succumbed to 'mediocrity' and the consumer ethic. 'In practice egalitarian policies have had the effect of weakening learning and criticism', he claimed.[12]

> So, either we have an education which is universal in the sense of developing standards of judgement but is not universal in the sense of being for everyone, or else we have a general education in which standards are lost, in which what are set up as standards are dictated by practical and local considerations.[13]

He agreed with Arnold that 'the mass of mankind will never have any ardent zeal for seeing things as they are; very inadequate ideas will always satisfy them', and he placed his fragile hope in a small élite, a righteous remnant, 'in whom the academic spirit survives'. The prospect was far from encouraging. Even science had become separatist, fragmented and rationalist, and these failings had infected modern philosophy itself:

> The decline of realism as a philosophical movement is not surprising in view of the growth of this substitution of quantity for quality, of 'illusions of progress' for the consideration

* Heraclitus 'was unremitting in his attack on subjectivist illusions, on the operation of desire or the imagining of things as we should like them to be, as opposed to the operation of understanding or the finding of things (including our own activities) as they positively are, with no granting of a privileged position in reality to gods, men or molecules, with conflict everywhere and nothing above the battle'.

> of what is permanent in human affairs, of the 'fresh start' for absorption in a tradition. The merely current, however, is as intellectually weak as it was in the days of the Sophists and can be as devastatingly exposed by objectivist criticism.[14]

Good judgement required authority, 'as having a certain weight as compared with the judgements of the first-comer, of someone entering the field for the first time', and Anderson advanced his notion of independent 'colleges' or 'schools' as 'the bearers of cultural traditions' within the university.[15] A continuous tradition of active study and positive standards was vital to inquiry. The good of 'inquiry' ceaselessly struggled with other extrinsic 'ends' and evils in the educational arena, and, depending on the outcome, certain societies were more cultured and civilised than others. But regression was always possible:

> We have to take a pluralist view of the university as well as of society in general and to see that, within any so-called academic institution, there are non-academic and anti-academic activities—that what is academic (for it is a question of movements and traditions, and not of 'individuals') has to fight for survival against pseudo-academic 'philistinism' as well as against the incult social mass, that the struggle of culture against 'bourgeois society' exists also on the campus.[16]

Thus in the debate about the future of university education in the 1950s Anderson stood for a conservative defence of academic standards and 'the major departments of human culture' against the 'external view' of the function of universities. He also fought to preserve the university from state interference and control, which he feared would come with increased government expenditure:

> The present is, of course, a period of the extension of State powers and is accordingly favourable to the conception of the 'running' of things from the centre; and, in particular, the invasion by the State of the *educational* field favours the development of schemes of educational organisation and reorganisation. But it makes all the difference to educational discussion if we recognise that it *is* an invasion, that the State

> does not create or own the interest in learning, that learning has its own history and traditions, and that in face of the State . . . it will operate to some extent as an opposition.[17]

The maintenance of standards and academic autonomy were Anderson's two greatest contributions to the debate, and they informed the submission by the Sydney Association of University Teachers to the Murray Committee in 1957:

> A University is a richly varied community of scholars in which free enquiry is insisted upon, in which no consideration of the interests, prejudices or fears of individuals or groups is allowed to impede or deflect the following of truth wherever it may lead. The initiative in this central aim must always be with the academic community itself. The effectiveness, and not merely the integrity of the University, is endangered if outside interests, from professional, industrial or commercial groups to governments, seek to tell the University what it should do and how, and what its values should be.[18]

For all his oppositional stance and defence of culture, in some ways Anderson was backward-looking and lacked a vision for the future. He failed to address the urgent issue of specialisation and postgraduate research, and what this might mean for the fragmentation of knowledge in an overcrowded curriculum. Ian Clunies Ross, a former colleague and a member of the Murray Committee, was more attuned to the problem:

> . . . we cannot doubt that the broad purpose of university education has been obscured in the pursuit of a narrow specialism, or by an increasingly exacting, if more diffuse, professional training. Less and less is the student able, even were it required of him, to concern himself with ideas about the meaning and purpose of life, or his place in society; less and less is it possible to see beyond the dense thicket of subject matter which dulls the intellect and clouds the vision.[19]

Anderson continued to see the university as essentially a teaching institution, and while deploring the Murray Committee's pedagogic rhetoric of 'efficiency', 'casualty rates', and manpower 'wastage', he refused to face up to the serious problems of high failure rates, poor teaching and unfavourable staff–student ratios. Ironically, the former Marxist chose to ignore the salient economic fact that, whereas private endowments and student fees comprised over half the university's income in 1939, they only contributed 34 per cent in 1957.[20] Inevitably, the state and federal governments had to increase their grants if the greatly enlarged university was to function at all. Yet he refused to consider the implications of the state's new role as paymaster and ignored the issue of public accountability altogether. Nor did he have anything to say about the issues of access and equity, apart from attacking 'meliorism' and 'the whole sickly apparatus of welfare'. He remained an unrepentant élitist, even becoming a somewhat crusty defender of 'privilege' in his last years.

What remains of perennial value in Anderson's educational theory, however, is the idea of a core of closely related departments of knowledge, distinct yet interrelated, that are central to a liberal education. As the Professorial Board declared in 1957:

> The study of language and literature, of philosophy, of mathematics, of history and of the physical and biological sciences demands the understanding and the discovery of general principles as well as acquaintance with an array of particular facts. It is a compound of such broad generality and exact particulars with the demand for certain free-ranging and enlightened attitudes of mind that characterizes these studies; it is not their extent, their utility or the difficulty involved in developing a technical facility in them that distinguishes them.[21]

According to Anderson, the study of these fundamental disciplines—philosophy, classics, literature and history—should be sequential and closely related to the unfolding talents and capacities of the student. In that sense, the education he proposes is architectonic and owes much to the Scottish humanist tradition transmitted through John Burnet, 'whose wholeness of view provides a striking contrast to the piecemeal "philosophies" which are now in vogue'. It is also an intellectual and general education that is opposed to narrow specialisation: 'Indeed, the most insidious foe to classicism and the objective outlook is the specialism which cuts some departments of culture off from the rest'.[22] Insofar as education is not concerned with extrinsic ends but solely with subjects in their intrinsic character, it is an aesthetic education and opposed to utility and vocationalism. 'Accordingly, vocational, professional training can never be at the centre of a University's concern, or constitute its aims', Anderson's colleagues argued:

> *The centre of the University must be the basic disciplines in the sciences and the humanities.* These constitute the creative central part of a University's life. It is from research into these that the most spectacular and influential contributions to knowledge come . . . It is very important, therefore, when discussing the future development of Australian Universities, that this primacy should be well understood, and that any plans should be so framed as to ensure its maintenance. Investigation, discussion, exploration, rigorous thinking in the central disciplines come first, operations and professional application come second.[23]

Today when the university has become so fragmented, impersonal and divided that the notion of what is central or marginal to a congested curriculum is problematic and fiercely contested, it may be time to consider again Anderson's conception of a coherent liberal education: 'Classicism, in short, stands for the unity of culture against all forms of subjectivism and interestedness, and for the unity, the common principles, of criticism against specialism and *ad hoc* devices'.[24] What can be said for such a general interdisciplinary view and for the role of objective and disinterested inquiry? Is it an anachronistic theory?

The quest for knowledge for its own sake seems as important as ever it was, but the obstructions and evils to be opposed are not so much prejudice and superstition as Mammon and a crude instrumentalism. As Anderson often said, culture is not secondary to economics—it is not epiphenomenal, as Engels claimed, but goes on simultaneously with earning a living: 'It is not the case that the winning of subsistence is antecedent to cultural ideas and activities; it is, for the most part, bound up with them and is frequently postponed or subordinated to them (i.e., men risk their subsistence for the sake of their "ideas")'.[25] Such active and co-operative enterprise remains the hallmark of a cultured and enlightened society. And even if the content of that culture is in dispute, can there be any serious argument about the central place of logic and criticism in the whole intellectual enterprise? 'What this involves', Anderson has said, 'is that there is a single logic which applies to all the sciences, a single way of being which all their objects have; we cannot divide reality into higher and lower orders, for the difference and the relation between them would alike be indefinable and indemonstrable'.[26] As he describes the process:

> . . . we apply the methods of 'implication and explication' to our beliefs, and, when we are working out the theory of these methods, it is the methods themselves, as far as we have grasped them, that we apply. Thus we use logic whenever we argue, and we apply logical criteria in determining that, *certain data being given*, certain arguments are valid or invalid, certain propositions are true or false, and certain definitions and solutions are or are not possible. And though we may make mistakes about them, the criteria themselves are perfectly objective, being expressions of the common characters of things. Thus, without pretending to have a final solution of logical problems, we set up criteria which are as definite as we can make them, since this is necessary both for precise application and for the possibility of further development of our theory.[27]

Socrates counselled his followers to guard against the danger of becoming misologic: 'No greater misfortune could happen to anyone than that of developing a dislike for argument'.[28] The sleep of reason brings forth monsters.

15

A Philosopher in Winter

DURING THE LAST YEARS of his chair and in retirement, Anderson became passionately embroiled in the 'Orr case' and the surrounding controversy about academic freedom. Sydney Sparkes Orr, the Professor of Philosophy at the University of Tasmania from 1952, was summarily dismissed by the university Council on 16 March 1956 'on the alleged ground that he had seduced one of his female students'.[1] Many, including Anderson and Alan Stout, came to believe that the sexual charge was a pretext and that Orr was 'victimised' by personal enemies for his political opposition to the university authorities. In 1954 Orr had played a vital part in exposing the shortcomings of the Council and Vice-Chancellor, and in persuading the state government to hold a royal commission into the university. The recommendations of the commission largely vindicated Orr's criticisms and called for important changes in the administration of the university but the Vice-Chancellor and Council were in no hurry to implement them. Then in February 1956, the father of a student alleged before the Vice-Chancellor that Orr had seduced his daughter, and for this 'despicable' offence he was dismissed after the briefest inquiry in which he was denied legal counsel and transcripts of the proceedings.

Anderson was among the first to see that the central issue at stake in the controversy was academic freedom and autonomy rather than a sex scandal or 'the sordid story of the sexual behaviour, or misbehaviour, of a particular professor'. It was an issue that raised the fundamental question of the relationship between the academic and the university. To the legalistic view 'that the relation between the University and a professor comes within the general legal conception of that of a master and servant',* Anderson was implacably opposed: 'it is the condition of the possession of any academic character by universities that the teaching staff (more properly, the thinking staff) should not be subservient to any body which is without competence in the subjects to be taught or, for that matter, in methods of teaching and examining'.[2] Throughout his life, Anderson had held an exalted view of the academic's public role as Socratic critic of society and 'opinion', but this essential function could not be performed unless the university authorities respected academic tenure and the professor's freehold. Security of tenure was the *sine qua non* of academic freedom; and, for Anderson, the latter did not mean 'that academics have the same rights, the same standing "before the law", as any other citizens; it means that they have a special province, a field in which they can say: "*We* are the experts here; *we* can tell you (the Law, the State) what has force, what *runs*, in this department of social activity" '.[3] Philosopher kings indeed.

In addition to his forceful advocacy of academic freedom, there were other elements in the drama that attracted his keen interest and sympathy. The action of a solitary philosopher goading a powerful and conservative establishment epitomised the Socratic task—'it is the business of a professor to be a "trouble-maker" in the sense of one who continually raises critical questions'[4]—and was bound to evoke Anderson's own early struggles with the university Senate in Sydney. It was Orr's open letter to the state premier in October 1954, charging 'the Council of the University of Tasmania' with 'apathy, neglect and maladministration', that led to the royal commission.[5] Orr also sought to be a charismatic teacher and publicist, and, in the

* 'Orr attacked the conception of the University Staff as servants, and upheld the alternative conception of them as the arbiters on academic matters. Here is an indication of the pointedness of Orr's criticism (carried on since he went to Tasmania) which has been not only brushed aside by most of his Tasmanian colleagues but also given no effective recognition by those on the mainland who profess to be guardians of academic interests'. (J. Anderson, *The Observer*, 28 June 1958)

Socratic manner, saw philosophy as both criticism and intellectual liberation. 'From this point of view', Anderson wrote:

> Orr fulfilled the requirements of an academic position immensely better than the mass of Australian 'academics', who have shown themselves to be either philistines, ready to accept the tradesmen's role of training for the professions, or conventional ditherers, trying to make the best of both worlds, having faith in the joint service of learning and of 'public interests', in the combination of academic freedom with government by worldlings—and resenting Orr's breaking through the reconciliatory pretences.[6]

Like Anderson, too, Orr was deeply interested in psychology and psychoanalysis, and for a time he even underwent analysis by one of his staff, Dr Milanov, a refugee from Yugoslavia. It seems very likely that his interest in psychoanalysis as therapy and his views on free love entangled him in a romantic relationship with Suzanne Kemp, a troubled and unhappy student of eighteen years. The nature of that relationship was strenuously contested in successive court cases and sensationalised in newspaper reports over the years, and inevitably the testimony and evidence were coloured and distorted by the adversarial nature of the legal proceedings. Assuming, as Anderson surely did, that Orr's relationship with the girl involved some sexual element, did this belief further strengthen his commitment to Orr's cause? Did it coincide with his own theory of freedom in love and his long hidden affair with Ruth Walker?

The principal justification provided by the university for its disciplinary action was the 'especially despicable' nature of Orr's offence. 'The relation of a university teacher to his students is one of very special privilege', declared the Vice-Chancellor, 'and such debasement of it, whatever the temptation, automatically in my opinion renders him unfit for his office. The University has an obligation, both to itself and to the public, to insist upon the observance of unimpeachable standards in this respect'.[7] Throughout the long and bitter dispute with the Vice-Chancellor and Council to reopen the case and obtain restitution and compensation for Orr, Anderson treated the 'seduction' of Suzanne Kemp as a sensational red herring to distract attention from the real issues of academic autonomy and natural justice. In the fullest expression of his views, he wrote on 28 June 1958:

> Professor Orr's answer to the question whether a professor who seduced one of his students should be dismissed—'Yes, of course, he should'—seems to me, while it is understandable enough, to confuse the issues. Presumably the suggestion of 'seduced' would be that the action in question related to the conduct of the professor's department; and it will be remembered that . . . no evidence was offered that Professor Orr's work as a teacher had been affected by his relations to any student.
>
> But prior to the question of dismissal is the question of what process of investigation the University authorities could follow in dealing with the charge and what proof of 'guilt' they could get. I suggest that no proof is possible which would not involve other charges of flagrant misconduct and neglect of duty. More broadly, it can be said that . . . 'students are not children' and that the personal relations of either staff or students are not the University's concern. What ensures high University standards is enthusiasm for learning; and no one has ever been able to question Professor Orr's devotion to his subject and to his educational work—in the interests of which his 'agitation' in Tasmania was consistently maintained. Such propagation of views on academic well-being is a prime essential of academic freedom and integrity, and a mark of a non-servile status for University teachers.[8]

Anderson himself contributed generously to the cost of Orr's appeal to the High Court and helped organise a fighting fund for this purpose. Concerning the 'legalism' of the appeal procedures, he sternly criticised the 'limitations of law'—'its rough-and-ready character, its lack of scientific exactness'—and the limitations of 'legal functionaries, who have no specific field of knowledge, but follow custom in their adjustments of disputes'.[9] He strongly supported the 'black ban' by the Council of the Australasian Association of Philosophy on Orr's vacant chair, which was implemented in August 1958. Considerable efforts also went into his reading and editing the draft of

W. H. C. Eddy's book on the Orr case, which was published in 1961.

As the seasoned old warrior led the fight for 'natural justice' and academic standards in the Orr case, he was also engaged on a much wider front against 'retrograde' aspects of 'modern philosophy'. 'Language is not meaning any more than paint is art', he once wrote as an angry young man, and now as he approached retirement he deplored the preoccupations of Oxford philosophy with language issues and mathematical logic, and for its eclecticism and subordination to science. All of these failings amounted to 'the subjection of logic to non-logical considerations'. In a series of important articles written during the 1950s, Anderson provided a ringing defence and masterly summing up of his view of traditional logic and empiricism as central to the concerns of philosophy. His enemies were no longer the idealists (indeed, on general culture, liberal education, classicism and the history of philosophy he held much in common with them) but the linguistic philosophers of Oxford, heavily influenced by the logical atomism of Russell and the language analysis of Wittgenstein. His particular target was Gilbert Ryle, Wayneflete Professor of Metaphysical Philosophy at Oxford, who in a provocative essay published in *The Australasian Journal of Philosophy* in December 1950, challenged the 'deflationist' arguments, the ambitious claims, and the 'exiguous' logic of Anderson's realism:

> Anderson's logical alphabet is so exiguous that one wonders where he got his 'logic' from. Not from Aristotle, who investigates other inferences than syllogisms and has ten 'categories' where Anderson has two; not from the Stoic logicians who investigated the inferences that hinge on conjunctions; not from Boole, De Morgan, Frege or *Principia Mathematica.* One is at least forcibly reminded of Bradley, who, though he spells the world very differently, spells it out of the same penurious selection of letters. Indeed the connection is, perhaps, more than accidental. For if a philosopher allows himself only an artificially limited set of logical cupboards and pigeon-holes, then when he finds that a lot of his belongings will not readily fit into them, he is tempted

> to solve his storage-problem by high-handed devices. Either he *deems* his articles to be of the required sizes and shapes, or, if intellectual scruples forbid this, he *deems* his cupboards and pigeon-holes to contain just those secret shelves and interior compartments which will afford the required fit. Sometimes repugnance for the latter device is the motive for resorting to the former, and then we get an Anderson. Sometimes repugnance for the former device . . . is the motive for resorting to the latter, and then we get a Bradley.[10]

In retirement and his last years, Anderson summoned up all his waning energies to vindicate his view of realism and logic, and to refute the criticisms of Ryle. He accepted that his arguments against all 'ultimates' and 'levels of reality' were 'deflationist', though they were still valid for that. He maintained that mathematics and ethics were essentially empirical subjects like any other; and he strongly defended his central metaphysical position that the conditions of logical discourse were the 'conditions of existence':

> . . . the logician is concerned not with a miscellaneous bunch of types of question which can be raised about this subject or that, but with a group of types of question which have a *common ground*, which hang together in any inquiry and thus apply to any subject-matter . . . Apart from such a common ground, there would be no such thing as logic, no sort of connection between one inquiry and another, and thus no inquiry.[11]

As a corollary Anderson restated his belief in the interdependence and connectedness of all subjects, especially philosophy and science:

> But this means that, if the work of inquiry is to be carried on, it must be *at once* scientific and philosophic, that if, in particular, the scientist is not philosophic, he will fall into confusions, he will rebuff philosophic criticism—he will lack a theory of categories, of sorts of problem, of 'method'—especially he will be carried away by practical interests, by the interest in producing something or implementing a programme instead of in finding something out.[12]

In his 1959 address to the Australian Humanities Research Council on 'Classicism', Anderson attributed the decline of liberal and classical studies in the university to the 'surrender' to the sciences and a present-minded 'practicalism'. He maintained, as he had always done, that philosophy had only been objective and disinterested while it had remained classical and true to its Socratic origins; to continue this tradition it had been necessary to fight against 'an even more debilitating modernism (or "up-to-dateness") than that of the Sophists'. The 'degradation of the subject, logic, to the status of an instrument or set of devices' and the 'contempt for syllogism' characterised 'the practicalist or instrumentalist outlook'.[13] Anderson's articles on 'Hypotheticals' (1952) and 'Relational Arguments' were vigorously argued attempts to refute Russell's logic and to rehabilitate the syllogism and the four forms. 'These "categorical" forms, then, are *the only* logical forms', he concluded, 'the only forms in which we can assert that *something is so*; and thus the logical form of "hypotheticals" (and similarly with "modals", etc.) must be found among the four forms'.[14]

Anderson saw Ryle's attack as symptomatic of modern philosophy's 'retrogression' and 'subservience' to a narrow and unreflective science: 'And it is this narrow, specialising and instrumentalist attitude that has infected the most influential schools of philosophy at the moment, leading them largely to ignore the history of philosophy, the "classics" of the subject which could provide them with an outlook at once broader and more critical'.[15] If Anderson's view of philosophy 'as the organisation or co-ordinating principle of science' or 'as science in general'—and not a second-order inquiry in Russell's sense—seemed naive, confused and old-fashioned to his Oxford critics, it was a conception that accorded much better with the history of European philosophy, and with the Scots humanist tradition he was steeped in. In seeing philosophy and 'the criticism of the categories' and of the foundations of our various systems of knowledge and belief, Anderson was once more fighting the battle of Scottish philosophy in the antipodes against the narrow specialisation, conservatism and 'technical exercises' of English analytic philosophy. Did his Australian students, freshly returned from Oxford, realise the fundamental national and cultural issues at stake in this contest, or the fierce passions it aroused in Anderson? His visit to Oxford in 1938 had confirmed his 'impression of the backward state of philosophical thought' in England 'and also of the intellectual feebleness and general dulness of Oxford'.[16] George Davie, writing from within the Scottish tradition of philosophy, places Anderson's stand firmly in its cultural and intellectual context:

> An ancient and proud movement of intellect such as Scottish philosophy does not give up provinces and pull down flags. Accordingly, round about 1960 . . . defences of the threatened tradition were put forward in Sydney and in Belfast, which, quite independently of one another, invoked the name and doctrines of John Burnet. The Australian arguments formulated by John Anderson in the last two or three papers written by him before he died in 1962, made the point that the sense of wholeness which was Burnet's great quality and which inspired his critique of specialisation was being emptied of meaning by a modern and superficial attitude to logic which destroyed the unity of science by developing a doctrine of every branch of science having its own logic. The way to defend what was valuable in the Scottish philosophical tradition was, according to Anderson, to renew the problem of Scottish logic . . . [and] to inaugurate a revised Aristotelianism, which by restoring the lost sense of the unity of logic, would at one blow reinstate Burnet's views of the whole, and frustrate Russell's efforts at atomising analysis.[17]

So strong was Anderson's feeling for, and attachment to, his intellectual institutions and traditions that when he retired late in 1958 he began to lose much of his personal identity and *raison d'être*. His psychological and social theory had consistently underplayed the role of 'the anxious and interfering ego'; the personality, according to Anderson, was 'a complex of interrelated processes', and the ego was not free or rational but 'adjudicated' between rival mental forces or passions, being merely a force or passion in its own right. Whatever identity the individual possessed came through membership of social movements, for, as Anderson wrote, ' "freedom" may be taken not in the metaphysical sense of release from causation but as a power of devoting oneself to what transcends oneself (a social movement or "cause")'.[18] Did Anderson largely ignore the existential claims of the self and submit too easily to the conformist demands of his social, institutional 'persona' and the 'common work' of his department and university as the solace for depression and melancholia? This was not such a difficult thing to do while he was a professor and public figure, but retirement and physical ageing revealed some of the self-deception and vanity of the man, even to himself. Without an institutional self, an official routine, access to power and influence and an admiring flock to shepherd he became a Lear-like figure in his last years. He failed to make any progress on the major work of philosophical synthesis he had hoped and promised to write. There was not even an appreciative audience for his ritual iconoclasm and habitual anti-clericalism.

Anderson had always objected to being described as a simple atheist or 'god-basher' because it discounted the positive aspects of his philosophy. He was a thorough-going empiricist or realist who, like Laplace, had no need of that hypothesis. From his earliest days, Anderson had rejected 'all ideals, ultimates, symbols, agencies and the like'. In the unpublished logic book of 1922, he had written:

> . . . logic postulates the existence of only one order of discourse. It is definitely opposed to the view that there is a region of unprovable things, as contrasted with that of proof. If this were so, there would be no logic; subjectively because any person might claim that his assertion belonged to the region of faith; objectively, because all that is common to things which are admitted to be subject to proof is common to all assorted things whatever . . . The possibility of logic, then, depends on there being only one sort of existence; and its scientific aim is to consider the nature and characteristics of things as existing.[19]

There was no place in Anderson's logic for mystery. To religious believers of whatever persuasion, Anderson always posed the 'problem of commensurability'—how could there be connections between different orders of reality? 'The chief, and

I think final, objection to any theory of higher and lower, or complete and incomplete, truth is that it is contrary to the very nature and possibility of discourse; that it is "unspeakable" '.[20] His logic had rendered God ontologically redundant. 'There are only facts, i.e., occurrences in space and time', and clearly God was not one of them: 'If there were anything either above or below the proposition, it would be beyond speech or understanding'.[21] In the Heraclitean doctrine of flux and conflict as permanent features of the world, Anderson found a classical pedigree for his atheism or 'pluralism without ultimates'.

Yet there were strong elements of transcendence in Anderson's philosophy, most notably in his ethical and aesthetic theory and in his life-long commitment to the 'goods' of inquiry, freedom and love. Did his unrelenting insistence on traditional logic and absolute space-time betray a mind divided against itself and given to '*folie de doute*'? If there was no God, was everything permitted? The question of values has been one of the most fiercely contested in modern philosophy and to maintain, as Anderson did, that ethical statements were just as factual and objective as scientific ones was, to say the least, an unusual position for an empiricist and one that sharply divided him from Wittgenstein, Ayer, Ryle and Oxford philosophy. His dismissal of Einstein's theory of relativity as 'utterly illogical' never changed and made him appear an increasingly conservative and old-fashioned figure. The desperate efforts to maintain belief in the unity of truth, the good and beauty suggest a thwarted Romantic beneath the classical and realist exterior. Drawing on the secular humanist tradition of Feuerbach, Marx and Freud, Anderson pitted his productive 'goods' against the 'compulsive moralism' and enslavement to dogma of conventional religions. Free inquiry was of necessity opposed to all religious authority, and free heterosexual love was bound to conflict with bourgeois Christian morality. 'If there *were* a master of the universe, then' Anderson, like Joyce,

> . . . would fight against him; he will not endure servitude, he cannot accept sacrifice and atonement, he rebels against the low conception of life, the base morality, which they imply. And this means that he is considering them in human terms (these being the only terms in which they are intel-

> ligible), that he recognises the arbitrariness of 'analogical reasoning', of the mystery-mongering which makes such things partly human and partly non-human. 'With me all or not at all'.[22]

Unlike other modern atheists, however, Anderson was not greatly troubled by the problem of suffering, and he repudiated most of the Christian virtues as fundamentally servile. At a party at Canberra in the 1950s he delighted an audience of academics by singing one of Joyce's parodies of the Christian religion:

> If anyone thinks that I amn't divine
> He'll get no free drinks when I'm making the wine
> But have to drink water and wish it were plain
> That I make when the wine becomes water again.
>
> Goodbye, now, goodbye! Write down all I said
> And tell Tom, Dick and Harry I rose from the dead.
> What's bred in the bone cannot fail me to fly
> And Olivet's breezy—Goodbye, now, goodbye!

Then, waving his right hand to heaven, he sang two more verses of his own composition:

> I get what I want without spinning or toil
> To all foolish virgins I give the good oil
> To the rich man who hopes he will go up on high
> I tell him it's all in a cam-u-el's eye.
>
> My methods are new and are causing surprise
> To make the blind see I throw dust in their eyes
> To make the lame walk I say get out of bed
> And there's no one to beat me at raising the dead.

However, one of the audience, Manning Clark, was less than enthralled by the performance:

> Towards midnight, after many tongue-looseners, and conscience-quieteners, John Anderson put on a turn. Don Baker . . . shook Anderson by the shoulders and told him he, Anderson, was the greatest academic in Australia. Anderson liked that. He offered to sing a song about the ascension of Christ—I do not remember any words now

> except the last line sung with Anderson waving his right hand towards the ceiling, 'Goodbye, goodbye'.
>
> I was dismayed by what had come up from inside John Anderson—I mean the old-hat blasphemy, and black humour about Christianity which belonged to the age of Bradlaugh, to the age of believers in progress, and not to the age of the atomic bomb. Why was his humour directed against such a target? I could understand any serious-minded man or woman rejecting the virgin birth, the claim to be God's only son, the resurrection, the post-resurrection appearances . . . and the ascension. What bothered me was that Anderson had neither reverence nor love for the man who had spoken the memorable words about love, belief, forgiveness and compassion. The previous day I had heard Anderson dismiss these words as trivial and superficial.[23]

For Anderson, Christ was not the supreme moral teacher or embodiment of humanity and although he admired the Christian 'rejection of revenge' he saw little evidence of its practice among Christians or the so-called Christian nations. An ethic of renunciation and consolation stood low in his scale of moralities. There was much in Nietzsche's view of Christianity as a slave morality that he accepted, and pity for the weak was not one of his virtues. 'There was no atom of tender-mindedness in Anderson's thinking', recollected David Armstrong, instead there was an 'utter absence of consolation and uplift'.[24] The realist philosopher was to be stoical, self-sufficient and strong. 'We must learn to bear our burdens', was one of his favourite sayings about psychoanalysis and suffering. 'Hell, the self-alienation of the spirit, occurs here and now; it is something that has to be fought through, not something that we can avoid by propitiating human or "cosmic" powers, not something that we can be protected from', he wrote.[25]

As Anderson lost his early faith in the 'proletariat', he turned with increasing intensity to the idea of an intellectual élite who would display in their work and lives the 'heroic values' of enterprise, initiative and disinterested inquiry. But it was a distinctly Nietzschean vision of the individual freethinker savagely at odds and in conflict with society. 'It will still be a main part of the work of those in whom the academic spirit survives', he wrote, 'to "scourge the errors of the age", to act as *critics* of modern society, to attack modernist ideology in the form of "the fresh start" . . . as against simple adherence to the cause of learning, to the continuity of culture'.[26]

When a prominent Roman Catholic layman and an English archbishop alleged a close association between Anderson's empiricism and 'moral corruption and political subversion' on the campus, the 68-year-old Anderson was stung into leading the forces of freethought and enlightenment in the last fierce battle of his career. Dr Gough, the Englishman who was Archbishop of Sydney and Primate of Australia, launched his attack on 6 July 1961 in a sermon at St Andrew's Cathedral. He was preaching to four hundred legal men and their wives at a service to open the Australian Law Council Convention. Much of the sermon was devoted to an attack on Communism but he included some remarks about the teaching of philosophy and its subversive effects on youth. 'Throughout the West—and in Sydney—men were shamelessly teaching in universities soul-destroying philosophies which could lead to Communism. I am not saying that they are Communists. But they are teaching ideas which are breaking down the restraints of conscience, decrying the institution of marriage, urging our students to pre-marital sexual experience and advocating free love and the right to self-expression'.[27]

Anderson's colleagues Stout and O'Neil, were quick to deny the charge and when the Vice-Chancellor, Professor S. H. Roberts, challenged the Archbishop to produce evidence 'to substantiate his charges', Gough cited a pamphlet 'Empiricism and Freedom', written in 1959 by Dr V. J. Kinsella, a Macquarie Street surgeon and Catholic layman. He also hinted darkly about confidential information soon to be submitted to the state government's Youth Policy Advisory Committee. Immediately, Anderson derided the cleric's charges and Kinsella's 'flimsy' pamphlet as 'rubbish'. 'Neither the Archbishop nor Dr. Kinsella has the right or intellectual background to criticise philosophy professors', he said: 'In my thirty-two years at Sydney University, I never heard a philosophy teacher advocate free love or pre-marital experience in the lecture-room. What he expresses in private is his own business, and not the Archbishop's or Dr. Kinsella's'.[28]

Although not in good health and suffering from the effects of a premonitory stroke, Anderson agreed to address a meeting of students at his old university on 14 July 1961 on the subject 'Academic Autonomy and Religion'. When he arrived, all available space in the lecture theatre was taken, the students sitting on steps, the floor and tops of desks. 'It is not for the university to amend its views and knuckle down to public opinion, even if it is church opinion', he declared to an audience of several hundred cheering stamping students. To their delight, he attributed the decline in morals at the university to 'the development of many student religious societies. Religious superstition should be deplored as much as loose living'. To counter such religious influences, 'the university should take the line that it is the supreme authority on education in this state. It is for the university to make its own case to the public in this matter, and not to submit to this outside judgement'.[29] As always, attack was the best means of defence.

Within the week Anderson spoke to another large meeting of students at the University of New South Wales to champion the cause of secular education and free inquiry against the clerical interest. 'The clerics are jealous', he said, 'they are antagonistic towards university workers and try to damage them. But they overrated themselves this time. Communism has stimulated men's minds far more than Christianity. Christianity is a conventionalism'.[30] In yet a further public address at Newcastle University College on 4 August he expounded his view of religion as a 'childish' and 'theatrical' escape from reality—Christianity did not make for freedom 'but for servility'. Sandy, who was now a philosopher at Newcastle, vigorously defended his father:

> The academic is concerned solely with inquiry—with established facts—and so must not bind himself by way of dogma. He forfeits his academicism if he takes anything to be superior to facts or believes there are assertions which he is not allowed to discredit. Again, he cannot accept as an 'explanation' of any fact an unobservable power (Divine

> or otherwise), for such a mystical position would end his inquiry and could lead only to scepticism. A fact can be explained only as following logically from other facts on the same level of observability: without this, there could be no theory.[31]

The issue of organised religion took up much of Anderson's time and energy in the last months of his life as he protested against its evil and corrupting influence on the university. For Anderson, there was a natural and necessary antipathy between the dogmatism, servility and meliorism of religion and the free life of inquiry and criticism at the university. In his last essay, published in November 1961 in *The Australian Highway*, he prophesied:

> But there seems little doubt that further encroachment of clericalism on the University will occasion the steepest drop in standards of academic work, that increased attention to religion will be seriously damaging to the study of ethics and increased attention to theology equally so to the study of logic and general philosophy, and that these are particularly *pressing* dangers now to what is left of the academic outlook.[32]

Despite these gloomy forebodings, Anderson had vanquished the prelates and the philistines and thereafter Dr Gough was a far less credible public figure. Moreover, there were still moments of great pleasure for the old warrior to savour. There was time to recall his socialist days in Scotland, when proudly he accompanied his father on a Sunday afternoon to Garrion Brig to expound the pure doctrine to the holiday crowd, or studying with his brother Willie in the university settlement in the Glasgow slums, his wooing of Jenny in the long summer twilight at Larkhall, and winning all the university prizes to the dismay of Professor Jones and the Christian idealists. Worthy, self-regarding Edinburgh was a dreary interlude between Glasgow and vibrant Sydney, but fortunately and unexpectedly the offer of the Challis chair came when he was in his youthful prime. There followed fierce struggles with the local idealists and entrenched conservatives like Todd and MacCallum, as alone he established his philosophical sway over Sydney. And savage battles with the Communist Party executive and the university Senate. Such academic and political in-fighting left their scars, but now that the wounds were healed it was pleasant to dwell on the unrelenting clash of ideas and convictions, the victories and self-aggrandisement, and the defeats and humiliations of his enemies. Through it all he had fathered a generation of distinguished Australian philosophers—they now spoke of 'Australian Realism' as if he had tutored a continent—and he fondly recalled his brightest students; in the 1930s Gaius MacIntosh, John Passmore and his wife Doris, Perce Partridge, Margaret and John Mackie, and in the 1940s Sandy, David Armstrong, Jim Baker and Eugene Kamenka. There were also many attractive and intelligent women to inspire and celebrate him. Above all, there had been Ruth, the impressionable 'rare *puella*', who had devoted her life to him and his philosophy. In spite of all her trials and suffering, she remained staunchly loyal. But he also valued the life-long companionship of Jenny and he told her that he had never loved her more than in these last years. He enjoyed chatting to the controversial Dobell while sitting for his portrait in the artist's Kings Cross studio. The approaching publication of his collected philosophical writings in one volume, *Studies in Empirical Philosophy*, edited by John Passmore, reassured him that the critical and realist philosophy he had practised and professed for a lifetime would be more widely diffused. Brennan's final lines from *The Wanderer* about the chill 'iron wind' are a fitting comment on Anderson in retirement:

> yet in that wind a clamour of trumpets rang,
> old trumpets, resolute, stark, undauntable,
> singing to battle against the eternal foe,
> the wronger of this world, and all his powers
> in some last fight, foredoom'd disastrous,
> upon the final ridges of the world:
> a war-worn note, stern fire in the stricken eve,
> and fire thro' all my ancient heart, that sprang
> towards that last hope of a glory won in defeat,
> whence, knowing not sure if such high grace befall
> at the end, yet I draw courage to front the way.

But John Anderson did not go gently into his dark night. When irascibility and anger threatened, he went outside the house and began to chop wood, a habit he acquired in the bitter years after the war. After a furious bout of wood-chopping one afternoon early in July 1962, he said to his wife, 'Oh Jenny I think I've overdone it'. He went inside to rest, Jenny worked in the garden until she was disturbed by strange inarticulate noises. She found him stretched out on the bed, almost unconscious except for the weird moanings. An ambulance took him to the Royal North Shore Hospital, where he remained in a coma for a few more days until he died on 6 July 1962. Jenny wept, but soon composed herself for the funeral. At first, she asked Stuart Watts, an ordained Anglican minister but latterly a convert to Andersonian realism, to conduct the service, but when Mrs Stout congratulated her on her good sense in choosing a non-practising clergyman, Jenny took umbrage at this interpretation. Instead, she invited Professor Bill O'Neil to deliver the valedictory address and tribute, which he agreed to do. Many friends and admirers attended the simple secular service at the Chatswood Crematorium. What Bill O'Neil chose to recollect and celebrate of Anderson's achievements on that occasion is not known, but later he delivered a handsome tribute before the Faculty of Arts. It is worth quoting in full:

> John Anderson was Challis Professor of Philosophy and a member of this Faculty for 32 years, from 1927 till his retirement at the end of 1958. He was beyond doubt the most distinguished and independent philosopher as well as one of the most remarkable men to work in an Australian university. He had early developed a systematic metaphysical (or, as he called it, logical) position, uncompromisingly empiricist and realist, having fruitful application to all branches of philosophy, including social theory. Central to this position is the view that there are no different levels of existence nor, consequently, degrees of truth. There is one way of being only, the way in which ordinary things exist in space and time. All talk of a spiritual, as distinguished from a mundane reality is therefore rejected. Ethics is the study of the way in which goods and evils in fact work in human

life; there is no possibility of a scientific study of what ought to be done.

Professor Anderson never accepted or even came to terms with the most recent developments in philosophy, such as linguisticism. He regarded these contemporary trends as piecemeal and superficial, and a betrayal of the traditional responsibilities of philosophy.

Professor Anderson's main activities outside the purely academic sphere—including his life-long fight for freedom of speech, his opposition to religion and his rearguard defence of the independence of academic work in all its phases against non-academic interference, particularly against its subjection to practical ends—were not separate from his philosophy, but followed logically from it. It is for these activities that he was best known (and widely misunderstood) in Australia.

Professor Anderson's work is not as well known overseas as it deserves to be. This is partly because almost all of it has appeared in the *Australasian Journal of Philosophy* (which he edited for twelve years and to which he was most loyal). Its circulation does not yet match those of the leading British and American philosophical journals. It is also because he never got round to writing a systematic account of his philosophy, and even in his articles he tends to argue *from* his position rather than *to* it, often developing his argument by trenchant criticism of opposing views . . . Even so, his eminence as a philosopher has not gone without overseas recognition. Shortly after his retirement the Court of Glasgow University, his *alma mater*, offered him an honorary degree. But such a degree cannot be conferred *in absentia*, and Anderson was unwilling to make the journey to Britain to receive it.

Professor Anderson believed in the Scottish tradition of formal lecturing as *par excellence* the best way of teaching philosophy. In his lectures, much of which he dictated, he presented a closely argued and coherent position and left it to his students, without further help, to wrestle with it. This sounds, on the face of it, an unpromising method, but its results and the testimony of successive generations of students show that it worked well. They speak of him as an inspiring teacher. It is, however, a method which would not work with such conspicuous success if employed by someone with a less comprehensive and penetrating doctrine, or with a less forceful personality to put behind it.

He had a remarkable memory for the names, faces, characters and abilities of his students past and present. His conscientiousness in academic matters set an example beyond the reach of his colleagues, and showed itself particularly in the painstaking care with which, as an examiner, he would consider and reconsider dividing lines and borderline cases.

He never accepted either the Deanship of the Faculty or the Chairmanship of the Professorial Board, no doubt believing that he could make a better contribution to the work of these bodies as an ordinary member. But he had a knowledge of the by-laws probably excelling that of any Dean we have had—a wide and detailed knowledge which he could bring to bear on the issue in hand. He had also an uncanny memory of what the Faculty had done last time, even when the last time was a number of years before.

But without doubt Anderson's main contribution as a member of the Faculty was his persistent and untiring defence of academic standards in the face of growing pressures to lower them. A notable example of this was his fight to the last ditch against the abandonment of a foreign language as a matriculation requirement.

In the part he played in meetings of the Faculty and its Committees, he was throughout actuated by his conviction that true education is 'liberal education', interpreted as a study of the *classics* of those cultural subjects which are this Faculty's chief concern. The 'classics' of any cultural subject, he said in his address on Classicism to the Humanities Research Council 'are those works which so fully expound and illustrate objective principles or expose subjective illusions that they have critical application in any age, and do not depend on passing fashions'.

He did what he could to warn us against these passing fashions.[33]

John Mackie, a former student and colleague of Anderson's who held the chair of Philosophy at the University of Otago in New Zealand, was appointed Anderson's successor to the Challis chair in 1959. Too independent to be a close disciple,

Mackie still believed that Anderson had done 'more for intellectual freedom, by his constant practice and defence of it, than any other one man in Australia'. But he also perceived the unfinished, incomplete nature of Anderson's philosophical achievement and 'the radical difficulties in the core of his system'. Mackie shrewdly observed that, for the most part, Anderson assumed his own position rather than argue towards it, and castigated his enemies rather than vindicate 'his most characteristic and most controversial views'.[34] Mackie attributed these failures to Anderson's impatience and his refusal to take contemporary philosophy seriously.

In 1964 another gifted ex-student of Anderson's took the Sydney chair when Mackie left for a chair at York in the United Kingdom. Such was the aura of Anderson that when David Armstrong first occupied the professor's large study, he half-expected the old man to enter and sternly ask him what he was doing there. Armstrong, who was to hold the chair until his retirement in 1991, appreciated 'how quintessentially Scottish' was the philosophic education he had received from Anderson, 'right down to the somewhat abstract, *a priori*, impression that it made':

> Anderson's thought, and the education he gave his students, was essentially generalist thought, and a generalist education. He was a philosopher of wide sweep, on the whole impatient of detail. He was concerned rather to take certain important principles—logical principles as he thought of them—through metaphysics, through epistemology, through ethics, social theory, aesthetics, and the theory of culture.[35]

From Sydney Anderson's influence now extended to Armidale, Newcastle, Kensington and Canberra. In the 1950s the Australian National University appointed three of Anderson's most distinguished students to senior positions in the Research School of Social Sciences. In 1951 P. H. Partridge became Professor of Social Philosophy, and from 1961 to 1968 served as Director of the Research School; in 1955 J. A. Passmore became a Reader in Philosophy, and Professor and head of the department in 1958; and in 1962 Eugene Kamenka joined the History of Ideas Unit to become its head in 1968. Kamenka's mature judgement was that 'Anderson was without question Australia's most original and creative philosopher. His public influence and student following were deeply rooted in the power of his philosophical mind . . . He exuded and attracted ability, sharpness of mind, penetration, theoretical force'.[36]

After Anderson's death Jenny continued to live at Turramurra and Ruth Walker to lecture at the university. When some years later Ruth approached her about establishing an Anderson Archive, she welcomed the idea and gave her every assistance with the project. Ruth occasionally visited the familiar old house with its sub-tropical garden in Nulla Nulla Street to work through Anderson's lectures and papers. As time passed there was a sort of reconciliation and understanding between the two women in their common task and devotion to the great philosopher. At one point Ruth declared her intention to destroy all her personal correspondence with Anderson. But Jenny was the better Andersonian and cautioned her against taking such drastic action. In the long run, only truth mattered. Jenny also helped to edit the book *Art and Reality*, published in 1982, which contained many of Anderson's unpublished writings on literature and aesthetics, the passion she had shared with him all her life. She kept up her interests in reading and current affairs and only left her home reluctantly when she was too old and frail to look after herself.

Sandy settled down at Newcastle, the gritty steel town north of Sydney, and for many years taught philosophy at the university. One of Anderson's students and a close disciple, Alec Ritchie, held the chair there. Sandy became the keeper of the Andersonian flame and continued to work closely within his father's system of realism, developing strong interests in logic, ethics, the pre-Socratics and psychoanalysis. Philosophically, he was an all-rounder, like his father, and a teacher devoted to his subject and students. He could also be exuberant and outgoing at parties, where he was noted for his 'turns'. At weekends, he often visited his mother, and after retirement returned to care for the family home at Turramurra.

In 1972 Ruth Walker retired from her senior lectureship at the University of Sydney. For many years she had lived at Pennant Hills before moving to Lawson in the Blue Mountains to spend her retirement. She died alone in 1986. Jenny died one year later in a Wahroonga nursing home at the age of ninety-four. Both women ended their lives with few doubts about the greatness of the man they had tried so hard to serve and love. Yet some doubts linger.

It has been said of Anderson that in university affairs and intellectual matters he became obstructionist and negative as he aged: his whole life and mind had crystallised around a negative. 'If you wanted to lose a motion in faculty', one professor observed, 'you only had to get Anderson to support it'. Such was his unpopularity. But Anderson was not interested in high office, his own advancement or popularity. He never lost the courage of his convictions and expressed them with vehemence and relish, particularly when they were least popular or fashionable. Only truth and arguments mattered.

To the more serious charge that as a philosopher he failed to produce the necessary systematic account of his realist position that he had always promised, the answer must be that Anderson chose to expend his time and energy on what he regarded as more important matters—to wage unrelenting war on thc evils of ignorance, prejudice and servility that he detected in society and contemporary philosophy. His own discipline was in danger of degenerating into eclecticism, trivialities and linguistic games. To arrest this decline, Anderson brought to bear a powerful mind that thought in large broad outlines rather than in detail, a character immune from the lures of power, wealth and social status, and a spirit whose standards of value were formidable. A passion to oppose had inspired him since his boyhood at Stonehouse and student days at Glasgow, and at Sydney he applied his great force of intellect to the university and society around him. Nothing was sacred or exempt from criticism; not patriotism, religion, politics or sex. 'I am the gadfly that God has attached to this city', Anderson's hero, Socrates, declared to his detractors, 'and all day long and in all places I am always fastening upon you, arousing and persuading and reproaching you. You would not readily find another like me'. If philosophy lost, the wider society gained.

> If often he was wrong, and at times absurd,
> To us he is no more a person
> Now but a whole climate of opinion,
> Under whom we conduct our differing lives.

To the last, he had a certain Scottish intransigence and all the oppositional virtues—courage in adversity, endurance, a savage gypsy wit, intelligence in overcoming obstacles, and the sheer refusal to yield. They are not redundant, least of all in our troubled and beleaguered universities. *Gaudeamus igitur*. Let us therefore celebrate.

Appendix

Anderson and Andersonianism

SINCE ANDERSON'S philosophical position developed as he responded to the many changes and challenges of his life, it is not easy to sum up his realist position. For this purpose, David Armstrong suggests an illuminating fragment of Heraclitus, which A. J. Baker has also chosen for the frontspiece of his study of Anderson's systematic philosophy: 'this world, which is the same for all, no one of gods or men has made; but it was ever, is now, and ever shall be an ever-living fire, with measures kindling, and measures going out'. Elsewhere, John Mackie attempts a more extended definition of Anderson's realist position.

> His central doctrine is that there is only one way of being, that of ordinary things in space and time, and that every question is a simple issue of truth or falsity, that there are no different degrees or kinds of truth. His propositional view of reality implies that things are irreducibly complex, that there can be no question of arriving at simple elements in any field. He rejects systematically all notions of entities that are constituted by relations: there can be no 'ideas' whose nature it is to be known, no 'consciousness' whose nature it is to know, no 'values' whose nature it is to be ends or to direct action. Knowledge is a matter of observing directly what is (objectively) the case. Ethics is a study of the qualities of human activities: there can be no science of conduct, considered as a study of what ought to be done. Aesthetics can only be a study of the characteristics of

> beautiful things, not a matter of judgements or feelings. Anderson takes a pluralist view alike of mind and of society: there is no ultimate 'self', and no inclusive social purpose, but only complexes of competing forces, diverse but on the same level as one another.[1]

From his occupation of the Sydney chair in 1927 to his retirement in 1958, Anderson exercised a profound influence on generations of students. Many of them came to the university with good matriculation results from city and country state schools; few came from Sydney's private schools. In the 1930s he taught J. A. Passmore, P. H. Partridge and J. L. Mackie, who were to become distinguished and productive philosophers and teachers in their own right. Passmore taught philosophy at Sydney for more than a decade until he left to take a chair in the University of Otago, returning to Australia in 1955 to join the Australian National University, where he held the chair of Philosophy from 1959 to 1979. Similarly, Partridge went from a lectureship and chair at Sydney to the chair of Social Philosophy in the Research School of Social Sciences at the Australian National University, which he occupied from 1951 to 1975. John Mackie graduated from Sydney in 1938. He later studied at Oxford and, after serving in the British army, became a lecturer and senior lecturer in Stout's Moral and Political Philosophy Department at Sydney. In 1959 he succeeded Anderson to the Sydney chair after spending four years in New Zealand as professor of Philosophy at Otago. In 1963 he took up a chair in the University of York and from 1967 until his death in 1981 was a Fellow at University College, Oxford, where he did important work in ethics. What Passmore, Partridge and Mackie got from their old teacher, writes Anthony Quinton, was 'an Andersonian spirit which combines business-like force and economy in tackling problems with ambitious boldness in taking on large topics and in seeing them as hanging together as parts of a single intellectual enterprise'.[2]

By contrast to professional philosophy, 'Andersonianism' was a fiercely Sydney cultural phenomenon of the 1940s and 1950s. It was closely associated with the later nihilist phase of Anderson, his rejection of 'moralism', 'meliorism' and his distrust of all forms of 'state authority', as well as with the bitter divisions of the cold war. As James McAuley saw the period:

> No worse age has ever been—
> Murderous, lying, and obscene;
> Devils worked while gods connived:
> Somehow the human has survived.[3]

The personal tie with Anderson became more attenuated and remote as the professor-patriarch, wearied by teaching in the post-war years, broke decisively with the Libertarian Society in 1951. 'He took offence fairly quickly', A. J. Baker commented; 'he did not like people close to him deviating from his position (as I myself found), and, in particular, he was unduly and unobjectively possessive about his philosophy, and discouraged or inhibited members of his school from tackling central issues in their writing'.[4] Among the 'loyal circle' of Andersonians, the best known philosophers have been A. J. Anderson and A. J. Baker. Their work has involved a vigorous restatement and endorsement of the master's realism rather than developing it in new and creative directions. The technical vocabulary of the Andersonians became more derivative, doctrinaire and exclusive, and was heavily influenced by Freudian theory and classical anarchism. There was a withdrawal from wider political and social issues to the bohemian, boozy *machismo* of the Sydney 'push':

> I believe: in the Proposition
> Wholly and indivisible trinity
> Three in one, one in three
> Subject, predicate, and copula!
> Especially the copula.
> Union is strength
> Strength thru' joy
> A thing of beauty is a joy forever
> Porphyry, Aristotle, Socrates![5]

John Docker's distinction between a left-wing 'libertarian' and right-wing 'Andersonian' camp (analogous to the left and right Hegelians of the 1840s) seems forced.[6] Apart from its vehement opposition to censorship and 'repressive' morality,

Andersonianism was a conservative social and political force. A shrewd student of Anderson's noted that, because of his corrosive effect on religious belief and 'the tradition of purposive activity', Anderson's political and ethical doctrines amounted to 'a theory of complete political and social quietism'. The improbable alliance between right-wing Catholics and Sydney freethinkers and atheists dates from this time. A distinction can be made between Andersonians like Peter Coleman, Donald Horne and James McAuley for whom anti-Communism was the major crusade, and those like A. J. Baker, John Maze and George Molnar who placed greater emphasis on civil liberties and sexual emancipation. But it was individuals and small groups who mattered, not the wider 'consumerist' society.

Neither David Armstrong nor Eugene Kamenka thought of themselves as Andersonians in the narrow sense, though both acknowledged a great intellectual debt to Anderson. They were distinguished students of the late 1940s. Kamenka, for all his affection and respect for his teacher, recognised the 'stultifying effect of proximity to Anderson', who became a philosophical Upas tree at Sydney. Anderson, he wrote, 'was jealously possessive of his theory, discouraging his students and followers in practice from criticising, amending, or even tackling independently views he had formed'.[7] Kamenka completed his doctorate at the Australian National University and in 1962, after a lectureship at the University of Malaya, joined the History of Ideas Unit in the Research School of Social Sciences, Australian National University, to become its head in 1968 and professor in 1974. Likewise, Armstrong disliked the discipleship and authoritarian atmosphere of the Andersonians; he later observed that while Anderson and Karl Popper 'preached the life of intellectual criticism so forcefully and effectively, yet [they] were unwilling to see it applied in their immediate intellectual environment'.[8] Armstrong, who occupied the Sydney chair from 1964 to 1991, went on to develop a realist theory of perception, mind and belief. He has also advanced some powerful arguments for a realist view of universals.

Beyond the immediate philosophical impact, Anderson had a more diffuse and elusive influence on the law (through his students F. C. Hutley and W. L. Morison), psychology (through W. M. O'Neil, D. J. Ivison and J. R. Maze), anthropology (L. R. Hiatt), political science (Douglas McCallum and W. H. C. Eddy), literary criticism (H. J. Oliver and W. Milgate) and education. Among the many women he taught, Margot Hentze became the first woman appointed to Sydney's History Department, Margaret Mackie has had a long and fruitful career as an educationist, Gwen Kelly is an important novelist, and Ruth Atkins had a notable career in Political Science at the University of New South Wales.

Given the varieties and tensions within Anderson's philosophy and those of his students and *epigoni*, what if anything do they have in common? John Docker has discerned strong elements of metaphysical dualism, social pessimism and cultural élitism. Eugene Kamenka emphasises the more positive values of objectivity, inquiry, liberty, independence and enterprise. He sees their finest expression in the words and work of J. A. Passmore: 'to defend rational inquiry against fanaticism and scepticism, imagination against pedantry, discipline against Romanticism, liberty against doctrinaire egalitarianism, culture against philistinism, compassion against heartlessness'.[9] Kamenka also specifies the 'evils' of censorship (whether religious, sexual or political), obscurantism and repressive morality. Andersonians 'believed, following Anderson (and Socrates), that the unexamined life was not worth living, that the life of prudence and precaution was a mean and base existence, that security-seeking was the enemy of intellectual enquiry, understanding, social enterprise and freedom'.[10] A. J. Baker discovers a shared set of doctrines and attitudes, such as social pluralism, the rejection of social atomism, voluntarism and all notions of the 'common good', a suspicion of planning and the welfare state, and the defence of academic traditions and interests in the university. Vincent Buckley, the Melbourne poet and critic, finds certain Sydney qualities writ large in Anderson and his followers—a tough-minded scepticism, the refusal to believe in any political or religious 'faith', the delight in disputation and argument for its own sake, an unquestioned individualism, and the air of amiable cynicism and hedonism:

> But much of Anderson is not characteristic of Sydney—or, if it is, becomes so in desiccated forms; I think of his rigorous insistence on logic, his intellectual stamina and persistence, his critical attraction to G. E. Moore, his interest in aesthetics as a formal discipline, his highly professional orientation to the publications of his contemporaries, and his ability to think in the perspective of the Greeks. Sydney is far too lazy for all that.[11]

Would worthy Melbourne, built 'from Scottish rigour and Victorian gold', have proved more fertile soil for Anderson's strenuous philosophising? I do not think it very likely.

If Anderson was one of the most thorough-going and uncompromising exponents of the secular humanist tradition in recent history, a sort of Scottish-Australian Zarathustra, then yet another irony is that as the practice of traditional theism has declined there has been a marked loss of faith in the militantly secularist creed by which Anderson lived, fought and died. And today in the citadel of academe, a company of postmodernist and feminist critics has been busy assailing, deconstructing and relativising his central values of disinterested inquiry, truth and independence. Simultaneously, powerful bureaucrats and ambitious politicians have applied the simple remedies of free market economics and utilitarianism to the universities, largely unopposed and unresisted. The tyranny of the present, the 'information revolution', new forms of political and ideological regimentation, and academic timidity or worse, have all obscured the most vital insight of Anderson—that education is a way of life characterised by inquiry, freedom and criticism. But, as Anderson so passionately proclaimed, 'liberty "has lived and always will live . . . a perilous and fighting life" '.

Notes

Prelude

[1] 'The Apology of Socrates', in Plato, *The Last Days of Socrates*, pp. 62–3.
[2] Peter Scott, *The Crisis of the University*, p. 115.
[3] Allan Bloom, *The Closing of the American Mind*, p. 312.
[4] Ibid., p. 340.
[5] *Higher Education: A Policy Statement. July 1988*, Canberra, 1988, p. 6.
[6] *Glasgow University Magazine*, Vol. 29, No. 4, 30 Jan. 1918.
[7] 'Socrates as an Educator', in *Studies in Empirical Philosophy*, p. 206.
[8] Ibid., p. 212.
[9] 'The University and the Public', in *Education and Politics*, p. 12.
[10] 'Socrates as an Educator', in *Studies*, p. 212.
[11] 'Classicism', in *Studies*, p. 202.
[12] 'The Conception of a Liberal Education', in *Education and Politics*, p. 55.
[13] 'Classicism', in *Studies*, p. 199.
[14] 'Socrates as an Educator', in *Studies*, p. 208.
[15] From the submission of the Professorial Board of the University of Sydney to the Committee on Australian Universities, June 1957, p. 1.
[16] Ian Clunies Ross, *Memoirs and Papers*, Melbourne, 1961, p. 177.
[17] J. H. Newman, *The Idea of a University*, pp. 33–4.
[18] Baker has also written a detailed monograph on Anderson's social philosophy and political life, *Anderson's Social Philosophy*, Sydney, 1979.
[19] 'Censorship', in *Education and Politics*, p. 19.
[20] George Davie, *The Crisis of the Democratic Intellect*, p. 62.
[21] Louis Hartz, *The Foundation of New Societies*, New York, 1964.
[22] Craig Beveridge and Ronald Turnbull, *The Eclipse of Scottish Culture*, p. 90.

1 The 'Dominie'

[1] *The Zincali*, Vol. 1, pp. 23–5, quoted in M. Collie, *George Borrow Eccentric*, Cambridge, 1982, p. 166.
[2] R. D. Anderson, *Education and Opportunity in Victorian Scotland*, p. 2.
[3] Ibid., p. 21. 'It is important to remember that the belief in a specific Scottish egalitarianism never implied that Scotland was in any sense a classless society. It held that the social gap between classes was never important and through societal encouragement and institutional means the "lad o' pairts" with ability and resolution could easily effect a crossing'. A. MacLaren (ed.), *Social Class in Scotland: Past and Present*, Edinburgh, 1976, p. 9.
[4] R. D. Anderson, *Education and Opportunity*, p. 282.
[5] James Scotland, *The History of Scottish Education*, Vol. 1, p. 230.
[6] George Wilson, *Hame*, Hamilton, 1969, pp. 57–8. Quoted in the *Hamilton Arts Journal*, No. 6, 1986, pp. 6–7.
[7] Ian D. Suttie, *The Origins of Love and Hate*, Peregrine, 1963 (first ed. 1935), p. 37.

2 Gypsy City—Divided Mind

[1] John Burnet, *Higher Education and the War*, p. 218. On the generalist tradition with philosophy as the cornerstone, see George Davie, *The Democratic Intellect.*
[2] William Buchan, *John Buchan: A Memoir*, London, 1982, p. 84.
[3] R. D. Anderson, *Education and Opportunity*, p. 260.
[4] Gilbert Murray, *An Unfinished Autobiography*, p. 96.
[5] Henry Jones, *Old Memories*, p. 38.
[6] H. J. W. Hetherington, *The Life and Letters of Sir Henry Jones*, p. 20.
[7] Henry Jones, *Idealism as a Practical Creed*, p. 101.
[8] Ibid., p. 7.
[9] Ibid., p. 209. 'By uniting nature to man, man to man, and all with God Idealism has involved all that exists, or that man can conceive, in one doubtful destiny' (p. 247).
[10] Hetherington, *Life and Letters*, p. 43.
[11] Ibid., p. 75.
[12] Jones, *Idealism*, p. 124. 'Herein is the ultimate achievement of the Spirit of Freedom. More cannot be demanded. Duty being the conscious accord and complicity of the individual's will with the whole scheme of things' (pp. 125–6).
[13] Henry Jones, *Social Responsibilities*, p. 21.
[14] S. G. Checkland, *The Upas Tree*, p. 6.
[15] *Report of the Royal Commission on the Housing of the Industrial Population of Scotland, Urban and Rural, 1917*, Cd. 8731, p. 346.
[16] T. C. Smout, *A Century of the Scottish People 1830–1950*, p. 262.
[17] J. Boyd Orr, *As I Recall*, London, 1966, p. 44.
[18] James Cunnison, 'Casual Recollections of the Students' Settlement', p. 33.
[19] William Boyd, 'Life Story', pp. 127–8, Glasgow University Archives.
[20] Henry Jones and J. H. Muirhead, *The Life and Philosophy of Edward Caird*, p. 115.

3 The Undergraduate

[1] *Glasgow University Court—Camera Minute Book No. 4*, Sept. 1912, Glasgow University Archives.
[2] 'Is the State a Moral Agent?', p. 39.
[3] John Anderson to Janet Baillie, 16 Nov. 1916.
[4] *Glasgow University Magazine*, Vol. 26, No. 8, 17 Dec. 1913.
[5] John Anderson to Janet Baillie, 30 Nov. 1916.
[6] 'Two Houses', *Glasgow University Magazine*, pp. 65–6.
[7] 'Thanksgiving', *Glasgow University Magazine*, p. 39.
[8] 'Sociological Tales', *Glasgow University Magazine*, p. 126.
[9] 'Tales for Men Only. II The Philanthropist', *Glasgow University Magazine*, pp. 252–4.
[10] 'A Fable', *Glasgow University Magazine*, pp. 50–2.
[11] 'A Vision of Beauty', *Glasgow University Magazine*, Vol. 28, No. 8, 25 May 1917, p. 250.
[12] *Glasgow University Magazine*, Vol. 29, No. 6, 27 Feb. 1918, pp. 140–1.
[13] *Glasgow University Magazine*, Vol. 29, No. 4, 30 Jan. 1918, p. 93.
[14] Ibid.
[15] 'Socialism on the Clyde', *The Times*, 28 Dec. 1922. Quoted in James D. Young, *The Rousing of the Scottish Working Class*, p. 202. For a more critical stance on these events, see Iain McLean, *The Legend of Red Clydeside.*
[16] Boyd, 'Life Story', p. 145.
[17] 'Prophet in a Gown', *Nation*, No. 9, 17 Jan. 1959, p. 11.

4 A Philosopher in Love

[1] John Anderson to Janet Baillie, Oct. 1918.
[2] John Anderson to Janet Baillie, Feb. 1919.
[3] Janet Baillie to John Anderson, 26 April 1921.
[4] Janet Baillie to John Anderson, 11 May 1921.
[5] Ibid.
[6] John Anderson to Janet Baillie, 6 March 1921.
[7] John Anderson to Janet Baillie, Oct. 1918.
[8] John Anderson to Janet Baillie, Feb. 1919.
[9] John Anderson to Janet Baillie, Feb. 1919.
[10] Janet Baillie to John Anderson, 12 June 1921.
[11] John Anderson to Janet Baillie, 21 June 1921.
[12] Janet Baillie to John Anderson, 17 Feb. 1922.
[13] John Anderson to Janet Baillie, 6 Dec. 1920.

5 The Making of a Realist

[1] 'Is the State a Moral Agent?, p. 20.
[2] Ibid., p. 46.
[3] Ibid., pp. 28–9.
[4] Ibid., p. 41.
[5] Henry Jones, *A Faith that Enquires*, pp. 63, 256.
[6] John Burnet, *Higher Education and the War*, pp. 66–7.
[7] Unpublished textbook on logic, p. 2.
[8] Henry Jones, *Social Responsibilities*, p. 30.
[9] 'Is the State a Moral Agent?', p. 45.
[10] The phrase, significantly, is Jones'. *A Faith that Enquires*, p. 51.
[11] Jones, 'Idealism and Epistemology', *Mind*, Vol. 2, N.S., No. 7, p. 293.
[12] John Anderson to Janet Baillie, 22 Feb. 1917.
[13] *Glasgow University Magazine*, Vol. 29, No. 6, 27 Feb. 1918, p. 146.
[14] N. Kemp Smith, *Prolegomena to an Idealist Theory of Knowledge*, p. 222.
[15] N. Kemp Smith, *The Present Situation in Philosophy*, p. 29.
[16] John Anderson to Janet Baillie, Feb. 1919.
[17] T. C. Smout, *A Century of the Scottish People, 1830–1950*, p. 114.
[18] John Anderson to Janet Baillie, 25 Oct. 1920.
[19] John Anderson to Janet Baillie, 23 Jan. 1922.
[20] John Anderson to Janet Baillie, Feb. 1919.
[21] Henry Jones, *Idealism as a Practical Creed*, p. 21.
[22] 'Empiricism (1927)', in *Studies in Empirical Philosophy*, p. 14.
[23] 'The Knower and the Known (1927)', in *Studies*, p. 29.
[24] 'Empiricism (1927)', in *Studies*, p. 4.
[25] Ibid., p. 12.
[26] Unpublished textbook on logic, p. 17.
[27] 'Realism and Some of its Critics (1930)', *Studies*, p. 59.
[28] 'Censorship', in *Education and Politics*, p. 19.
[29] 'Realism and Some of its Critics (1930)', in *Studies*, p. 53.
[30] 'Socrates as an Educator', in *Studies*, p. 203.
[31] J. Burnet, *Early Greek Philosophy*, p. v.
[32] 'The Place of Hegel in the History of Philosophy', in *Studies*, p. 80. See also his later essay on 'Classicism'.
[33] Ibid., p. 86.
[34] Ibid., p. 80.

6 Sea City—Provincial Mind

[1] H. E. Barff, *A Short Historical Account of the University of Sydney*, Sydney, 1902, p. 5. See also C. Turney, U. Bygott and P. Chippendale, *Australia's First*, Ch. 2.
[2] Ibid., p. 34.
[3] H. J. W. Hetherington, *The Life and Letters of Sir Henry Jones*, p. 209.
[4] *Australasian Journal of Psychology and Philosophy*, Vol. 1, No. 1, 1923, p. 60.
[5] J. Passmore, 'Philosophy' in A. L. McLeod (ed.), *The Pattern of Australian Culture*, p. 140.
[6] Ibid., p. 140. Compare Morris Miller's assessment in 1929: 'The adherence to idealism in some form or other in opposition to naturalism and materialism on the part of philosophical thinkers in Australia is a highly significant fact when viewed in relation to the great effort of a small population to grapple with the material resources of an immense unsubdued continent'.
[7] Henry Jones, *Idealism as a Practical Creed*, pp. 298–9.
[8] G. V. Portus, *Happy Highways*, Melbourne, 1953, pp. 63–4.
[9] S. Fitzgerald, *Rising Damp*, p. 23.
[10] A. Davidson, *The Communist Party of Australia*, p. 16.
[11] J. Klugman, 'Marxism, Reformism and the General Strike', in J. Skelley (ed.), *The General Strike 1926*, London, 1976, p. 77.

7 Founding a School

[1] John Anderson to Janet Baillie, 24 Nov. 1917.
[2] 'The Working Class', Sydney University Labor Club, 15 June 1932, pp. 5, 8.
[3] MS. on history of Communism in Australia by James Normington-Rawling, p. 456, ANU Archives of Business and Labour, N57/2.
[4] 'The Working Class', *Proletariat*, p. 3.
[5] 'Freedom and the Class Struggle', *Proletariat*, pp. 2, 4.
[6] 'The Working Class', p. 3.
[7] 'Freedom and the Class Struggle', p. 3.
[8] 'The Working Class', p. 4.
[9] 'Freedom and the Class Struggle', p. 5.
[10] 'The Working Class', p. 6. 'Socialisation appears, then, as an example of social philanthropy, and, like all proposals of this sort, it is of no effect in improving the position of the workers (i.e., their fighting position, but equally their "lot"), but rather makes it worse' (p. 4).
[11] Margaret Mackie to John Mackie, 1 Oct. 1937, Mackie Papers P. 69, University of Sydney Archives.
[12] 'The Conception of a Liberal Education', in *Education and Politics*, p. 63.
[13] 'Politics and Publicity', *The Workers' Weekly*, 14 Oct. 1927.
[14] 'Censorship', in *Education and Politics*, p. 22.
[15] 'Ulysees (1930)', in *Art and Reality: John Anderson on Literature and Aesthetics*, p. 95.
[16] 'Leadership and Spontaneity'.
[17] Ibid.
[18] Kavanagh's criticisms are included in a typed version of Anderson's 'Leadership and Spontaneity' held in the James Normington-Rawling Collection, ANU Archives of Business and Labour, N57/206.
[19] 'Some Questions in Aesthetics'.
[20] 'Realism versus Relativism in Ethics', in *Studies in Empirical Philosophy*, p. 241.
[21] 'Realism and Some of its Critics', in *Studies*, pp. 41–2.
[22] 'The Non-Existence of Consciousness', in *Studies*, pp. 60–1.

[23] See 'Discussion: Some Features of Professor Anderson's Logic' and 'Reply by Professor Anderson', *Australasian Journal of Psychology and Philosophy*, Vol. 7, No. 2, June 1929, and 'An Examination of Realism', Vol. 7, No. 4, Dec. 1929.
[24] 'Realism and Some of its Critics', in *Studies*, p. 42.
[25] Ibid., p. 59.
[26] 'The Working Class', p. 6.
[27] 'Determinism and Ethics', in *Studies*, p. 225.
[28] Passmore, 'Philosophy' in A. L. McLeod (ed), *The Pattern of Australian Culture*, p. 149.
[29] Anderson's statement to Vice-Chancellor, 6 Sept. 1933, University File G3/158, University Archives.
[30] Turney *et al.*, *Australia's First*, p. 526.
[31] 'University Reform', in *Education and Inquiry*, pp. 148–9.
[32] P. H. Partridge, 'Anderson as Educator', in *Education and Inquiry*, p. 4.
[33] 'The University and the Public', in *Education and Politics*, p. 11.
[34] 'Censorship', in *Education and Politics*, p. 21.
[35] Ibid., p. 23.

8 Socratic Gadfly

[1] Anderson Papers, Series 4, University of Sydney Archives.
[2] *Honi Soit*, 15 July 1931, quoted in A. J. Baker, *Anderson's Social Philosophy*, p. 90.
[3] *N.S.W. Parliamentary Debates*, Second Series, Vol. 128, p. 4966.
[4] Anderson's submission to the Senate, p. 6, P. 42, Anderson Papers, Series 4, University of Sydney Archives.
[5] Minutes of special meeting of Senate, 20 July 1931, G3/158, University of Sydney Archives.
[6] Anderson Papers, Series 4, University of Sydney Archives.
[7] 'Socrates as an Educator', in *Education and Politics*, pp. 37–8.
[8] From *Capital*, Vol. 1, quoted in David McLellan, *The Thought of Karl Marx*, p. 132.
[9] Anderson Papers, Series 4, University of Sydney Archives.
[10] From Mr Henry's speech, 1 Sept. 1931, *N.S.W. Parliamentary Debates*, Second Series, Vol. 129, p. 5819.
[11] Anderson Papers, Series 4, University of Sydney Archives.
[12] John Thornton, 'University or Technical College?', *Honi Soit*, 22 July 1931. *N.S.W. Parliamentary Debates*, Second Series, Vol. 128, p. 4969.

9 A Realist 'Til it Hurts

[1] 'Affairs in Russia Today', radio talk on 2BL, 17 Sept. 1936, published in *The Militant*, Oct. 1936.
[2] 'Marxist Philosophy', in *Studies in Empirical Philosophy*, p. 292.
[3] Ibid., pp. 299–300.
[4] Ibid., p. 312.
[5] Ibid., p. 293.
[6] Ibid., p. 313.
[7] See 'Production, Distribution and Exchange', *Australasian Journal of Psychology and Philosophy*, Vol. 13, 1935, pp. 136–42.
[8] 'Marxist Ethics', in *Studies*, p. 314.
[9] 'In Defence of Revision', a paper presented at the Workers' Party Conference, Feb. 1937, p. 5, James Normington-Rawling Collection, ANU Archives of Business and Labour, N57/510.

[10] Ibid., p. 5.
[11] The Present Position of the Workers Party, 12 April 1937, p. 3. Normington- Rawling Collection. N57/511.
[12] Political Theory (1942), p. 42, University of Sydney Archives.
[13] Ibid., pp. 47–8.
[14] Ibid., p. 48.
[15] 'The Servile State', in *Studies*, p. 331.
[16] Political Theory (1942), p. 52.
[17] Ibid., p. 54.
[18] 'Marxist Philosophy', in *Studies*, p. 301.
[19] The Present Position of the Workers Party, 12 April 1937, pp. 2–3, Normington-Rawling Collection, N57/511.
[20] Political Theory (1942), p. 55.
[21] Ibid., p. 8.
[22] Ibid., p. 10.
[23] Ibid, p. 14.
[24] John Burnet, *Early Greek Philosophy*, p. 134.
[25] Political Theory (1942), p. 4.
[26] Ibid., p. 37.
[27] Ibid., p. 21.
[28] See 'Freudianism and Society', in *Studies*, pp. 340–58.
[29] Ethics and Aesthetics (1942), p. 6, University of Sydney Archives.
[30] 'Freudianism and Society', in *Studies*, p. 342.
[31] Ethics and Aesthetics (1942), p. 7.
[32] 'The Meaning of Good', in *Studies*, p. 267.
[33] Ibid., p. 266.
[34] Ibid., p. 267.
[35] Ethics and Aesthetics (1942), p. 10.
[36] Ibid., p .15.
[37] 'Art and Morality', in *Art and Reality*, p. 90.
[38] 'The contrast of rationalism and empiricism, or the contrast between metaphysics and logic', p. 64, M237, Item 2, University of Sydney Archives. On the separation of logic and history, Anderson said in a lecture on Hegel 'to have a developing logic is not to have a logic at all'.
[39] Samuel Alexander (1944), p. 145, University of Sydney Archives.
[40] John Passmore, 'John Anderson and Twentieth-Century Philosophy', in *Studies*, pp. xii–xiii.

10 Love and Strife

[1] Private Diary of Ruth Walker, 1935–36, entry for 19 Aug. 1935, held by Alexander Anderson.
[2] Ibid.
[3] Ibid., 'Christian Scientists perhaps more than any other people resolutely shut their eyes to reality. They are a splendid example of that type of mind that sees unpleasant things about them, dislikes these and turns to religion for help—for a means to shut these things from their sight'.
[4] Ibid.
[5] Ibid., entry for 13 March 1936.
[6] John Anderson to A. R. Walker, 15 March 1938, Walker Papers.
[7] John Anderson to A. R. Walker, 8 Feb. 1947.

[8] John Anderson to A. R. Walker, 14 Jan. 1938.
[9] John Burnet, *Early Greek Philosophy*, p. 147.
[10] Most of the poems were written in 1941, Walker Papers.
[11] A. R. Walker to John Anderson, 18 Feb. 1950, held by Alexander Anderson.

11 Sydney's Wars

[1] John Robertson, *Australia at War*, 1939–45, p. 22.
[2] M. Barnard, *Sydney: The Story of a City*, pp. 77–8.
[3] R. G. Menzies, *The Forgotten People and other Studies in Democracy*, Sydney, 1943, p. 5.
[4] 'Religion in Education', in *Education and Inquiry*, p. 203.
[5] Hegel (1941), p. 15, Anderson Papers, University of Sydney Archives.
[6] Ken Gott, 'Student Life: The Forties . . . That Other R.S.L.', *Melbourne University Magazine*, 1961, p. 25.
[7] Manning Clark, *The Quest for Grace*, p. 193.
[8] *Art and Reality*, p. 3.
[9] Leonie Kramer (ed.), *James McAuley*, p. xxiii.
[10] Robin Gollan, *Revolutionaries and Reformists*, p. 135.
[11] Ibid., p. 137.
[12] Ibid., pp. 138–9.
[13] M. Barnard Eldershaw, *Tomorrow and Tomorrow*, Melbourne, 1947, p. 364.
[14] David Washington, 'A Call to Regain Lost Independence', *National Graduate*, Autumn 1993, p. 10.
[15] R. Carnap, *The Logical Syntax of Language*, London, 1937, p. xiii.
[16] O. P. Wood and G. Pitcher (eds.), *Ryle: Modern Studies in Philosophy*, London, 1970, p. 11.
[17] P. H. Partridge, 'Anderson as Educator', p. 51.
[18] Hegel (1941), pp. 9–10, University of Sydney Archives.
[19] John Anderson to Ruth Walker, 19 Jan. 1952, Walker Papers.

12 War, the University and the Servile State

[1] Donald Horne, *The Education of Young Donald*, p. 205.
[2] Ibid., pp. 205–6.
[3] E. Kamenka, 'The Andersonians', p. 60.
[4] [George Munster?], 'Prophet in a Gown', *Nation*, No. 9, 17 Jan. 1959, p. 13.
[5] Radu J. Bogdan (ed.), *D. M. Armstrong*, p. 7.
[6] Horne, *Education of Young Donald*, p. 212.
[7] Bodgan (ed.), *D. M. Armstrong*, p. 7.
[8] Jill Ker Conway, *The Road From Coorain*, London, 1989, p. 221.
[9] E. Morris, 'The Patriarchal Push', *Quadrant*, Jan.–Feb. 1979, pp. 76–7.
[10] Selwyn Grave, *A History of Philosophy in Australia*, p. 66.
[11] Merle Thornton, Review of A. J. Bakers's *Anderson's Social Philosophy*, pp. 116–28.
[12] P. H. Partridge, 'Anderson as Educator', p. 52.
[13] D. R. V. Wood, *Stephen Henry Roberts*, p. 37.
[14] P. H. Partridge, 'Anderson as Educator', p. 52. Also in *Education and Inquiry*, p. 10.

[15] P. H. Partridge, 'Some Thoughts on Planning', in *Australasian Journal of Psychology and Philosophy*, Vol. 19, 1941, p. 238.
[16] 'The Servile State', in *Studies in Empirical Philosophy*, p. 334.
[17] Ibid., p. 333.
[18] John Anderson's introduction to W. H. C. Eddy (ed.), *Prospects of Democracy*, pp. 11–12.
[19] 'The Future of Education', a review of Eric Ashby's *Universities in Australia* (Melbourne, 1944) was first published in *Australasian Journal of Psaychology and Philosophy*, Vol. 21 1943, and later in *Education and Inquiry*, p. 173.
[20] 'Education for Democracy?', a review of J. D. G. Medley's *Education for Democracy* (Melbourne, 1943) was first published in *Australasian Journal of Psychology and Philosophy*, Vol. 21, 1943, and later in *Education and Inquiry*, p. 162.
[21] 'The Future of Education', in *Education and Inquiry*, p. 179.
[22] 'Education and Practicality' was first published in *Australasian Journal of Psychology and Philosophy*, Vol. 22, 1944, and then in *Education and Inquiry*, p. 156.
[23] 'Religion in Education' was published by the New Education Fellowship in 1943 and in *Education and Inquiry*, pp. 203–13.
[24] 'University Rcform', in *Education and Inquiry*, p. 150.
[25] 'The Servile State', in *Studies*, p. 339.
[26] 'The Future of Education', in *Education and Inquiry*, pp. 179–80.

13 Love and Freedom

[1] Ruth Walker to John Anderson, held by Alexander Anderson.
[2] Ruth Walker to John Anderson, Saturday, held by Alexander Anderson.
[3] John Anderson to Ruth Walker, 24 Feb. 1947, Walker Papers.
[4] R. F. Walker to Prof. J. Anderson, 15 March 1950, held by Alexander Anderson.
[5] A. J. Baker, 'John Anderson and Freethought', *The Australian Quarterly*, Vol. 34, No. 4, Dec. 1962, p. 62.
[6] D. M. McCallum, 'Anderson and Freethought', p. 75.
[7] John Anderson to Ruth Walker, 11 Aug. 1952, Walker Papers.
[8] John Anderson to Ruth Walker, 14 March 1952, Walker Papers. 'They (the Libs.) had a silly meeting on Tuesday at which (I am given to believe) a certain June Wilson gave vent to the remarkable aphorism that love is the basis of life and therefore free love is the basis of free living!' (John Anderson to Ruth Walker, 3 April 1952).
[9] John Anderson to Ruth Walker, Friday, held by Alexander Anderson.
[10] John Anderson to Ruth Walker, 5 Sept. 1952, Walker Papers.
[11] Virginia Woolf, *Three Guineas*, London, 1952 (first ed. 1938), p. 258.
[12] John Anderson to Ruth Walker, 8 July 1952, Walker Papers.
[13] John Anderson to Ruth Walker, 13 Nov. 1952, Walker Papers.
[14] 'The contrast of rationalism and empiricism', p. 76, M237, Item 2, University of Sydney Archives.
[15] John Anderson to Ruth Walker, 28 Feb. 1952, Walker Papers.

14 Education and Inquiry

[1] *Report of the Committee on Australian Universities*, Sept. 1957, p. 27.
[2] 'Utilitarianism', in *Studies in Empirical Philosophy*, p. 229.
[3] 'Art and Morality', in *Australasian Journal of Psychology and Philosophy*, Vol. 19, 1941, p. 265, and *Education and Inquiry*, p. 201.
[4] 'Classicism', in *Education and Inquiry*, p. 44.

[5] Ibid., p. 62.
[6] 'Lectures on Spencer and Dewey', *Dialectic*, Vol. 14, 1977, p. 38.
[7] 'Lectures on the Educational Theories of Spencer and Dewey', in *Education and Inquiry*, p. 102.
[8] Paul Selver, *Orage and the New Age Circle*, pp. 97–8.
[9] 'Lectures on the Educational Theories of Spencer and Dewey', in *Education and Inquiry*, pp. 117–19.
[10] 'Classicism', in *Education and Inquiry*, p. 50.
[11] 'Lectures on the Educational Theories of Spencer and Dewey', in *Education and Inquiry*, p. 103.
[12] Ibid., p. 128.
[13] 'Lectures on Spencer and Dewey', *Dialectic*, pp. 43–4.
[14] 'Realism', *The Australian Highway*, p. 56.
[15] 'Lectures on the Educational Theories of Spencer and Dewey', in *Education and Inquiry*, pp. 112–13.
[16] 'The Place of the Academic in Modern Society', in *Education and Inquiry*, p. 216.
[17] 'Education and Practicality', in *Education and Inquiry*, p. 155.
[18] Submission by the Sydney Association of University Teachers to the Committee on Australian Universities, 7 June 1957, pp. 3–4.
[19] Ian Clunies Ross, *Memoirs and Papers*, Melbourne, 1961, p. 175.
[20] Submission by the Vice-Chancellor and Principal to the Committee on Australian Universities on the Financial Needs of the University of Sydney, June 1957, p. 5.
[21] From the submission of the Professorial Board of the University of Sydney to the Committee on Australian Universities, June 1957, pp. 1–2. The chairman of the Professorial Board was Prof. W. M. O'Neil, a keen admirer of Anderson.
[22] 'Classicism', in *Education and Inquiry*, p. 63.
[23] Submission by the Sydney Association of University Teachers to the Committee on Australian Universities, 7 June 1957, pp. 4–5.
[24] 'Classicism', in *Education and Inquiry*, p. 63.
[25] 'The Servile State', in *Studies*, p. 330.
[26] 'Socrates as an Educator', in *Studies*, p. 212.
[27] Unpublished textbook on logic, pp. 207–8.
[28] 'Phaedo', in Plato, *The Last Days of Socrates*, p. 144.

15 A Philosopher in Winter

[1] *The Dismissal of S. S. Orr by the University of Tasmania*, Hobart, 1958, p. 1.
[2] 'The Place of the Academic in Modern Society', in *Education and Inquiry*, p. 217.
[3] Ibid., p. 220.
[4] Ibid., p. 217.
[5] W. H. C. Eddy, *Orr*, pp. 10–11.
[6] 'The Place of the Academic in Modern Society', in *Education and Inquiry*, p. 218.
[7] *The Dismissal of S. S. Orr by the University of Tasmania*, pp. 2–3.
[8] 'The Orr Case and Academic Freedom', *The Observer*, 28 June 1958.
[9] 'The Place of the Academic in Modern Society', in *Education and Inquiry*', pp. 219–20.
[10] Gilbert Ryle, 'Logic and Professor Anderson', pp. 146–7.
[11] 'Empiricism and Logic', in *Studies in Empirical Philosophy*, p. 172.
[12] Ibid., p. 183.
[13] 'Classicism', in *Studies*, pp. 194–5.
[14] 'Hypotheticals', in *Studies*, p. 139.
[15] 'Classicism', in *Studies*, p. 201.
[16] John Anderson to Ruth Walker, 20 July 1938, Walker Papers.

[17] George Davie, *The Crisis of the Democratic Intellect*, pp. 170–1.
[18] 'The Meaning of Good', in *Studies*, p. 267.
[19] Unpublished textbook on logic, p. 4.
[20] 'Empiricism', in *Studies*, p. 4.
[21] Ibid., p. 4.
[22] 'Art and Morality', in *Education and Inquiry*, p. 196.
[23] Manning Clark, *The Quest for Grace*, pp. 194–5.
[24] Radu J. Bogdan (ed.), *D. M. Armstrong*, p. 7.
[25] 'Art and Morality', in *Education and Inquiry*, p. 196.
[26] 'The Place of the Academic', in *Education and Inquiry*, p. 221.
[27] *Newcastle Sun*, 6 July 1961.
[28] *Sydney Sun*, 7 July 1961.
[29] *Sydney Morning Herald*, 15 July 1961.
[30] Ibid., 21 July 1961.
[31] *Newcastle Morning Herald and Miners' Advocate*, 11 August 1961.
[32] 'Religion and the University', *The Australian Highway*, p. 54.
[33] The tribute was made at a meeting of the Faculty of Arts on 1 August 1962, and was communicated to Mrs Anderson soon after. University File G3/158.
[34] J. L. Mackie, 'John Anderson', p. 125.
[35] D. M. Armstrong, 'Metaphysical Scotland', p. 78.
[36] E. Kamenka, 'John Anderson', in *The Greats*, p. 228.

Appendix: Anderson and Andersonianism

[1] J. L. Mackie, 'John Anderson', pp. 124–5.
[2] A. J. Baker, *Australian Realism*, introd. by Anthony Quinton, p. ix.
[3] James McAuley, 'Explicit', in L. Kramer (ed.), *James McAuley*, p. 228.
[4] A. J. Baker, 'The Andersonians', p. 10.
[5] J. S. Rybak, 'Credo', *Broadsheet*, No. 33, Sept. 1963.
[6] John Docker, *Australian Cultural Elites*, Ch. 8.
[7] E. Kamenka, 'The Andersonians', pp. 60–4.
[8] Radu J. Bogdan (ed.), *D. M. Armstrong*, p. 13.
[9] Kamenka, 'The Andersonians', p. 62.
[10] E. Kamenka, 'John Anderson', in L. Kramer *et al.* (eds), *The Greats*, p. 223.
[11] Vincent Buckley, 'Unequal Twins', in Jim Davidson (ed.), *The Sydney-Melbourne Book*, pp. 148–58.

Bibliography

Primary Sources

1. Published Works by John Anderson

Most of Anderson's published writings appeared as articles in Australian journals. They fall roughly into three categories. The first, and most important, consists of his philosophical articles, discussions with colleagues, and reviews. It includes 82 items, 64 of which were published in the *Australasian Journal of Psychology and Philosophy*, which Anderson edited for twelve years between 1935 and 1946. The remainder appeared in *The Australian Highway*, the *Australian Journal of Politics and History* and other periodicals. The major essays are collected in *Studies in Empirical Philosophy*.

His papers on political, social and literary topics comprise the second group. It includes over 60 pieces published in political journals such as *The Workers' Weekly, The Communist* and *The Militant*, and in university magazines like *Honi Soit, Hermes* and *Freethought.* Most of the summaries of his addresses to the Freethought and Literary Societies published in the *Union Recorder* and *Honi Soit* were written or approved by Anderson himself. Many of them have been published in *Art and Reality*.

The third group consists of letters to Sydney newspapers and polemical pieces in *The Workers' Weekly* and *The Militant*, some of which were probably written by Jenny Anderson, and some of which appeared pseudonymously.

Collections

Education and Politics—Essays. Sydney, 1931.

Studies in Empirical Philosophy. Sydney, 1962.

'Anderson on Education', *Dialectic*, (journal of the Newcastle Philosophy Club, 14, 1977), ed. by Brian Birchall and Norelle Evans.

Education and Inquiry: John Anderson, Ed. by D. Z. Phillips. Oxford, 1980.

Art and Reality: John Anderson on Literature and Aesthetics, ed. by Janet Anderson, Graham Cullum and Kimon Lycos. Sydney, 1982.

Selected Individual Works

From *Glasgow University Magazine*

'Thanksgiving', Vol. 27, No. 2, 2 Dec. 1914.

'Sociological Tales', Vol. 27, No. 4, 27 Jan. 1915.

'Russia as I Saw It', Vol. 28, No. 1, 22 Nov. 1916.

'A Disquisition', Vol. 28, No. 3, 20 Dec. 1916.

'The World to Come', Vol. 28, No. 5, 14 Feb. 1917.

'The Evolution of a Literary Artist', Vol. 28, No. 7, 9 May 1917.

'Tales for Men Only. II. The Philanthropist', Vol. 28, No. 8, 25 May 1917.

Editorial and 'Ghosts', Vol. 29, No. 1, 5 Dec. 1917.

'Goats' and 'A Fable', Vol. 29, No. 2, 19 Dec. 1917.

'Two Houses', Vol. 29, No. 3, 16 Jan. 1918.

Editorial and 'Blind to the World', Vol. 29, No. 4, 30 Jan. 1918.

'The Cult of Immaturity', Vol. 29, No. 5, 15 Feb. 1918.

Editorial and 'Oatmeal', Vol. 29, No. 6, 27 Feb. 1918.

Editorial and 'Double or Quits', Vol. 29, No. 8, 15 May 1918.

Australia

'The Working Class', *Proletariat* (organ of the University of Melbourne Labour Club), April 1932.

'Freedom and the Class Struggle', *Proletariat*, July 1932.

'Leadership and Spontaneity', published as *Censorship in the Working-Class Movement*, Sydney University Freethought Society, 1932.

'Some Questions in Aesthetics', Sydney University Literary Society, 1932.

Introductory essay to W. H. C. Eddy (ed.), *Prospects of Democracy*, Sydney, 1945.

'Realism', *The Australian Highway*, Sept. 1958.

'Classicism', in Australian Humanities Research Council, fourth annual report, 1960.

'Religion and the University', *The Australian Highway*, Nov. 1961.

2. Unpublished Writings of John Anderson

University of Glasgow Archives

'Is the State a Moral Agent?', 1916–17 Silver Medal Prize Essay.

University of Sydney Archives

A valuable collection of material on and by John Anderson is held in the University Archives, Fisher Library, University of Sydney. It was largely assembled by Ruth Walker and Tom Rose, with the active support of Jenny Anderson, David Armstrong and many others. The personal papers of John Anderson (P 42) include written and typed lecture notes, letters, notes, university correspondence concerning the 1931 controversy etc., photographs, and some publications.

It should be noted that many of Anderson's writings do not present his realist position in a complete or fully developed form. A good deal of his philosophy was presented in conversation or discussion with students. His stance, as expressed in his writings, is often negative and critical. Moreover, as he aged a certain impatience and 'rigidity' made him unwilling to defend his doctrines in detail.

Lectures in Anderson's Own Hand

Aristotle (1928).
Modern Philosophy (1929).
Phaedo (1933).
Reid's 'Inquiry' (1935).
Nature of Mental Science (1940).
T. H. Green's 'Principles of Political Obligation' (1941).
Ethics and Aesthetics (1942).
Political Theory (1942).
Introduction to Philosophy (1943).
Samuel Alexander (1944).
Logical Atomism (1954).
Greek Theories of Education (1954, 1955).

Student Lecture Notes

Like the famous *Zusätze*, written by Hegel's students, the lecture notes taken by Anderson's students are an important source for tracing stages in the latter's developing thought. Lectures were carefully dictated in the Scottish manner, and students were expected to assimilate their content for study and close examination. In addition, the pressures of undergraduate teaching meant that Anderson often incorporated the notes, borrowed from good students, into his own later lectures on the subject. Anderson's annotations occasionally appear in the margins. The present Archivist has placed most of the student lecture books in Miscellaneous Series 237, 240, 242 and 243. There are notebooks by F. C. Hutley (1932–34), J. A. Passmore (1931–33) L. C. Rodd (1931), T. A. Rose (1941–47), and A. D. Sumner (1929–32).

Reserved File

One of the boxes of Anderson's personal papers is not available for research until 1998. It contains letters sent by Ruth Walker to Anderson, 1936–61, and now forms part of the Walker Papers.

Papers in the Possession of Mr Alexander J. Anderson at 'Levenshulme', 2 Nulla Nulla Street, Turramurra

Manuscript of a textbook on logic, prepared for publication about 1922 but never published.

Correspondence between John Anderson and Janet Anderson née Baillie, 1917–23.

Private Diary of Alice Ruth Walker, 1935–36.

3. Alice Ruth Walker Papers

P 158. University of Sydney Archives, Fisher Library. Most of Anderson's letters to Ruth Walker are in this collection. Letters sent by Ruth Walker to Anderson, 1936–61, will not be available for research until 1998, at Ruth Walker's request.

4. University Records

University of Glasgow Archives

Matriculation Albums, Class Roll Books, 1907–18; Glasgow University Court—Camera Minute Books, Nos 4–6; Students' Representative Council Minute Book, 1904–19; Dr William Boyd's unpublished manuscript 'Life Story'; Financial and Statistical Reports by the Universities of St Andrews, Glasgow, Aberdeen and Edinburgh, 1913–18.

Registrar, University of Sydney

Staff file of Professor John Anderson, G3/158.

University of Sydney Archives

Senate minutes, 1951.

5. ANU Archives of Business and Labour, Canberra

MS. on history of Communism in Australia and other papers in the James Normington-Rawling Collection, N 57.

Secondary Sources

Alexander, S. *Space, Time and Deity: the Gifford Lectures, 1916–18.* 2 vols, London, 1920.

Anderson, R. D. *Education and Opportunity in Victorian Scotland: Schools and Universities.* Oxford, 1983.

Armstrong, D. M. 'On Metaphysics', in 'Fifty Years of John Anderson', *Quadrant,* 21 (7), July 1977.

——— 'Metaphysical Scotland, *Quadrant,* May, 1987, pp. 77–8.

Arnold, Matthew, *Culture and Anarchy,* ed. by J. Dover Wilson. Cambridge, 1963.

Ayer, A. J. *Language, Truth and Logic,* London, 1946 (first ed., 1936).

——— *Philosophy in the Twentieth Century.* London, 1982.

Baker, A. J. *Anderson's Social Philosophy: The Social Thought and Political Life of Professor John Anderson.* Sydney, 1979.

——— *Australian Realism: The Systematic Philosophy of John Anderson.* Cambridge, 1986.

——— 'The Andersonians', *Heraclitus,* No. 15, April 1988.

Barnard, M. *Sydney: The Story of a City.* Melbourne, 1956.

Beveridge, Craig and Turnbull, Ronald *The Eclipse of Scottish Culture: Inferiorism and the Intellectuals.* Edinburgh, 1989.

Bloom, Allan. *The Closing of the American Mind.* New York, 1987.

Bogdan, Radu J. (ed.). *D. M. Armstrong* (Profiles, Vol. 4). Dordrecht, 1984.

Boucher, David. 'Practical Hegelianism: Henry Jones's Lecture Tour of Australia', *Journal of History of Ideas*, 1990, pp. 423–52.

Buckley, Vincent. 'Unequal Twins: A Discontinuous Analysis', in Jim Davidson (ed.), *The Sydney–Melbourne Book*, Sydney, 1986, pp. 148–58.

Burnet, John. *Early Greek Philosophy*. London, 1892.

——— *Higher Education and the War*. London, 1917.

Caird, E. *Hegel*. First ed. 1883; Edinburgh, 1896.

——— *Essays on Literature and Philosophy*, Vol. 1. Glasgow, 1892.

Carswell, J. *Lives and Letters*. London, 1978.

Checkland, S. G. *The Upas Tree: Glasgow 1875–1975*. Glasgow, 1976.

Checkland, S. G. and Olive. *Industry and Ethos: Scotland 1832–1914* (Vol. 7 of the *New History of Scotland*). London, 1984.

Clark, Manning. *The Quest for Grace*. Melbourne, 1991.

Cunnison, James 'Casual Recollections of the Students' Settlement', *College Courant*, Martinmass, 1955.

Davidson, A. *The Communist Party of Australia: A Short History*. Stanford, Calif., 1969.

Davie, George. *The Democratic Intellect: Scotland and Her Universities in the Nineteenth Century*. Edinburgh, 1961.

——— 'John Anderson in Scotland: 'Tis Sixty Years Since', *Quadrant* 21 (7), July 1977.

——— *The Crisis of the Democratic Intellect: The Problem of Generalism and Specialisation in Twentieth Century Scotland*. Edinburgh, 1986.

Docker, J. *Australian Cultural Elites: Intellectual Traditions in Sydney and Melbourne*. Sydney, 1974.

——— 'Sydney versus Melbourne Revisited', in Davidson (ed.), *The Sydney–Melbourne Book*, pp. 159–67.

Eddy, W. H. C. (ed.). *Prospects of Democracy*. Sydney, 1945.

——— 'Ethics and Politics', *The Australian Highway*, Sept., 1958.

——— *Orr*. Brisbane, 1961.

——— *Understanding Marxism*. Oxford, 1978.

Findlay, J. N. *Hegel: A Re-examination*. New York, 1958.

Fitzgerald, S. *Rising Damp: Sydney* 1870–90. Melbourne, 1987.

Gollan, Daphne. 'The Balmain Ironworkers' Strike of 1945—Part I', *Labour History*, No. 22, May 1972, pp. 23–41; 'The Balmain Ironworkers' Strike of 1945—Part II', *Labour History*, No. 23, Nov. 1972, pp. 62–73.

Gollan, Robin. *Revolutionaries and Reformists: Communism and the Australian Labour Movement 1920–55*. Canberra, 1975.

Grave, Selwyn A. *A History of Philosophy in Australia*. Brisbane, 1984.

Hetherington, H. J. W. *The Life and Letters of Sir Henry Jones*. London, 1924.

Holland, J. A. B. 'A System of Classical Atheism', *Scottish Journal of Theology*, August 1973.

Horne, Donald. *The Education of Young Donald.* Melbourne, 1975 (first ed. 1967).

——— *Confessions of a New Boy.* First ed. 1985; Melbourne, 1986.

Jones, (Sir) Henry. *Social Responsibilities: Lectures to Business Men.* Glasgow, 1905.

——— *Idealism as a Practical Creed: Being the Lectures on Philosophy and Modern Life Delivered before the University of Sydney*. Glasgow, 1910.

——— *The Working Faith of the Social Reformer and Other Essays.* London, 1910.

——— *Morality and Its Relation to the War*. Oxford, 1915.

——— *A Faith that Enquires: The Gifford Lectures 1920–21*. London, 1922.

——— *Old Memories*. London, 1922.

Jones, (Sir) Henry and Muirhead, J. H. *The Life and Philosophy of Edward Caird.* Glasgow, 1921.

Jones, Thomas. *Welsh Broth.* London, 1950.

Kamenka, E. *The Philosophy of Ludwig Feuerbach.* London, 1970.

——— 'John Anderson', in *The Greats: The Fifty Men and Women who Most Helped to Shape Modern Australia*, ed. by L. Kramer *et al.* Sydney, 1986.

——— 'The Andersonians: Philosophy and Criticism in Australia', *Quadrant*, July 1987, pp. 60–4.

Kelly, Gwen. *There is No Refuge*. London, 1961.

Kemp Smith, N. *The Present Situation in Philosophy—Inaugural Lecture, University of Edinburgh, 16 Oct. 1919*. Edinburgh, 1919.

——— *Prolegomena to an Idealist Theory of Knowledge*. London, 1924.

Kramer, L. (ed.) *James McAuley: Poetry, Essays and Personal Commentary*. Brisbane, 1988.

McCallum, D. M. 'Anderson and Freethought', *The Australian Highway*, Sept. 1958.

Mackie, J. L. 'Anderson's Theory of Education', *The Australian Highway*, Sept. 1958.

——— 'The Philosophy of John Anderson', *Australasian Journal of Philosophy*, Vol. 40, No. 3, Dec. 1962.

——— 'John Anderson', *Australasian Journal of Philosophy*, Vol. 40, No. 2, Aug. 1962.

——— *Ethics: Inventing Right and Wrong*. Harmondsworth, 1990 (first ed. 1977).
McLean, Iain. *The Legend of Red Clydeside*. Edinburgh, 1983.
McLellan, David. *The Thought of Karl Marx*. London, 1982 (first ed. 1971).
McLeod, A. L. (ed.). *The Pattern of Australian Culture*. Melbourne, 1963.
Mairet, P. *A. R. Orage: A Memoir*. New York, 1966 (first ed. 1936).
Molesworth, Voltaire. *Landmarks in Logic*. Sydney, 1958.
Munster, George (?). 'Prophet in a Gown', *Nation*, No. 9, 17 Jan. 1959, pp. 10–13.
Murray, Gilbert. *An Unfinished Autobiography*. London, 1960.
Newman, J. H. *The Idea of a University*. New York, 1966 (first ed. 1853).
O'Neil, W. M. 'Some Notes on Anderson's Psychology', *The Australian Highway*, Sept. 1958.
——— 'John Anderson', in *Australian Dictionary of Biography*, Vol. 7. Melbourne, 1979.
Partridge, P. H. 'Anderson as Educator', *The Australian Highway*, Sept. 1958.
Passmore, John A. *A Hundred Years of Philosophy*. London, 1957.
——— 'John Anderson', in Paul Edwards (ed.), *The Encyclopedia of Philosophy*, New York, 1967, pp. 119–21.
——— 'Commemorating John Anderson', *Times Literary Supplement*, 9 April 1976.
Plato. *The Last Days of Socrates*. Trans. and introd. by H. Tredennick. Harmondsworth, 1986.
Pybus, Cassandra. *Gross Moral Turpitude: The Orr Case Reconsidered*. Melbourne, 1993.
Robertson, John. *Australia at War 1939–45*. Melbourne, 1981.
Rose, T. A. 'Logic', *The Australian Highway*, Sept. 1958.
Russell, B. *My Philosophical Development*. London, 1959.
Ryle, Gilbert. 'Logic and Professor Anderson', *Australasian Journal of Philosophy*, Vol. 28, No. 3, Dec. 1950.
Scotland, James. *The History of Scottish Education*. 2 vols, London, 1969.
Scott, Peter. *The Crisis of the University*. London, 1984.
Scruton, R. *A Short History of Modern Philosophy: From Descartes to Wittgenstein*. London, 1985 (first ed, 1981).
Selver, Paul. *Orage and the New Age Circle: Reminiscences and Reflections*. London, 1959.

Smout, T. C. *A Century of the Scottish People 1830–1950*. London, 1987.

Suter, Geraldine. 'Bibliographic Study on the Philosophy of John Anderson'. *Australian Historical Bibliography*, No. 10, Sept. 1984.

Thornton, Merle. Review of A. J. Baker's *Anderson's Social Philosophy*, *Bowyang*, No. 4, Aug.–Sept. 1980.

Turney, C., Bygott, U. and Chippendale, P. *Australia's First: A History of the University of Sydney*. Vol. 1 (1850–1939). Sydney, 1991.

Wood, D. R. V. *Stephen Henry Roberts*. Sydney University Monographs No. 2, 1986.

Young, James D. *The Rousing of the Scottish Working Class*. London, 1979.

Index